D0906096

Conscience and Power

An Examination of Dirty Hands
and Political Leadership

Stephen A. Garrett

St. Martin's Press

New York

ISBN 0-312-15908-0

Library of Congress Cataloging-in-Publication Data

Garrett, Stephen A., 1939-
  Conscience and power : an examination of dirty hands and political leadership / Stephen A. Garrett.
    p. cm.
  Includes bibliographical references and index.
  ISBN 0-312-15908-0
  1. World War, 1939-1945—Moral and ethical aspects. 2. Political leadership—Moral and ethical aspects—Czechoslovakia—Case studies. 3. Political leadership—Moral and ethical aspects—France—Case studies. I. Title.
  D744.4G35 1996
  940.53-1—dc20   95-51501
                                                                CIP

Book design by Acme Art, Inc.

First edition: August 1996
10 9 8 7 6 5 4 3 2 1

Contents

Preface

Politics will, to the end of history, be an area where conscience
and power meet, where the ethical and coercive factors
of human life will interpenetrate and work out their
tentative and uneasy compromises.

Reinhold Niebuhr, *Moral Man and Immoral Society*

Some years ago, the journalist Merle Miller conducted a series of interviews
with former President Harry Truman. The subsequent book was widely
praised for providing a provocative insight into the thought processes of a
major contemporary political leader.[1] Inevitably, Miller asked Truman about
his decision to drop the atomic bomb on Hiroshima and Nagasaki. The former
president replied in his normally direct, even gruff, manner that he had never
lost any sleep over this decision. Moreover, he was impatient with those who
were prone to moral agonizing over the matter. The scientist J. Robert
Oppenheimer, for example. Oppenheimer had been the scientific director of
the Manhattan Project, the code name for the development of the atomic
bomb. After the war, when there was a debate within the American government over whether to proceed with the development of the much more
powerful H-bomb, Oppenheimer requested a personal audience with President Truman to urge that the project not go ahead. He advanced a mea culpa
with respect to his own role in the creation of atomic weapons: "Mr.
President, I feel as if I have blood on my hands." Truman's cool response
was to remove his handkerchief from his breast pocket and offer it to
Oppenheimer: "Would you like to wipe them off?" Oppenheimer, according
to Truman, had "turned into a crybaby. I don't want anything to do with
people like that."[2]

Given the enormous consequences of the decision to drop the atomic
bomb on two Japanese cities—most importantly in terms of the citizens of
Hiroshima and Nagasaki, but also in terms of its implications for the whole
future of humanity—Truman's dismissal of the notion that he should feel
guilt or even an uneasiness about his decision may strike a good many as

exceptionally callous and unfeeling. Whatever stance one takes here, Truman's attitude toward the dropping of the bomb serves as an introduction to the central focus of this essay, which has to do with what may be called "political morality" or the ethical considerations that should, can, and perhaps sometimes do affect the calculations of statesmen in their conduct of affairs. Such a topic, of course, has many ramifications and may be applied to various settings, including relatively mundane matters of domestic policy. For our purposes, however, the emphasis is on the international arena and, more than this, on political leadership in wartime, which may rightly be regarded as the most severe and complicated test of the political morality of powerful individuals.

I would suggest that anyone with even a casual interest in international affairs, and with at least normal ethical sensitivities, has to be bothered at times by the following deceptively simple question: How can they do it? How can foreign policy leaders (especially the leaders of powerful countries) make the sort of decisions involving life and death, suffering or salvation, that seems to be their standard lot? Presumably some of them, or most of them, are reasonably decent in individual circumstances. They treat those around them with respect, recoil from the notion of using violence to achieve their personal aims, and have at least some regard for the standard virtues of honesty and decency in private life. Yet somehow in their professional capacity, they sign off on pieces of paper that consign thousands to an early death or, by a murmur, refuse help for those in desperate need.

There are various ways in which we can attempt to sort out this paradox, including the application of insights from individual or group psychology. The emphasis of this essay, however, is not so much on the inner lives of statesmen as it is on how we as citizens can rightly evaluate the morality of their conduct, and what standards and criteria we should employ in so doing. It is taken as a given that such an enterprise is worth undertaking on its own merits, not least because politics is ultimately *about* moral judgment, but also because those for whom political leaders claim to act have not only a right but even a duty to hold them to moral inspection.

The first of these assumptions holds that political activity is hardly conducted for its own sake, that it is not simply an exciting or intriguing game—or, in Macbeth's darker phrase, "a tale full of sound and fury, signifying nothing"—but rather is a purposive enterprise directed toward the achieving of certain goals through certain means. Both goals and means can ultimately be understood only in moral terms. As to the second premise, if we deny its force we accept that our leaders are essentially immune from ethical judgment, that they are free actors capable of (and perhaps prone to) committing all sorts of crimes without fear of denunciation. This invitation to moral anarchy is not one that even the most cynical of citizens would be likely to—or should—embrace on close analysis.

In rejecting it, one has to deal with a standard theme that appears in discussions concerning the morality of statesmen. It is sometimes suggested that even if statesmen do evil, they are not acting in their own interests, after all, but in our own. Absent a selfish motive, therefore, we ought to go easy on them. An official with the Lyndon Johnson Administration, Townsend Hoopes, displayed this attitude in discussing some of the decisionmakers involved in the Vietnam War: they "were struggling in good conscience . . . to serve the broad national interest according to their lights."[3] Such an attitude, however generous, is really a non sequitur. The individuals of whom he spoke had hardly come into high office by accident. They desired and sought political power and in this sense laid themselves open to appropriate moral judgment, especially since their actions affected such a broad segment of both the domestic and international community.

To be on the receiving end of a negative moral judgment about one's behavior is, to be sure, an unpleasant and unsought experience, especially since it seems to call into question one's very bona fides and character. For this reason, politicians very often regard moral criticism of their actions as being essentially political opportunism, offered not in the way of genuine ethical concern, but as a tactic to discredit and to gain political advantage. This may very well be the case in a number of circumstances, but it does not alter the fact that in assuming political office, and especially high political office, statesman must accept as an integral part of their brief answering morally for their actions. It was Truman himself who (perhaps ironically) offered the best response to those politicians who bridle at moral evaluation on the basis that they are simply attempting to serve the country and not themselves: "If you can't stand the heat, get out of the kitchen."

In discussing the issue of political morality, the central organizing concept here is that of "dirty hands." Reduced to its essentials, the notion of dirty hands suggests that political authority may be required to do things—or to tolerate things—that would be regarded both by them and by others as unacceptable, even as genuinely evil, if they took place in their private lives. It is sometimes suggested that political leaders actually have little choice in the matter: if they *are* to exercise leadership, they must set aside their standards of personal morality in those cases where insisting on such standards may be obstructive in advancing the broader public interest (to paraphrase Hamlet, they "must be cruel only to be kind"). Stated in its most direct form, the political leader has no other alternative and moreover *should* have no other alternative.

The notion that political leaders, especially those in supreme authority, must accept having "dirty hands" has a long pedigree. In Jean-Paul Sartre's play of that title, the Communist leader Hoerderer proclaims rather impatiently, "I have dirty hands right up to the elbows. I've plunged them in filth and blood. Do you think you can govern innocently?"[4] Perhaps the best-known reference to dirty hands in real life came from Count Camillo di Cavour, the great Italian statesman, who once suggested that "if we had done for ourselves the things that we are doing for Italy, we should be great rascals."[5]

The basic thrust of this book is to subject the concept of dirty hands to a systematic analysis in terms of its implications, its limitations, and its ambiguities. In offering such an analysis, we will be entering into the realm of what is generally called "applied ethics." Particularly as it relates to international affairs, applied ethics straddles both the concerns of the moral philosophers and the political theorists and those of actual policymakers and political operatives. It represents an attempt to attach some of the insights of the former to the practical concerns of the latter. Above all, it endeavors to marry some generally accepted principles of moral conduct to the real world of affairs, and to offer judgments on the degree to which a decisionmaker may or may not have demonstrated an appropriate ethical probity given the constraints operating on him or her or *as* decisionmaker. It is evident from this description that if applied ethics is to mean anything, it has to have some ultimate utility in shaping actual conduct. As the British philosopher Peter Singer says, "An ethical judgment that is no good in practice must suffer from a theoretical defect as well, for the whole point of ethical judgments is to guide practice."[6]

As defined above, the field of applied ethics almost inevitably involves the use of case studies, and the majority of this book is in fact taken up with two specific events from World War II that involved the problem of dirty hands in a particularly dramatic way. The first has to do what was called "Operation ANTHROPOID," a plan developed by the Czech government-in-exile in London to assassinate the top Nazi official in occupied Czechoslovakia, Reinhard Heydrich. The operation was a success in that Heydrich was killed, but the consequences of this action were formidable. Thousands of Czechs lost their lives as a result of Nazi reprisals; in particular the small village of Lidice outside Prague was totally destroyed by the Germans and virtually all of its inhabitants—including 100 children—were murdered. Eduard Beneš was the president of the London Czech government, and the prime mover behind ANTHROPOID. Attention will therefore focus primarily on him and on his moral responsibility for the destruction of Lidice.

The second case study concerns the so-called "Darlan deal." Admiral Jean François Darlan was a top official in the wartime French Vichy government, which had a record of collaboration with the Germans and of complicity in the rounding-up of Jews in France for shipment to Nazi concentration camps. As part of the Allied plan for the invasion of North Africa, code named TORCH, American officials agreed to recognize Darlan as the chief political authority in the area in return for his cooperation in TORCH. The American willingness to work with Darlan raised a storm of controversy at the time and was particularly criticized because it seemed to be such a cynical negation of the whole moral purpose of the war. In this particular examination of dirty hands, attention will be given to various individuals, including Secretary of State Cordell Hull and President Franklin Roosevelt, but also some others, such as General Dwight Eisenhower, overall commander of TORCH, who were not "political leaders" in an official sense, but were nevertheless heavily involved in the politics of the Darlan affair.

The reason case studies form such an important part of the literature of applied ethics is that the judgments emanating from this literature almost inevitably involve some sort of "situational ethics," or what has been called "nonperfectionist ethics." That is, they depend on a close reading of the particular circumstances facing a decisionmaker at his or her moment of choice, which in turn dictates the actual range of moral options available to him or her at the time. The British statesman Edmund Burke made the essential point a long time ago:

> A statesman differs form a professor in a university; the latter has only the general view of society; the former, the statesman, has a number of circumstances to combine with those general ideas, and to take into his consideration. Circumstances are infinite, and infinitely combined; they are variable and transient. . . . A statesman, never losing sight of principles, is to be guided by circumstances; and judging contrary to the exigencies of the moment, he may ruin his country forever.[7]

It is indeed a lamentable but perhaps understandable phenomenon that philosophers and practitioners typically spend relatively little time addressing the concerns of the other: the former emphasize the importance of abstract principles, the latter emphasize the pressures of the moment. In responding to (and perhaps ameliorating) this failure to communicate, it is necessary to start by examining a set of facts and only then proceed to an assessment of the moral implications of those facts.

Of course, assembling such detail is only the first step in the enterprise, and in many, though not all, instances the easier part of the job. The tricky aspect of case studies in applied ethics is the development of the moral argument based on the details offered. This argument will depend in part, to be sure, on the facts presented but necessarily has to involve some sort of systematic ethical framework as well. The first two chapters of this essay are an attempt to suggest just such a working framework for analysis. Any effort of this sort should have as its goal the establishment of a set of general moral guidelines that can be adapted or applied to a special set of conditions. It is not supposed to be a catechism of rigid moral rules that says to the statesman, "Always do this regardless of the circumstances." Rather, it says, "If certain circumstances permit, you ought to do this." This definition of the "ethical framework," however, does not simply equate to unrestrained moral relativism, in which anything goes depending on the situation or perhaps special political or cultural environments. It does establish that there are moral principles that exist on their own terms and must rightly be reflected in each political judgment. The principal question is not whether they exist, but how and to what extent they can be realized in discrete situations. Applied ethics, in sum, deals with what the late scholar Arnold Wolfers once called "the best moral choice that circumstances permit," but it is ethics just the same.[8]

To accept that political leadership involves nonperfectionist ethics is also to suggest the need for prudence, modesty, and sometimes even compassion in assessing the moral conduct of statesmen. As we have already suggested, the student of applied ethics is not (or should not be) in the business of simply offering ex cathedra pontifications about how statesmen "should" behave, and how if necessary they must bend reality to conform to certain unchanging moral principles. This does not mean that there are not, occasionally, true villains who are running the affairs of a state and who deserve unambiguous condemnation. The history of the twentieth century provides an unfortunately ample roster of such individuals. It is to say, however, that even in our lamentable era the majority of statesmen deserve at least some understanding and benefit of the doubt from outside observers, academic or otherwise, who are critiquing their conduct. One is struck in particular by the essential tragedy of the statesman's position in many instances. No morally attractive alternatives present themselves, and the individual must weigh a formula essentially based on the lesser of two (or more) evils. Perhaps he or she takes some comfort in Machiavelli's comment that "the act may accuse but the result may excuse." Even so, the burden on individual conscience and self-image must at times be oppressive. Nobody escapes totally unscathed from the responsibilities of high public office.

It so happens that I have serious doubts about the moral justification of President Truman's ordering the atomic destruction of Hiroshima and Nagasaki. Even so, there is an interesting bit of information provided by Merle Miller in his oral history that casts a somewhat different light on Truman's action. Miller was perusing the president's private library one day and discovered that there was one whole section devoted to books about the atomic bomb. At the end of one of these books, the speech from Horatio in the last scene of *Hamlet* was reproduced:

> . . . let me speak to the yet unknowing world
> How these things came about: So shall you hear
> Of carnal, bloody, and unnatural acts,
> Of accidental judgements, casual slaughters,
> Of deaths put on by cunning and forced cause,
> And, in this upshot, purposes mistook
> Fall'n on the inventors' heads. . . .
> But let this same be presently perform'd,
> Even while men's minds are wild; lest more mischance,
> On plots and errors, happen.

The President had underlined the entire speech; he had underlined the last sentence twice.[9] What this suggests is that Truman's apparently indifferent public stance toward the moral issues presented by the bomb perhaps was not fully indicative of how he really felt about the matter, at least in the sanctuary of his own thoughts. Even if he did have private doubts, of course, they did not have much effect in sparing the citizens of Hiroshima or Nagasaki. Still, one of the prime requirements of moral statesmen is that they at least recognize and accept that a moral issue is presented by their actions. This acknowledgment of what Max Weber described as the "ethic of responsibility" may indeed be regarded as the first step on the road to appropriate moral conduct in statecraft.

PART I

THEORY

1

The General Problem of Dirty Hands

One of the more unprofitable—at times, even banal—aspects of contemporary writing on international affairs is the often fractious debate between the so-called "idealists" and "realists" as to the role of ethics in foreign policy. In its most extreme variation, the discussion is reduced to whether there is really anything to debate. When things reach this stage, the participants are, in effect, talking not to each other but past each other.

Both sides bear their own responsibility for this occasional "dialogue of the deaf." A good deal of commentary on foreign affairs by the "idealists" is characterized by a self-assurance that at times borders on arrogance. Sissela Bok offers a very apt description in this regard of what she calls the "moralizers," those who are "high-handed in the face of human complexity".[1] Their tendency is to belittle the genuinely difficult, even agonizing dilemmas that often face the policymaker. The primary emphasis instead is on establishing at the outset certain moral precepts as virtually self-evident, after which a (generally negative) verdict is passed on the degree to which the decisionmakers lived up to these moral absolutes. Much of the effort is spent on hunting and pecking through the details of the situation in order to find substantiation for certain moral conclusions already firmly held. The debate over the moral issues presented by the Vietnam War was a lamentable example of this phenomenon in action.[2]

The intellectual sins committed in that debate were not just confined to the idealists; the "realists" were guilty of their own over-simplifications. As a group they are often accused (sometimes justly) of assuming that

4 Conscience and Power

politics, and especially international politics, is a realm essentially immune to the claims of ethics, given the evident emphasis in foreign policy on power and violence and the protection of state interests. In making their arguments, the realists often seize (rather effectively) on simplistic analyses by the idealists as to what states or statesmen "should" do, and in the process they dismiss out of hand *any* connection between ethics and international affairs. In describing the discussions that took place among high government officials at the time of the Cuban missile crisis, former Secretary of State Dean Acheson exemplified this approach. He wrote that the emphasis was on an "appraisal of dangers and risks, the weighing of the need for decisive and effective actions against considerations of prudence. . . . Moral talk did not bear on the problem." In response to a colleague who did raise certain moral concerns, he stated that "on the Day of Judgment his view might be confirmed . . . [but] it was not a view which I could entertain as a public servant."[3]

This seems to be as close-minded an approach to the issue as that of the naïve idealists for whom Acheson had such disdain. Sometimes the pure realism of an Acheson is reinforced by the argument that, after all, all values are relative. What may be right for one culture may be considered irrelevant or even wrong by another. Thus the effort to establish universally accepted standards of human rights founders on the conflict between the socialist or Third World countries, who tend to regard social and economic values (such as full employment, guaranteed health, housing, and old-age benefits) as the essence of human rights, and the position of the Western industrial democracies, who may place more emphasis on political, religious, and civil liberties.

Certainly there is considerable difficulty in these terms in establishing a universally applicable theory of human rights. Nevertheless, the moral relativist argument seems, on final analysis, to be more of a denial of reality than an interpretation of it. Any reasonable examination of the world's cultures and main religious movements reveals a set of core values that transcend place and time, among them a need to give meaning to individual existence, pleasure and sometimes sorrow at family life, striving for security and freedom from want, and perhaps, above all, a sense of anticipated "proportionality" in which suffering will eventually produce some commensurate reward. From a somewhat different perspective, simply because a certain culture may regard a given practice as "ethical" does not make it so. Thus female infanticide was at one time (and to a limited extent is still) regarded by some cultures as an appropriate response to unwanted female births. That such a principle is accepted does not make it worthy of equal moral weight compared with more enlightened behavior. The point is that ethics is not merely a matter of subjective judgment: in the final analysis, it receives at least part of its definition from certain enduring, and intuitively identifiable, standards of conduct.

In practical terms, the influence of ethics on foreign policy takes three distinct forms. The values of the particular society that the foreign policy leadership is serving plays its own role in policymaking. There is also the impact of "international norms", that is, generally accepted standards of conduct in international relations, however tentative or uncertain. Finally, and for purposes of this essay most important, there is the "conscience" of the individual decisionmaker, those spurs to appropriate behavior that represent his or her internalized values and principles.[4] Except for the genuine psychopath (fortunately rare in international affairs), political leaders as a group presumably do have private voices speaking to them of good and evil. Assuming this to be the case, how do they square the unpleasant—and sometimes very unpleasant—things they have to do in their public lives with their consciences? Perhaps even more important, how do *we* as their subjects regard the matter? In short, what are we to make of the dirty hands of the politician?

It is striking in this respect how the notion that dirty hands is actually the prevailing and normal characteristic of political leadership, especially in foreign policy, is almost taken for granted by many people. Lord Acton put it more directly than most with his assertion that "all great men are also bad men." In part such an attitude may be a reflection of the prevailing cynicism that exists concerning political life, especially in the contemporary age. Many feel that the idea of a "moral politician" is an oxymoron, a contradiction in terms. Yet, as we have already observed, there is sometimes a rather less negative connotation here: not only do we not expect politicians to behave in accordance with standard definitions of morality but it may even be wrong to argue that they should do so. At first glance this seems to represent a startling paradox: Why should we allow, even endorse, our political leaders undertaking or tolerating behavior that we would reject in other circumstances? Why do we set for them a different standard of judgment than we do for ourselves?

Two assertions are typically advanced to spare top officials from the burden of moral judgment, to allow them a realm of "freedom from morality" that is supposedly their special preserve and even right. The first has to do with their identity as representatives of the "collective." The idea is that a social unit, especially a nation, has needs and demands that perforce require the leader to set aside any personal moral doubts he or she may have about either these needs themselves or the means necessary to attain them. In this sense the foreign policy leader is not a creature of free choice but rather the servant of the primordial demands of his or her constituency, whether they be for territorial security, economic advantage, religious or ideological influence, or whatever. If the leader feels uneasy with what is necessary to achieve these, or with the goals themselves, the only legitimate recourse is to stand down from leadership of the nation and pass authority on to someone with less delicate sensitivities.[5]

Another argument advances the special nature of the international system. It asserts that international relations is a peculiarly brutal and anarchic enterprise. Considerations of justice, fairness, or moderation that might be appropriate in dealing with domestic affairs have little if any place in confronting the realities of the world beyond one's shores. The English writer E. M. Forster put the point rather vividly:

> The man who is selling newspapers outside the Houses of Parliament can safely leave his papers to go for a drink and his cap beside them: anyone who takes a paper is sure to drop a copper into the cap. But the men who are inside the Houses of Parliament—they cannot trust one another like that, still less can the Government they compose trust other governments. No caps upon the pavement here.[6]

It was Machiavelli, however, who is perhaps best known for supplying the basic proposition. He cast scorn on those who dreamt of "imagined republics and principalities which have never been seen or known to exist in reality." As far as political leadership is concerned, Machiavelli argued, "a man who wishes to make a profession of goodness in everything must necessarily come to grief among so many who are not good. Therefore it is necessary for a prince, who wishes to maintain himself, to learn how not to be good, and to use this knowledge and not use it, according to the necessity of the case."[7]

The implications of such an argument are rather melancholy. They suggest that even the most well-meaning individual necessarily must set aside personal moral convictions in dealing with the grim realities of the world on behalf of the nation. Would that the world were a better place so that saints could direct the affairs of state. Since the world is not a better place, and indeed is a worse place than any but the most vivid imagination could conceive, effective leaders have to accept the essential tragedy of their position, which is that political power essentially *equates* with dirty hands. Not incidentally, they must also then accept the corruption of their own selves that accompanies this fact. As Max Weber put it, "Whoever wants to engage in politics at all . . . must know that he is responsible for what may become of himself under the impact of these paradoxes. . . . He lets himself in for the diabolical forces lurking in all violence. . . . Everything that is striven for through political action operating with violent means following an ethic of responsibility endangers the 'salvation of the soul.'"[8]

THE ISSUE CONSIDERED

Several questions immediately come to mind in weighing the notion of dirty hands. The first has to do with whether the conflict between public ("official") and private morality is really an issue at all. Is there actually any inherent contradiction between appropriate moral conduct in private life and the conduct of statesmen? In theory, there can only be two answers to this important query. Either the two moralities are really indistinguishable, or on the contrary the principles of the second cannot be derived from the first. The question has both an empirical and a prescriptive aspect, and may be raised either by us as citizens or by statesmen themselves. On the one hand, do we or they feel that such a tension exists? On the other hand, do we or they feel that such a tension *need* exist (assuming that the answer to the first question is yes)? Must statesmen indeed set aside their personal predilections as to appropriate moral conduct in order to serve the interests of the state?

The Right of Self-Sacrifice

Perhaps the ultimate test of this proposition involves a situation in which the statesman is convinced or persuaded that the position of another nation on a certain matter is actually more just than his or her own. This surely cannot be that unusual a phenomenon. Nobody but a fanatic would suggest that one's country is invariably in the right when a conflict with others develops. It hardly seems surprising or objectionable that the statesman involved may privately view others as holding the moral high ground on a particular issue; indeed, a person's capacity for doing so may be regarded as a mark of virtue. The far more contentious issue is whether the leader has the right to *act* on it, to translate this conviction into concessions to the other party even if so doing may deprive his or her own country of certain advantages (no matter how undeserved).

The German philosopher Immanuel Kant offered his own straightforward answer to this conundrum. He asserted that the truly moral politician must be willing to sacrifice state interests, even valuable state interests, in obeisance to a moral principle: "The natural right of men must be held sacred, regardless of how much sacrifice is required of the powers that be. [For] it is impossible to figure out a middle road, such as a pragmatically conditional right, between right and utility."[9] The realists, on the other hand, such as Hans Morgenthau, tend to dismiss such self-abnegation as contradictory to the essence of political leadership. As Morgenthau argues, "The moral problem of politics is posed by the inescapable discrepancy between the commands of Christian teaching, of Christian ethics, and the requirements of political success. It is impossible, if I may put it in somewhat extreme and striking terms, to be a successful politician and a good Christian."[10]

This may strike some (presumably Kant would have been one of them) as a rather curious approach to the definition and duties of a "good Christian." Nevertheless, it is not easily resolved. What is involved here is the perennial issue between "duties of station" and "duties of conscience." In our individual lives we may well sacrifice—at times, even be expected to sacrifice—our own comfort, income, or even our very existence in order to serve others. From the parable of the Good Samaritan to the universally admired figure of Mother Theresa, such behavior has been celebrated. But do statesman have the right to indulge in good works at the expense of their fellow citizens? Not surprisingly, it is not easy to identify specific historical cases in which a political leader openly admitted to sacrificing his or her own country's position to the morally superior claims of others. Such admissions, while apt to be praised by the moral philosopher, are not generally seen by those involved as likely to further their political popularity.

Perhaps one example that can be cited of the Kantian leader in operation involves Robert Kennedy's role during the Cuban Missile Crisis. In the early days of that crisis, a clear majority of the Executive Committee of the National Security Council (EXCOM), focusing simply on what was necessary for the security of the United States, favored a massive air strike, without warning, against the Soviet missile installations in Cuba. Robert Kennedy, in sharp disagreement, said that he did not want his brother to be seen as another Tojo (the Japanese prime minister at the time of the attack on Pearl Harbor). The United States, he said, had always eschewed the idea of surprise attacks against another country. Moreover, a great many innocent civilians would likely be killed as a result of an American air strike on Cuba and this in itself would not be in accord with American values (not to mention the rights of Cuban civilians). Evidently, in large part because of Kennedy's intervention on the matter, the EXCOM turned to a consideration of less drastic solutions to the problem of the missiles.[11]

Now it should be noted that Kennedy's argument was offered within the secrecy of the EXCOM's deliberations and that it only became known later. Moreover, he never went out of his way to make a public point concerning his ethical reservations about the air strike against Cuba, although he did discuss the matter in his brief memoir of the crisis.[12] Moreover, it could be argued from a pragmatic point of view that for the United States to undertake an unannounced air strike against the missile installations was actually not in this country's self-interest (particularly since there was no guarantee that all the missiles would actually be destroyed). Still, there was a feeling within EXCOM at one point that bombing the missile sites in Cuba was the preferred course of action, and the evidence suggests that Kennedy objected to it, at least in part, because of its violation of the legitimate and higher interests of others (that is, of Cuban civilians).

As it turned out, the United States was able both to do good and to do well in those tense days in October 1962. The option that was eventually chosen—a quarantine of Cuba—succeeded in getting the missiles out while sparing the lives of Cuban civilians. This suggests that oftentimes the challenge facing political leaders may not necessarily be an either/or one in which a decision to serve their country's interests means remaining indifferent to the just rights of others. There can be numerous occasions in which the statesman is confronted with alternative ways of securing his or her country's needs, and in such situations due consideration for the welfare of others may be regarded as a legitimate factor in policymaking. Even Morgenthau seems to accept this point: "To choose among several expedient actions the least evil one is moral judgment. [In this way] man reconciles his political nature with his moral destiny."[13]

Leaders and Led

Morgenthau's reference to "man's political nature" introduces yet another item for discussion. Consider the following comment from former president Jimmy Carter about morality and statecraft shortly before he assumed the presidency: "As it has related to such areas as Pakistan, Chile, Cambodia, and Vietnam, our government's foreign policy has not exemplified any commitment to moral principles. . . . A nation's domestic and foreign policy actions should be derived from *the same standards of ethics, honesty, and morality which are characteristics of the individual citizens of the nation.*"[14] There are two things of particular interest in this statement: Carter's dismissal of the notion that there was any real discrepancy between the demands of public and private morality, and his assertion that

"ethics, honesty, and morality" were in fact the distinguishing characteristics of the American citizenry.

Assume for the moment that we accept his first argument. Whether the
American people were indeed the repository of "ethics, honesty, and morality" then becomes a pretty important question, at least insofar as their elected
representatives are seen as simply reflecting their basic values. Depending
on one's response to this question, we might (ironically) have here a
stumbling block to Carter's optimistic vision of a moral foreign policy.
Suppose that the views of the masses *were* accurately reflected in the
behavior of their leaders, but that the morality of the general population was
not quite as elevated as Carter suggested. In this case, a flawed foreign policy
(at least in moral terms) would simply be symptomatic of the inadequate
ethical foundations of the nation's citizenry. On the other hand, perhaps the
nation's citizens were as principled as Carter suggested, yet the demands of
office were such that the president (whether Carter or anyone else) would
necessarily be forced to behave in ways that contradicted these ethics, that
is, he or she would have to accept having dirty hands.

It would be, in my view, an optimistic person indeed (maybe a fool-
hardy one) who would assume that the morals of the "people" are always
such that they constitute pressure on their leaders to behave in exemplary
ways. There are numerous examples in which the influence of public opinion
has not flowed in quite such beneficent channels. To take only one example,
the American government's refusal to admit large numbers of Jewish refu-
gees into the United States fleeing Nazi persecution in the late 1930s was
heavily conditioned by the general public hostility to such a program (one
public opinion poll ranked the Jews only behind the Germans and Japanese
as "threats" to the United States).[15]

At the same time, it does seem idle to suggest that statesmen can,
should, or will conduct themselves with precisely the same rectitude in public
life as they may display in private circumstances. Without going as far as
Lord Acton's comment about great men always being bad men (in their
unscrupulous political methods), the fact remains that individuals who
subject themselves to the stress and frequent indignities involved in climbing
the "greasy pole" toward great political power can hardly be considered
"normal" in any commonly accepted definition of the term. These individuals have an unusual lust for power; although such power may be sought in
order to do good, it is a lust just the same. It is inherent that in order to satisfy
this craving, the person involved will adopt a single-mindedness that is
foreign to the vast majority of their fellows. Such a focus on the attainment
of power implies a willingness to do all sorts of things to attain and keep that

power that most would find, at the least, uncomfortable and unpleasant. Moreover, we are all familiar with another aphorism from Lord Acton to the effect that power corrupts and absolute power tends to corrupt absolutely. Even if the degree of corruption may vary depending on individual character and goals, it is hard not to agree with Hazlitt's statement from "On the Spirit of Monarchy" that "he who has the greatest power put into his hands will only become the more impatient of any restraint in the use of it." High office, in fact, seems to be a peculiarly liberating or even intoxicating experience that can easily lead to a presumption that one is (or should be) free from normal standards of judgment or restraint as long as one is serving the public. To this extent, the existence of and willingness to have dirty hands does indeed seem implicit in the character of great leaders.

The Appeal to Necessity

Despite this truism, it is curious how defensive such leaders become when confronted with evidence of their dirty hands. They seem to have a compulsion for explaining away their apparent misdeeds. In the next chapter we will be considering in some detail the formal and informal excuses that politicians offer for getting their hands dirty (quite aside from the inherent tendency toward such a condition as a consequence of their ambition). At this point it might be appropriate to refer to one particular excuse because it raises some general theoretical questions central to this discussion.

At the outbreak of war in August 1914, the German chancellor, Theobold von Bethman Hollweg, made the following statement to the Reichstag concerning the violation of the neutrality of Belgium:

> Gentleman, we are now in a state of necessity, and necessity knows no law. Our troops have already entered Belgian territory.
>
> Gentleman, that is a breach of international law. . . . The wrong—I speak openly—the wrong we thereby commit we will try to make good as soon as our military aims have been attained.
>
> He who is menaced as we are and is fighting for his highest possessions can only consider how he is to hack his way through.[16]

Bethman Hollweg's mea culpa for the moral offense that his nation had committed can hardly be taken as a serious defense of an admitted wrong. Germany had a host of other possibilities open to it at the time that involved no serious threat to the nation and would have reflected the moral imperative to continue to respect the Belgium neutrality that the Reich had in fact agreed to for almost 100 years. What he was saying, however, is common enough in the parlance of statecraft, which attempts to explain away morally problematical actions by reference to the "law of necessity." The reason for regarding such an excuse with skepticism is that only rarely does a decision actually involve an absolutely vital interest of the state, for example, its very survival. The vast majority are considerably less dramatic, which in turn means that some *choice* is available without drastic harm to the nation. Moreover, as we have already noted, it is rare that any single alternative can clearly be identified as in the national interest. Typically there may be several possible interpretations of how to serve the nation's cause, and thus the individual conscience of the statesman may (rightly) tip a decision one way or the other.[17] This does not mean, of course, that the argument of necessity must always be spurious. Situations may indeed exist in which necessity forces a (temporary) setting aside of moral standards. The trick as always is to determine what constitutes such a situation and to separate the false from the real in this respect.

The question of necessity needs to be considered in terms of the classic levels-of-analysis issue in contemporary research on international politics. As first formulated by J. David Singer and elaborated on almost endlessly by subsequent writers, the argument is that we can explain or interpret decisionmaking in foreign policy from any one of three perspectives: systemic, national, or idiosyncratic.[18] In the first paradigm, states are no more than "billiard balls" (having the same basic characteristics) reacting to external pressures and behaving in relatively uniform ways, for example, by attempting to maintain a balance of power with their potential enemies. The second approach concentrates on the particular characteristics of different states, and argues that policymaking will vary depending on these characteristics, for example, democracies will be reluctant to make war whereas totalitarian countries will be prone to aggression. The idiosyncratic model, finally, argues that the identities and personalities of individual leaders or decisionmaking institutions are critical to policy outcomes.

Obviously none of these three approaches need be mutually exclusive. Different writers may place varying emphasis on each of the variables, but accept that each has its influence. For present purposes, however, the importance of the levels-of-analysis debate is in how it may effect our attitude toward dirty hands. To the extent that we tend toward a systemic approach to analyzing international relations, dirty hands fades into relative insignificance: *all* leaders in a given situation will react (or be forced to react) in approximately the same way, and thus it is idle to pretend that they have real moral choices. But the idiosyncratic paradigm is a lot more significant for dirty hands. If we accept the basic premise, leaders *do* have choices, and maybe in some variety. To this extent, we can hold them responsible for what they decide. They are not simply impersonal agents representing the state as "billiard ball," but have a range of opportunity and challenge. Between the systemic and the idiosyncratic approach to analyzing foreign policy lies the nation-state paradigm, which tends to emphasize the objective factors (such as geography or political system) of a particular community as well as its institutions, history, and social values in assessing the conduct of its leaders.

All this may seem like the usual wearying social science jargon, but there is an important substantive point that underlies the abstractions. It has to do with how much credit we give to the very plea of necessity. The first two "levels-of-analysis" argue that such a claim ought to be taken very seriously, either because leaders are simply reacting to the international system in which they must operate or because they are compelled to reflect closely the value and other demands of their own constituency. If we have reservations about either of these approaches, however, then quite a different environment of moral evaluation emerges. For whatever it is worth, the premise (or perhaps the bias) of the current study is that political leaders do normally have a good deal of latitude in foreign policy, and for a variety of reasons, not least among them being their constituency's relative lack of interest in or expertise on international politics. More fundamental is the general philosophical proposition that little in individual or state affairs is predetermined, and that the concept—and availability—of choice is central to any morally significant view of our existence. The plea of necessity, in short, is treated here as only a very limited and often quite unconvincing excuse for morally problematical decisions.

WHOSE DIRTY HANDS?

Taking such a position obviously implies a somewhat stiffer standard in our judging of dirty hands, but there does remain the nettlesome problem of actual responsibility. Assuming that we can identify an ethically indefensible action, on whom should we focus an accusing glare? The problem of dirty hands would be a lot simpler if we could identify in every case whose hands are actually soiled. In actuality, the complexity of many political decisions, especially in foreign policy, often makes it difficult to figure out to whom we ought to assign blame (or credit). It is a curious phenomenon that the legal heads of state or government often go out of their way to pronounce that "the buck stops here" and that whatever good or ill may have resulted from a particular policy, they accept full responsibility for it. In some instances, this may represent an admirable willingness actually to accept responsibility. In many other cases, however, it represents only a subtle type of *denial* of responsibility and, more than that, an attempt to protect a political position.

Rote expressions of responsibility for an action may be offered amidst other language that suggests that actually the policy adopted was a complex one that bore the imprint of many hands. A heroic statement that despite this fact "I alone am accountable" for the initiation and outcome of the policy—given my political status—is calculated to arouse admiration for the probity of one's behavior and bona fides. In the case of policies that have gone badly awry, this amounts to a case of having one's cake and eating it too. President Kennedy was privately bemused by the fact that public opinion polls gave him the highest approval rating of his administration immediately following the disastrous Bay of Pigs invasion. In this instance, however, Kennedy was presumably receiving credit for the graceful way in which he accepted full responsibility for the operation ("victory has a hundred fathers, defeat is an orphan"), even though it had been initiated and developed by the preceding administration and strongly pushed on him by the CIA.

Despite the pretense (or hypocrisy) that may attend the question of multiple dirty hands, the issue still remains a serious one. According to a traditional or hierarchical model, moral responsibility for dubious conduct properly lies with the person who has ultimate power of command or authority. Others may advise, or carry out instructions, but it is that person who has the keys to the kingdom who must eventually stand in judgment.[19] As Weber says, "The honor of the political leader . . . lies precisely in an exclusive political responsibility for what he does, a responsibility he cannot and must not reject or transfer."[20] Despite the comforting precision of such a formula, however, it hardly conforms to the realities of modern political systems and, more important, to the development of a system of moral judgment. Leaders, to be sure, always bear their share of credit or blame for what has been done, but the range of input into important policy judgments is such that other hands have to be legitimately considered as well.

Take the case of political advisers. When things go wrong, it is not an uncommon occurrence (and indeed is almost to be expected) that some advisers will discreetly or more openly adjure moral responsibility for what has happened since they were only "making suggestions" to their masters, and that it was they who made the actual bad decisions. Yet in many instances the formulation of the message contains an implicit, and sometimes not so implicit, suggestion that there is only one appropriate course for their superiors to follow. In this instance, the adviser has in effect crossed over into the realm of the policymaker, at least to the extent that the boss is left with few or no attractive alternatives to what the adviser is arguing for. Hobbes identified the duties of a legitimate counselor as one devoted to "true reasoning" in contrast to those who "vehemently pressed . . . common passions and opinions."[21] The point is that the statement of the factual background, the available choices open to the decisionmaker, and the pragmatic and even moral consequences of adopting differing alternatives establishes parameters for choice by the leader that inevitably—and rightly—opens the adviser to examination in terms of moral responsibility. In particular, they place that individual within the causal chain that produced the morally problematical decision.

We can bring all this down to earth by considering two specific cases. The first involves the role that Professor Walt Rostow played in decisions on the Vietnam War. Rostow was never a "line officer" with specific responsibilities for operational matters. He first served on the State Department's Policy Planning Staff and later became National Security Adviser to President Lyndon Johnson. For those offering a moral query against the Vietnam War, Rostow—given his roles—might well escape much inspection. In reality, his moral responsibility for Vietnam would have to be regarded as considerable. So convinced was he of the essential correctness of American policy that he carefully concealed from President Johnson negative information on the course of the war or the views of dissenters. He even went so far as to edit telegrams coming in from the American mission in Saigon, as well as intelligence assessments from the CIA, to make them more congenial to Johnson's (and his) view of the prospects for success in the struggle. Now it was certainly President Johnson himself who issued the orders that escalated the war and caused so much suffering. Like a shadow over his shoulder, however, Rostow was ever in the background. Can we say that he should remain free from moral examination even as his boss was subject to the ethical denunciation of the critics?[22]

Then there is the case of Professor F. A. Lindemann, later Lord Cherwell, the principal scientific adviser to Winston Churchill in World War II, and in particular on matters having to do with British bombing of German cities. The adoption of what came to be called "area bombing" in early 1942 resulted over the course of the war in the death of over 500,000 German civilians, the serious wounding of another million, and the destruction of about three million homes. British area bombing has been widely condemned since the war as a morally offensive blurring of the legitimate distinction between combatant and non-combatant in wartime.[23] It is instructive in this regard to recall Lindemann's role in British bombing policy, for which Churchill was later to receive so much criticism.

In a famous minute to the British prime minister on March 30, 1942, Cherwell concentrated on the impact on German morale of a major British area bombing campaign. Based on his analysis of the German bombing of British cities, he argued that "having one's house demolished is most damaging to morale. People seem to mind it more than having their friends or even relatives killed." He went on to estimate that, with adequate resources and by concentrating on the 58 major German population centers, Bomber Command could by 1943 render a third of the German people homeless. "There seems little doubt that this would break the spirit of the people." The concept of the shattering of the German people's morale, and thus of Germany's will or ability to continue the war, was enshrined henceforth as one of the guiding premises of British bombing policy. As the official history of Bomber Command puts it, "Because of the position which he occupied and the time at which he submitted his minute, Lord Cherwell's intervention was of great importance. It did much to insure the concept of strategic bombing in its hour of crisis."[24]

At the time of Cherwell's minute, Churchill was going through some considerable doubts about the wisdom of the city-bombing of Germany. At the same time, he had great respect for Cherwell's acumen, and as the official history says, he seems to have been greatly influenced by Cherwell's advice on bombing policy. It is important to note that Cherwell's "scientific" calculations on the effects of city-bombing were disputed by a number of other prominent British scientists, but he nevertheless continued to have an almost fanatical intuitive belief in the efficacy of such bombing. As it happened, he was able to deflect the doubts of others and persuade Churchill of the soundness of his views. If we are to criticize the morality of British bombing of German cities, then, should not Cherwell be as open to condemnation as Churchill, even if the latter had the formal power of command?

Both the Rostow and the Cherwell cases, in any event, suggest the complexity inherent in identifying where dirty hands may lie, and how we evaluate the degree of culpability for such hands. As it happens, the noted scientist Freeman Dyson had his own answer to this question. During World War II, Dyson worked for the British Royal Air Force in the area of operations research. He was a scientific analyst for Bomber Command, and thus had extensive knowledge of the strategy behind British air strikes against Germany. Dyson's description of his contribution to the British war effort is rather striking: "I felt sickened by what I knew. Many times I decided I had a moral obligation to run out into the streets and tell the British people what stupidities were being done in their name. But I never had the courage to do it. I sat in my office until the end, carefully calculating how to murder most economically another hundred thousand people."[25]

His mea culpa extends even further than this. He recalls reading reports after the war about the men who had worked in the Adolf Eichmann organization, and admits that he had a certain sympathy for these individuals. "Probably many of them loathed the SS as much as I loathed Bomber Command," Dyson reflected, "but they, too, had not had the courage to speak out." When it came down to it, the main difference between his work and that of Eichmann's operatives "was that they were sent to jail or hanged as war criminals, while I went free."[26] This is about as dramatic, or, as some would suggest, overly-dramatic a description of the responsibility of an adviser as we are likely to get. In any case, Dyson's lament reinforces the earlier point that in trying to establish the location of dirty hands, we may have to do more than simply focus on those at the top level of decisionmaking.

The Responsibility of Society

For some, this requires a look not just at the formal institutions of government but at the broader community that that government represents. We discussed earlier President Carter's assertion that American foreign policy would be morally sound to the extent that it reflected the basic values of the American people. Whether or not American society can be regarded as the repository of special virtue is an issue in itself, but the question of the complicity of a community in the actions of its leaders stands as a matter worthy of general consideration.

It would seem important in this regard to distinguish between political leadership in democratic as opposed to authoritarian societies. The main distinction is that the former supposedly have an overall writ for their actions and to this extent perhaps should be considered less liable for condemnation when they dirty their hands. After all, they have been put into office through popular selection, and the public (perhaps more in parliamentary than presidential systems) continues to exercise some supervision over their activities. If cruel deeds are then performed by democratic politicians, can their guilt be said to be greater than those who elected them and continue to support them? Perhaps the main instance in which a clear divide can be established between the moral responsibility of leader and led concerns policies that involve secrecy, deception, or disinformation. In such a case, one might argue, the people cannot be considered to be complicit in the action since they had no knowledge of it and thus could not have approved of it, even indirectly.[27] The bombing of Cambodia by the Nixon administration during the latter phases of the Vietnam War has been widely criticized as an abuse of American power, but the fact is that this policy was carefully concealed from the American public, perhaps because Nixon and those around him feared that it would be condemned if openly announced.[28] In any event, Nixon's dirty hands over Cambodia would seem in this case to be uniquely his own, and to the extent that the policy may be justifiably criticized, such criticism should properly attach to him alone.

The innocence of a democratic society in the committing of wicked acts by their leaders involving secrecy can be taken too far, however. In selecting their politicians, it would seem morally incumbent on the electorate to give due attention to the general character and tendencies of the individual in question, particularly since it is unlikely that in a modern and complex political system the citizenry will have full knowledge of everything that is being done in its name (meaning that it cannot give its approval or dissent to every individual action). Take, for example, Hitler's program for the extermination of the European Jews. This policy was held in the closest confidence among the Nazi leadership, and consequently a defense is sometimes offered for the German people that they can hardly be blamed for the Final Solution since they did not have any specific knowledge of it. On the other hand, Germany was a reasonably functioning democratic system in 1932 when the Nazis emerged as the largest single party in the Reichstag with Hitler as their leader and soon to be the German Chancellor. Hitler was on record both in his speeches and in his writings (notably *Mein Kampf*) as being a fanatical anti-Semite who considered a "solution" to the "Jewish question" as a prime goal of his ideology. It is unlikely that if the German people had been presented with a clear choice on the physical extermination of the Jews that they would have given a majority assent to such a program. But the overall direction of Hitler's thinking was such that at least a substantial degree of moral responsibility for the Final Solution would seem to be properly assignable to the general German population for putting Hitler into power in the first place, even if they remained generally unaware of the details of this particular atrocity.

The Possibility of Judgment

None of what we have said above is meant to suggest that it is not possible, at least for purposes of moral judgment, to identify a certain individual or individuals as having meaningful responsibility for a particular action. The difficulty that sometimes arises in locating such responsibility leads some essentially to abandon the hunt. They either posit that *all* members of a particular government, in whatever capacity, have to bear responsibility for that government's policies, or they go even farther and suggest that the collective that the government serves has equal culpability for evil actions. In either case, no single individual bears *special* responsibility for such actions; the existence of dirty hands is part of a seamless web.[29]

To adopt such an approach is essentially to abandon the very concept of dirty hands. If all are guilty, then none are guilty, at least insofar as the prospect of some meaningful sanction for dirty hands is concerned or even the very concept of responsibility. How do we punish an entire government or society? The result can only be a type of moral anarchy in which ethical judgment concerning political conduct becomes impossible in any meaningful sense. In actuality, there are two criteria that can be used to identify the special moral responsibility of certain actors within the context of a given policy.

The first of these has to do with whether the individual's acts—either of commission or omission—were a direct cause of a particular political outcome, and the second with whether these acts were a result of either ignorance or compulsion. In the first instance, we must establish that the outcome would not have taken the form it did save for the individual's decisions (or lack of same). In the second, the premise is that the individual is responsible to the degree that he or she could have done otherwise. The former basically sets out a threshold of responsibility; the latter is important in determining *degrees* of responsibility. These principles, to be sure, are only general guidelines, and they must accommodate a number of specific problems, including the politician's usual appeal to the force of necessity in his or her decisionmaking. At the very least, employing the two criteria demands that we be as specific as possible in examining the circumstances of a given action. That it may often be quite complicated to determine these circumstances, however, does not mean that such a task is beyond doing.

2

The Judging of Dirty Hands

The assertion that dirty hands is an inherent feature of political leadership cannot be easily set aside. Indeed we have already accepted that it stands as a convincing proposition concerning some aspects of the world of statecraft. Despite President Carter's optimism on the matter, it is hard to feel that leaders of nations can apply exactly the same moral standards to their activities as public servants as they do in their own private lives. Yet the essential argument of this essay is that the dirty hands construct represents only a partial truth about the duties and, even more, the opportunities of statesmen. The public and private realms are indeed different, but that does not mean they are totally unconnected. The real challenge is to establish what special moral principles may rightly be applied to public life in contrast with more intimate circumstances. Even Machiavelli, in our earlier quote, recognized that a knowledge of how "not to be good" should sometimes *not* be used (or need not be used) depending on the circumstances of the case.

In examining the issues presented by the conflict between private and public morality, however, it bears repeating that we have to go beyond essentially sterile observations about the "agony" of power, or the dilemmas of trying to do good in an imperfect world. There is a need for a more detailed set of standards by which we can judge specific political actions. Assuming that a tension between public and private morality is indeed an inevitable accompaniment of statecraft, how is this conflict to be resolved or assessed? In particular, under what circumstances can we deem legitimate the statesman's plea that he or she had to *set aside* personal moral convictions because of the overriding demands of the state?

In considering the latter scenario, it is important to be alert to those situations in which the *private* morality of statesmen is quite reprehensible in itself. This may mean that these leaders' public acts are no more than reflections of their flawed personal ethics. In this instance, the individuals involved may attempt to disguise how reprehensible they really are by arguing that their more visible public conduct has been forced on them by force of (political) circumstances. In such a case, however, the tension inherent in the general problem of dirty hands hardly exists. The latter assumes the rectitude of private conduct, and thus sets aside cases such as Hitler, Stalin, or Saddam Hussein, for whom there is amply documented evidence of quite repugnant individual personalities who behaved as brutally in more intimate circumstances as in their public life.

For purposes of this essay, such cases are of relatively little interest. It is hardly a breakthrough in analysis to suggest that generally evil people produce evil policies. The far more important question, certainly a far more compelling one, is how "good" people may wind up being responsible for evil policies (or policies that at least have evil side effects). Given our basic premise that political leaders (especially in international relations) will indeed have dirty hands on occasion by virtue of their position, the further premise is that there are certain circumstances in which this may be morally justifiable whereas there are other situations in which a moral defense is much more problematical. In arriving at a judgment as to whether a specific manifestation of dirty hands is only a regrettable but understandable function of a leader's position, or, on the contrary, an abuse of his or her power, I would suggest that three factors are of special importance.

CRITERIA FOR EVALUATION

Intuitive Values

The first of these has to do with what may be called the "intuitive values" or ethical first principles of the leader. An intuitive value judgment regards a certain action as intrinsically wrong (or right) regardless of its effects, and reflects the pure dictates of conscience.[1] Even given the heavy responsibilities of leadership, one has the right to suggest that there are inherent differences between various ends and means in policy, and that some are inherently more ethical than others. Saint Thomas Aquinas defined proper intuitive values for the statesman as "a correct appreciation of an ultimate principle assumed as self-evident." The whole foundation of moral statecraft, he argued, rested on this "insight or understanding."[2] In somewhat broader language, we can describe intuitive values as a set of principles, guidelines to action, or general moral temperament (such as a commitment to compassion, truth, justice, honor, or courage) that argues against the adoption of certain policies or, on the contrary, is an *inducement* for adopting certain policies.

Assessing the intuitive values of political leaders becomes particularly important when the practical effects of their actions turn out to be (at least partially) bad ones. In such instances, an appropriate set of bona fides may shield them from our condemnation in a way that might not obtain in the absence of such values. Take, for example, the virtues of truthfulness or candor on the part of the politician. An honest expression, from the beginning, of his or her calculations and expectations may well provide him or her a certain benefit of the doubt when things go wrong. Clearly, one of the reasons that President Lyndon Johnson became such a target of moral criticism during the Vietnam War was that he systematically concealed his real intentions and methods in conducting that struggle. When the war went badly, few were inclined to be generous with him given his previous record of dissimulation.

In its purest form, the claim that behavior—whether political or otherwise—should be governed by certain immutable values or principles is called deontological ethics (or sometimes intuitionism). Deontology, or the "science of duty," asserts that certain acts are morally obligatory regardless of their practical outcomes, and that they may be intuitively identified. To some degree, therefore, a full-fledged deontological definition of ethical behavior rests on an essentially nonrational foundation that asserts a priori that some things are good and some are bad. In this sense, such principles are in themselves underivative and independent, that is, they do not flow out of other propositions nor are they subject to empirical tests of their positive effects. The admonition "let justice be done though the heavens fall" summarizes the basic credo. Kant is perhaps the best-known spokesman for deontological ethics. He went so far as to argue that it would be illegitimate to tell a lie even if this would save another person's life. A variation on deontology is what is called "rule utilitarianism." This asserts that a primordial moral principle has to be first defended in terms of its beneficent effect on the human condition. This nod to utilitarianism, however, does not mean that any subsequent violation of the moral principle can be defended in utilitarian terms.[3]

For purposes of this essay, the appeal of deontology, while tempting, provides an inadequate basis on which to judge the actions of statesmen. When all the philosophical abstractions are set aside, it seems almost impossible to offer a convincing model for judging political dirty hands on the basis that the leader must *always* do this or that regardless of its practical consequences. In the real world of affairs, as opposed (perhaps) to individual life, the people being studied hardly seem to have such latitude in their actions, nor should they have such latitude. Another problem with deontology that bears directly on the topic at hand is that "basic principles" may conflict with one another—for example, respect for human life versus respect for freedom—and may require that choices be made between or among principles. As the philosopher Peter Singer states, deontologists attempt to extricate themselves from this dilemma "by finding ever more complicated and more specific rules which do not conflict with each other, or by ranking the rules in some hierarchical structure to resolve conflicts between them."[4] The basis for making such choices, however, would logically seem to involve some standard of utilitarianism.

This is not to dismiss, however, the importance of intuitionism or deontological ethics in judging dirty hands. Hans Morgenthau once suggested that standards of morality in foreign policy in the nineteenth century were higher than in the twentieth because there was an interlocking set of elites with similar value systems. Many, if not most, came from approximately similar upper-class or aristocratic backgrounds, and felt a certain obligation to the observance of moral norms common to this class of individuals. Morgenthau regretted the "democratization" of foreign policy leadership in the twentieth century to the extent that it had destroyed this unifying element. There is no doubt an element of truth in Morgenthau's proposition, even though it was patently elitist in character and rather dismissive about the possibility of ethical leadership in our own time.[5] One piece of self-evident wisdom that is suggested by his analysis, in any case, is that in the age of democratic foreign policy, it is important to elect or choose "good people" rather than bad to lead our affairs.

One example of the proper influence of intuitive values in operation may be taken from the practice of war: the slaughter of innocents, that is to say, of noncombatants, may rightly be regarded as an evil in itself quite aside from whatever utilitarian calculations may be advanced for the necessity of violating this principle. A moral leader in wartime, thus, is one who constantly has the protection of innocents as a major consideration. Even more than this is the general sanctity of life itself: it is an intuitive requirement that leaders conduct military operations in such a way that not only their own troops but even those of the enemy suffer the least harm consistent with the search for victory. Enemies in uniform—just as enemy noncombatants—do not lose all of their rights. It cannot be said that they are subject to idle or vengeful slaughter simply because they are the enemy. This principle is also widely accepted. It accounts for the standard injunction that enemy prisoners of war are entitled to certain basic protections, even though their murder might actually be of some military utility to their opponent. In passing moral judgment on leaders in wartime, therefore, a first test is the degree to which they display an appropriate commitment to and awareness of the intuitive values discussed above. Such a test, for example, helps us to assess the ethics of a Napoleon Bonaparte, who is said to have boasted to Metternich that he could afford to "spend" 30,000 men a month. Also relevant was his comment that "I do not care a fig for the lives of a million men."[6] Whatever his other qualities, this virtual moral nihilism disqualifies (or should disqualify) Napoleon from our admiration.

It is important to stress that the expression—indeed the existence—of an individual's intuitive values has an impact and can be identified mainly in terms of their "nonenforceability." The basic concept was conveyed by a certain Lord Moulton of Bank, a nineteenth-century British parliamentarian, writing in the twilight of his career. In an essay for *The Atlantic* published in July 1924, Moulton distinguished among "three great domains of human action." The first was governed by "positive law," standards established by the lawmakers and enforced by the coercive power of the state. A second arena of conduct involved the "domain of free choice," such as the choice of a marriage partner, in which the law had no voice and the individual enjoyed complete freedom. Finally, there was a domain in which adherence to standards could not be compelled but in which obligations were nevertheless recognized and accepted ("the obedience of a man to that which he cannot be forced to obey [but where he is] the enforcer of the law upon himself"). In a compelling conclusion, Lord Moulton asserted that "the real greatness of a nation, its true civilization, is measured by the extent of . . . obedience to the unenforceable."[7]

In the realm of foreign policy, there are various treaties, conventions, international rules, and customary norms that can reasonably be identified and described as formal strictures governing the conduct of statesmen. To be sure, they may not be enforceable in the same way that domestic legal precepts are, but they exist nonetheless, particularly since their violation may in fact involve some sort of international sanction. The concept of intuitive values, however, goes beyond such international standards and is wider in content. It embraces those forms of conduct that may or may not be subsumed under currently accepted principles of, say, international law but which we can reasonably regard as important in arriving at a moral judgment on the behavior of the individual statesman. The point is that moral conduct in foreign policy is not just (or only) a matter of adherence to what may be fairly narrow positivist standards of international conduct. The argument may even be offered that, in certain circumstances, following such standards may itself be morally problematic, for example, a rigid adherence to respecting state sovereignty even when the state in question is committing great crimes against its own people. Historian Robert McElroy is almost certainly right when he says that "one cannot automatically assume that the policy option indicated by an international moral norm is the morally correct policy option."[8]

Consequentialism

A focus on the intuitive values of politicians means that we judge them not just in terms of how much they "accomplish" in the world of affairs, but also in terms of what means they have adopted to achieve their ends, and what the character of those ends themselves has been. Implicit in such a standard, for example, is the idea that sometimes the pursuit of worldly success must be sacrificed to respect for certain moral principles. Utilitarian or (more broadly) consequentialist standards are, however, important in their own right in judging the ethics of leaders. As one study puts it, "awareness of the consequences of one's actions seems a necessary if not sufficient condition for moral conduct. . . . The principle seems [especially] beyond dispute for public officials deciding important policy issues. Officials have a duty to anticipate the important consequences of policies they advocate or implement."[9] We have a right to expect from this perspective that statesmen will examine all possible alternatives in dealing with a policy problem, and, more than this, make a careful assessment of the likely positive outcomes of certain actions balanced against their negative side effects. The moral statesman is thus a person who not only means well but does well—or at least as well as possible, taking into account the constraints facing him or her.

    It may be observed that in discussing the consequentialist standard for ethical political action, there may arise cases in which the refusal to adopt a certain "immorality" may in itself be (in consequentialist terms) an immoral act. This of course is the central issue in the argument between Creon and his daughter in *Antigone,* and it can raise some perplexing questions. The demands of moral utilitarianism may indicate, for example, that one has to sacrifice the rights of a certain group for the larger welfare of the many. Such a step is justified, according to utilitarian theory, "if it produces as much or more of an increase in the happiness of all affected by it than any alternative action, and wrong if it does not."[10] Certainly there are many situations in the mundane circumstances of peacetime to which this rule applies, for example, the principle of the progressive income tax. In the far more stressful environment of war, the principle becomes even more compelling. Thus 60,000 casualties were accepted by the British government on the first morning of the Battle of the Somme in 1916 in order to deal a blow to German militarism, which was seen as a threat to all that the British held near and dear. In this instance the immorality of imposing such suffering on the British soldier was (it could be argued) outweighed by the contribution such suffering made to protecting the welfare of the entire British nation. In effect, British leaders made (or thought they had to make) a choice between two moral standards in order to achieve what they saw as the higher moral good.

In some ways, an attention to consequences may seem like a fairly commonplace injunction. Certainly most, if not all, leaders do consider different ways of achieving their goals, and pick the course of action that seems best calculated to contribute to the desired end. In the case of international relations, however, the consequentialist principle has a special application. Decisions taken in this realm are often going to result not just in grumbles from some dissatisfied interest group but in considerable human suffering, even (in wartime) death and destruction. It is thus that the principle of proportionality intrudes itself. Simply put, this requires that for any given action taken in a (presumably) just cause, the positive returns from that action must outweigh the evil side effects that it may produce. This standard is particularly germane to those inclined to pursue one moral good at the expense of all others, which may lead to a situation in which "the best becomes the enemy of the good," that is, the *net* moral return from the actions undertaken is less than could have been achieved.

To be sure, the principle of proportionality is often a difficult one to apply in practice, particularly in establishing a set of criteria for judging relatively better or relatively worse outcomes. How *much* of a contribution does a specific action have to make to a just cause in order to counterbalance certain evil side effects? How do we define what *are* "evil side effects"? In the special case of war, the second question is perhaps more easily answered. On an intuitive basis, all human death or suffering is ipso facto an evil effect. The issue thus becomes how one can choose actions that are productive or necessary in the search for victory while at the same time limiting death or suffering as much as possible. From a somewhat different perspective, the standards of utility require that if the latter is to be great, the value of the former must be pronounced and unmistakable.

Even in the case of warfare—but especially in less violent circumstances—there is another complication that intrudes in judging the actions of statesmen from a consequentialist perspective. What time frame is appropriate in arriving at a final evaluation? It is an obvious but important point that what may seem like a morally defensible decision in the short run may prove to be a lamentable one in the longer term. Thus certain steps taken to bring Allied victory in World War II—for example, the dropping of the atomic bomb on Hiroshima—might well be defended as ethically sound in terms of their immediate effect, that is, the saving of both American and even Japanese lives (assuming that this action ended the war sooner than might otherwise have happened). From a more extended perspective, however, the use of atomic weapons against Japan might easily be regarded as having introduced a dolorous precedent into international relations that outweighed whatever short-term good it achieved. If this dilemma applies in times of war, it is hardly less prevalent in peacetime. A standard example concerns the offering of food aid by the developed countries to the Third World. Such assistance meets the immediate problems of a potentially starving population, but in the longer term also tends to disrupt the economics of the local agricultural production system, which is ultimately the best guarantor of a reasonable food supply for the country's population.[11]

Even having said all this, however, it remains that judging the morality of statesmen has to depend, at least in part, on weighing not just their bona fides but also the actual outcomes of even well-meant decisions made by them.[12] In suggesting a consequentialist standard for the evaluation of political morality, what we are really asserting is what Alberto Coll calls the "tradition of normative prudence." Such a tradition argues that the melding of politics and moral principles is hardly a vain enterprise, even though it does present its special difficulties. "Normative prudence" does, however, require some special qualities on the part of statesmen. It dictates an ability to make discriminating judgments between the achievable and the utopian in the practice of politics, that is, in the actual selection of political goals. Just as important is the choice of the means to attain just ends. In making decisions on both these matters, the statesman who displays normative prudence will recognize the inherent difficulty of choosing a particular policy that will maximize the moral good, and be alert to the ever-threatening paradox that one may set out to do good and end up by doing bad. He or she will control his or her (perhaps irrational) impulses to move in one direction or another without adequate consideration of the connection between proposed means and anticipated ends. Above all, the tradition of normative prudence asserts that in achieving a moral politics, it is not enough simply to put "good and decent" people into power. The intuitive values of such individuals are a necessary prerequisite to ethical conduct in politics, but they are not in themselves sufficient to attain such an outcome. Close reasoning on cause and effect, on the possible and the improbable, and on the actual impact of given policies constitute equally important aspects of moral statesmanship.[13]

From this perspective, the classical notion of the "virtues" provides a critical guide in judging the morality of statecraft. The statesman possessed of such virtue will demonstrate a capacity to set aside pressures from those seized with a fever for immediate but inadequately considered action, to mute his or her own temptation toward the decisive (although perhaps disastrous) step, and to steadily insist on a cool consideration of the positive and negative aspects of a given course of conduct. The concept of prudence is, once again, inevitably linked to the classical definition of political virtue. Prudence in this sense does not simply mean a focused attention on what is good for one's own selfish interests or even for those of the community that one represents, but for all those for whom one's decisions may have an impact. Such a demonstration of virtue requires a close appreciation of the details of a particular situation, and an equal appreciation of the various consequences likely attendant on different courses of action.[14]

To ignore or set aside such considerations is to invite a legitimate condemnation of the statesman as lacking in moral stature. Edmund Burke regarded prudence as a general virtue but especially compelling in the realm of politics, where it was the "first of virtues." He went on to spell out his criteria for the virtuous leader, especially in times of great crisis or peril for the nation: "To dare to be fearful, when all about you are full of presumption and confidence, and when those who are bold at the hazard of others would push your caution and disaffection, is to show a mind prepared for its trial."[15]

Universalization

There is a third test that may be applied in the moral evaluation of political leaders, although it may be argued that it has somewhat less force than the other two. A standard philosophical principle in establishing moral conduct is the requirement of "universalization." This means that the action undertaken must reflect an appropriate sensitivity to the interests of *all* concerned parties—not just one's own personal interests, or those of the special community one represents.[16] Such a standard, as noted, is in itself an aspect of the concept of political prudence. Real ethics in this sense demands that the statesman adopt, at least in some measure, the role of the "impartial spectator" or the "Ideal Observer," and in so doing accept that "the justification of an ethical principle cannot be in terms of any partial or sectional group. Ethics takes a universal form."[17] What is right (or necessary) for me is equally so for all others. What is implicitly involved here is Kant's famous categorical imperative, which dictates that one should "act only on that maxim whereby thou canst at the same time will that it should become a universal law."

In its most pronounced form, the concept of universalization equates to what is called "cosmopolitan" ethics, in which the inalienable rights of each human being, regardless of nationality, is (or should be) the primary focus of all political action.[18] Each person is an equal member of the world community, and has their own rights and duties. Kant in these terms spoke of an ethic in which "the duties of virtue apply to the entire human race [and] the concept of ethical commonwealth is extended ideally to the whole of mankind."[19] The inherent rationale for the principle of universalization is its role in contributing to an ultimate sense of personal self-worth and even happiness, which in turn requires a connection to a larger purpose and a larger community beyond self. At the same time, the concept of universalization may be at least partly based on straightforward prudential considerations as well. By considering the effects of one's actions in their totality, one may contribute to a more positive or stable collective environment that in itself will benefit the specific community that one represents.

The requirement of universalization, or of the categorical imperative, of course presents complications when we consider the conduct of states as opposed to that of individuals. Some would assert the relevance of these concepts to individual life while at the same time doubting whether they really apply to the life of collectives, given the semi-anarchic and self-interested character of international politics. Even if we partially concede the point, however, it seems reasonable to suggest that, by definition, a leader of great moral authority will attempt to go beyond an exclusive focus on the narrow interests of his or her own society and give at least some attention to the broader welfare of the international community as such. This does not mean that the very life and future of one's country has to be mortgaged to the welfare of others; it does imply that there are numerous situations in which a little less for me means a great deal more for others, and there is considerable moral imperative for recognizing such situations and designing appropriate policies as a result.

Take, once again, the challenge to the statesman presented by a state of war. Even in wartime, the enemy population still retains certain rights and interests that require attention. To be sure, it seems reasonable to suggest that these may rightly be regarded as less compelling than the rights and interests of one's own soldiers and civilians, or those of allied nations. Yet they hardly disappear even in the carnage of war. The idea that the welfare of even the enemy should be a subject of concern inevitably rests (as we have already argued) on the premise that there is no essential difference between sides in the sanctity of life. If this applies even in terms of the treatment of enemy soldiers, the principle seems especially important in balancing the welfare of, say, one's own combatants with that of the enemy civilian population who are not combatants. By what moral calculus can we say that the death and injury of enemy civilians is essentially irrelevant as long as there is at least some prospect that such suffering will marginally reduce the danger to one's soldiers? Merely because a state of war exists does not remove the legitimate claims of enemy civilians for a reasonable chance to go on living. In order to protect such rights, it may be necessary for one's soldiers to accept—and perhaps be ordered to accept—a somewhat higher degree of risk (no one is demanding that they simply be directed to sacrifice themselves for the sake of enemy non-combatants).

Aristotle stressed this imperative in listing "sympathetic understanding" as a prime requisite for moral statesmanship: "To say that a person has good judgment in matters of practical wisdom implies . . . that he has sympathetic understanding; for equitable acts are common to all good men in their relation with someone else."[20] What this means in practice is that moral statesmen have the capacity to put themselves in someone else's shoes and to appreciate how their decisions may look from the other's perspective, and, even more, what effect their policies may have on the other's legitimate interests. In somewhat different language, the philosopher Thomas McCollogh speaks of the "moral imagination," the existence of which is a prima facie attribute of the ethically sensitive leader:

> The moral imagination may be understood as the capacity to empathize with others and to discern creative possibilities for ethical action. The moral imagination considers an issue in the light of the whole. . . . [It] broadens and deepens the context of decision-making to include the less tangible but most meaningful feelings, aspirations, ideals, relationships. It encompasses the core values of personal identity, loyalties, obligations, promises, love, trust and hope. Ethical judgment consists in making these values explicit and taking responsibility for judging their implications for action.[21]

In a world of widely diverse cultures, different historical experiences, and conflicting social and economic demands, it is no doubt more difficult for statesmen to display a "moral imagination" in foreign policy than to demonstrate such a quality with respect to their own citizens. This does not release them, however, from the general obligation to regard the citizens of other nations as the subjects and not just the objects of their decision-making.

THE EXCUSES OF POLITICIANS

It has been rightly said that "the great modern crimes are public crimes. . . . the growth of political power has introduced a scale of massacre and despoliation that makes the efforts of private criminals, pirates, and bandits seem truly modest."[22] Given this gloomy circumstance, it is hardly surprising that analyses concerning the proper relationship between morality and political behavior should be greeted with such skepticism by so many. Often they are simply regarded as equivalent to Don Quixote's enterprise in tilting at windmills, an idle exercise hardly worthy of our attention or effort.

Yet there is a surprising source of evidence for the proposition that the actions of statesmen *are* legitimately subject to moral examination, and that the phrase "moral statecraft" is not an oxymoron. The source of this evidence lies with the politicians themselves. It is a most striking phenomenon that most if not all political leaders display a palpable concern with being viewed not just as "successful" and "hard-nosed" practitioners of government but also as morally admirable in the bargain. When was the last time that we heard a prominent leader (at least in a reasonably democratic society) openly admit to all sorts of brutalities in his or her methods but boast that at least the methods had been effective? On the contrary, when such brutalities occur, the consistent pattern is for the leader either to disguise them, or at least attempt to explain them away as being regrettable but necessary, or perhaps even inevitable.

The first type of behavior, of course, involves political hypocrisy, and the widespread existence of such hypocrisy is offensive to many, if not most, and no doubt accounts in large part for the low opinion in which politicians and the political profession are held. At the same time, the prevailing existence of political hypocrisy is somehow reassuring, in that it suggests that almost all in positions of great power do have some nagging moral qualms. Such hypocrisy is prima facie an acceptance of the fact that virtue does exist and that as a general matter it should be adhered to. Otherwise, why engage in hypocrisy? This consideration is critical in reacting to the spurious commonplace assumption that there are no real binding limits to what is legitimate in achieving the ends of the state. If this were indeed the way in which most people (including the typical statesman or even the military professional) actually regarded their society's conduct of affairs, there would be no need for disguising the character of various activities if they seemed to be efficient in gaining the goals of the nation.

To be sure, there may be statesmen who actually have no understanding or appreciation of certain moral principles but nevertheless cover their actions by paying lip service to what they feel is expected of them. Kant made the essential point a long time ago when he distinguished between "the moral politician" and "the political moralist." The former was one who "employs the principles of political prudence in such a way that they can coexist with morals" whereas the latter was one "who would concoct a system of morals such as the advantage of the statesman may find convenient."[23] Thus Hitler disguised his real intentions to go to war in the late 1930s by piously referring to his terrible experiences as a front-line infantryman in World War I. Did the German people, he asked, really feel that he would take them once again into the hell of war, given his personal knowledge as to what war was like?

Still, hypocrisy in statecraft remains a curiously important piece of evidence that political leaders themselves do fret about their dirty hands, and that in doing so they implicitly accept the relevance of the debate over morality and public policy. One of the most striking aspects of the British government's public statements on British bombing policy in World War II, for example, was their consistent denial that Bomber Command was actually targeting German civilians.[24] What was particularly interesting in this regard was the assumption on the part of leading figures that the public was morally sensitive to indiscriminate air attacks on Germany and would protest if their existence was revealed. Whether this would generally have been the case is a matter perhaps open to debate, but one is reminded of the famous French sage La Rochefoucauld's aphorism that "hypocrisy is the tribute that vice pays to virtue." The British people seemed to have been credited with considerable virtue, and the government's hypocrisy paid tribute to it.

One way in which political leaders attempt to deal with the problem of their dirty hands is through disguise or denial. There is a considerably broader range of what might be called "excuses" that they also bring to the fore when the former strategy is denied to them or at least seems unavailing. In this instance, the effort is to explain away their dirty hands as being logically, and thus morally, defensible. It is important to examine these mea culpas not only in terms of their (occasional) legitimacy, but also in terms of how much weight we give them in our final judgment on the moral probity of their conduct. There are essentially two varieties of such excuses that may be identified: the first deals with the general character of political decisionmaking, and the second with the types of challenges that powerful leaders may have to face.[25]

The Essence of Decision

There is, for example, what is called the "excuse from alternative cause," which amounts to saying that "if I hadn't done it, someone else would have," or would have been found to do so. Sometimes this rationale is extended by saying that "someone else" would have done even worse, so I should be applauded for my relative moderation. Such a stance is common among officials who are belabored for not having resigned from a government doing evil. The argument here asserts that by staying, the person prevented even worse crimes. Of course this assertion need not always be spurious. Albert Speer was sentenced to 20 years' imprisonment at the Nuremberg trials for his participation in the Nazi regime. One of his defenses was that, particularly in the last days of the war, he was able to impede some truly draconian steps that Hitler was contemplating, including the wholesale destruction of Germany's infrastructure that would have made post-war life for Germans and occupiers alike virtually unbearable. Perhaps in partial recognition of this defense, the court spared him the gallows, even though it did punish him for his participation in other of Hitler's schemes.

Then there is the plea of "unintended consequences." Simply put, this states that "even though evil may have resulted from my actions, such evil was in no way intended and indeed was quite unanticipated. Thus I cannot be held responsible for such an unexpected outcome given my original good intentions." A good example of this defense in action might be Chancellor Helmut Kohl's much-criticized decision to offer early recognition to the breakaway states of Slovenia and Croatia in the former Yugoslavia. There is evidence that this step goaded Belgrade into a general program of expansion and war in order to meet what they saw as a threat to the Serb nation represented by Kohl's action. The German chancellor, on the other hand, defended his position by saying that it was intended to stabilize the Yugoslav situation by convincing the Serbs to accept the fait accompli of the breakup of the former Yugoslavia. Whatever final verdict is appropriate on Kohl's stance in this particular case, simply having "good intentions" is, as already noted, hardly a complete defense against a charge of moral culpability. Officials have a duty to examine in full detail the possible effects of their actions for good or ill, no matter how pure their bona fides may be, and there is at least a presumptive case that Kohl did not do so in this instance. Sometimes the political leader accused of moral dereliction in his policies offers a "defense from ignorance," not in terms of his lack of knowledge of basic facts (presumably an embarrassing admission to make) but rather in terms of the actions that subordinate officials took quite without his knowledge. This was the original cover assumed by President Eisenhower in 1960 when news of the shooting down of the U-2 spy plane over the Soviet Union was revealed. Many considered the U-2 mission a reckless and even immoral violation of standards of international law, but at first Eisenhower simply protested his personal innocence of such charges on the grounds that he was unaware that the CIA had undertaken this particular mission and that he had certainly not given specific authorization for it.

The "defense from ignorance" is problematical in two ways. Oftentimes a powerful leader will purposely shield himself from doubtful activities even if he suspects their existence, so that he will have what is called "deniability" should things go badly. There is also the fact of "Murphy's law" ever bearing down on the actions of statesmen: if things can go wrong, they will go wrong. In this instance, if a leader sets out and supports a general course of action, he can hardly escape responsibility if his underlings stumble in interpreting or implementing his general policy. In the case of the U-2, Eisenhower had long supported an aggressive intelligence program against the Soviet Union, and not incidentally had given his basic approval to overflights of that country. He may not have been responsible for the particular U-2 flight in May 1960, but this hardly exculpated him. As it happens, the president seems to have recognized the essential falseness of his position, and he soon openly accepted responsibility for what had happened.

Finally, there is the "excuse from compulsion." This doesn't refer to the general issue of "necessity" in foreign policy decisionmaking but rather to the cumulative effect of past decisions by one's predecessors in office that supposedly push its current occupant in a particular direction, no matter how objectionable. This was perhaps the main tacit or explicit moral defense offered by President Lyndon Johnson and his supporters for the doubtful aspects of American policy in Vietnam during the Johnson administration. The consistent refrain was that the administration was only responding to the commitments made by earlier American leaders, from Kennedy through Eisenhower to Truman. Once again, such a defense cannot simply be set aside: considerable momentum had indeed built up by the start of the Johnson administration in terms of regarding the defense of South Vietnam as a vital American interest.

At the same time, it is well to recall that Johnson was a powerful American senator during the Eisenhower years and even had some role in influencing Vietnam policy during the Kennedy period. His responsibility for the war thus partakes of more than simply his presidential decisions. There is an even more fundamental point, which is that "compulsion" in politics is almost never a truly irresistible factor. It may be difficult to reverse or change past policies, but that doesn't mean that it can't be done. Indeed, there is some evidence that Kennedy himself was planning to reverse the momentum of previous policy on Vietnam after his anticipated reelection in 1964 and began a gradual drawdown of the American role in that country. Johnson, if he had felt strongly enough about it, could presumably have done the same. That he chose not to can only partially be expiated by the argument of compulsion.

The Burden of History

Sometimes political leaders attempt to excuse their dirty hands not just in terms of the inherently complex circumstances that bear on political choice, but also in terms of the particular character of the choices open to them. The core of the argument here is that sometimes the choices available are such that there are at the least mitigating circumstances for adopting brutal policies.

Two themes are prominent in this regard. The first involves what has been called the theory of the "sliding scale." This suggests that the more just the cause, the greater latitude one has in ignoring, or at least temporarily setting aside, standard principles of moral conduct. The eminent theoretician John Rawls puts the point somewhat indirectly with respect to the practice of violence: "Even in a just war, certain forms of violence are strictly inadmissible; and when a country's right is questionable and uncertain, the constraints on the means it can use are all the more severe. Acts permissible in a war of legitimate self-defense, when these are necessary, may be flatly excluded in a more doubtful situation."[26]

The argument of the sliding scale was (and is) very common in the moral defense of certain Allied military policies in World War II, particularly as they related to aerial bombardment of civilians. The problematical aspect of such an assertion obviously has to do with the fact that the Allied war effort was after all a defense of certain basic values, among which was a decent respect for the individual. In the ultimate sense this was the political purpose of the war (in the Clausewitzian sense), that is to say, the defense of a whole way of life. One of the prime requisites of a truly "just war" is that the peace and justice to be achieved must not be compromised by the measures used to gain military victory. One of the leading historians of Allied, and especially British, bombing in World War II observes that a great many people (among whom he presumably numbers himself) "felt that by embarking on a systematic attack on cities . . . the Allies sacrificed something of their own moral case and that they contributed substantially to the terrible moral collapse that took place in the Second World War, most especially in the treatment of prisoners and civilians."[27] To this argument the sliding scale thesis can present few rebuttals. The melancholy truth seems to be that in combating a great evil, the British (and the Americans) condoned other evils that significantly lessened the whole moral purpose of the struggle.

There is also a defense for dirty hands that is sometimes subsumed under the rubric of the "supreme emergency." The argument is that, in such a situation, even humane and civilized statesmen may be forced (temporarily) to set aside commonly accepted moral guidelines in the interests of the survival of the nation—and, moreover, they have a (temporary) right to do so. An important assumption is that one's state is devoted to the pursuit of a just cause. How to define a supreme emergency? Two ingredients seem to be necessary: there must be a clear and imminent danger of defeat by the enemy, and the consequences of such a defeat must appear to be truly catastrophic. In practical terms, this would mean that losing the struggle would threaten the very essence of the nation, would involve one's society and values being subjugated to a completely repugnant rule, and would perhaps even put one's existence as a separate state at risk. Notice that both elements have to be present in order for there to be a supreme emergency: if the threat of defeat is imminent but the consequences of defeat are limited, or if the potential consequences are dire but there is no immediate danger of defeat, then no supreme emergency exists. If such a peril does exist, however, Machiavelli for one argued that with "the entire safety of our country . . . at stake, no considerations of what is just or unjust, merciful or cruel, praiseworthy or blameworthy must intervene."[28]

The argument from supreme emergency was very common in an earlier and perhaps more innocent age in which the activities of the American Central Intelligence Agency (CIA) came under question. As a consequence of the Church Committee's investigations in the 1970s, it was revealed that the CIA had engaged in all sorts of morally problematical activities, including experiments with hallucinogenic drugs on a number of unsuspecting individuals as well as a series of assassination plots against foreign leaders. The general defense offered for those in authority who had approved such activities was that the United States had in past years faced a "fundamental" challenge to its institutions and even survival from the Communist bloc, and thus doubtful measures were rendered legitimate by the severity of this threat. The basic problem with the idea of supreme emergency, of course, is that it seems inherently elastic, and thus can be expanded to cover or make legitimate almost any sort of morally dubious activity. Certainly it was used in this way often enough during the height of the cold war, and not just by members of the CIA. Perhaps the abuse of the concept during this period is one reason why it is rarely offered today as an excuse for doubtful political decisions, although the end of the Cold War itself presumably has had its own effect as well.

CRIME AND PUNISHMENT

We have only touched on a partial list of the rationales that political leaders may offer for their dirty hands. Presumably we can or should accept some of these excuses, but there are others that remain problematical. In the latter instance, there arises an important and separate issue in considering politicians with dirty hands, and it has to do with whether or not they should be "punished" in some way for their transgressions. It was remarked earlier that at least part of the citizenry may not only *expect* that statesman will not be totally bound by the moral principles of private life, but may even *insist* that they not be so bound, if such is necessary in pursuit of the public interest. Still, there remains a widespread notion that the politician's wickedness has to result in at least some sanction, even if the bad things done were in service to a good cause. The paradox here may perhaps be explained in part by our uneasiness at granting our leaders as much moral latitude as we do. In holding them accountable for their actions, we are in effect reaffirming our belief in the existence of a certain moral coherence to life. This demands that even though cruel methods on the part of our leaders are to be expected, and are perhaps even necessary, politicians cannot be allowed to simply walk away from their actions without challenge. Even so, this insistence on accountability presents a number of murky questions, among them the matter of who should be punished (assuming a decision was authored by more than one individual), what types of punishment can be realistically identified, and who should be the judge as to what punishment is appropriate.

Michael Walzer identifies three traditions in Western thought concerning accountability for the dirty hands politician. The first is the Machiavellian argument that the prince who learns "how not to be good," and in so doing successfully serves the interests of his state, is rewarded with the pleasures of power and glory but need pay no price for his sins, since they were committed not in his own interests but in the interests of the community. Then there is the Weberian tradition of the "suffering servant," which posits the political leader as an essentially tragic figure who will inevitably be subject to remorse at the wicked things he or she must do and in the process must accept the corruption of his or her own character which great power entails. Finally, there is a line of thought associated with Catholic theology in which the sins of the leader can only be made good through the effect of some external agency (in the most extreme example, his or her own death). From this perspective, wickedness may be a regular ingredient of political power, but it always requires penance.[29]

Each of these approaches presents its own problems. An unalloyed adoption of the Machiavellian credo would seem to invite a type of moral anarchy in which statesmen are free to do anything they want without fear of judgment so long as they are "successful" in utilitarian terms. To adopt such a standard is to eliminate the inherent connection between moral principles and the ends and means of politics. The Weberian ethos runs the risk of introducing all sorts of pretentiousness and even hypocrisy into political discourse. Politicians may perceive that they are *expected* to be a "suffering servant" and thus proclaim on the agony of the soul that they felt in making cruel decisions, even if such sensitivities were in reality quite absent at the time. Upon being offered the Democratic nomination for the Presidency in 1952, Adlai Stevenson said that he had prayed that "this cup would pass from my lips." General Eisenhower, who had been an admirer of Stevenson before this comment, henceforward regarded the Illinois governor as a poseur and a fake who had attempted to disguise the fact that he had a considerable thirst for presidential office. Finally, the doctrine of the Catholic theologians may be appropriate in attending to the immortal soul of political leaders, but it doesn't help very much in dealing with the evil effects of their current or future actions. There is more than one powerful leader who might not be amiss to a Faustian bargain in which they could do entirely as he wanted in this life on the proviso that they somehow suffer in the next.

Despite these caveats it bears repeating that the essential concept of punishment, that is, of accountability, remains a powerful and perhaps even central ingredient in the argument that moral principles have their rightful place in political conduct. Even if a particular individual may escape specific sanction, the notion that the potential application of such sanction is always present seems essential to any morally coherent view of public life. This sort of threat is premised on the idea that there are wicked—and *indefensibly* wicked—steps taken by statesmen, and that a due accounting of these may be in the offing. Without such a shadow over their actions, powerful leaders may be comforted by the notion that they alone are the only true judge of appropriate conduct, and "comfort" is not a condition that we want our leaders to feel, especially those in supreme authority.

But what sorts of punishment can be realistically identified for the dirty hands politician? What are the sanctions that have historically been applied, or could be applied, to such an individual, not just in terms of their merit as a form of retribution, but also in terms of their tutelary value? The most obvious of these perhaps consists of formal legal proceedings, the best examples of which were the Nuremberg trials dealing with the major Nazi war criminals. The key principle established by these trials was that individuals remain responsible for their actions regardless of any putative claim that they were only carrying out orders from higher authority in the commission of crimes. Moreover, Nuremberg has not been the only example of legal punishment applied to those committing misdeeds in wartime. The Turkish government held trials after World War I for those involved in the massacre of the Armenians, and the German courts in the early 1920s themselves dealt with a number of cases of supposed war crimes by German nationals. More recently, the United Nations has established a formal legal tribunal to deal with atrocities committed in the war in Bosnia by all of the parties involved.[30]

Sometimes legal sanctions for dirty hands can take less drastic but at the same time equally pointed or effective forms. In democratic systems there is, for instance, the threat of electoral retaliation—not all that common, perhaps, but nevertheless evident on at least some occasions. Thus one of the main reasons for President Johnson's announcement on March 31, 1968 that he would not seek another term as president was his clear recognition that popular disillusionment with his Vietnam policy (not all of it based on moral grounds, to be sure) made it highly unlikely that he would be successful in another campaign. Even more dramatic was the Republican loss of the White House in 1976. The public's anger at President Ford's pardoning of Richard Nixon almost certainly was the deciding factor in this very close race. The popular perception among a majority of the American people was that Nixon had unjustly escaped a formal settling of accounts for his role in Watergate, and Ford was forced to pay the price for this discontent.[31]

A more subtle form of punishment for dirty hands can fall under the rubric of what we might call social ostracism, and here we can refer again to the case of British area bombing. At the end of World War II, there seems to have been a widespread uneasiness within British public opinion, and the British government itself, concerning the legitimacy of such bombing. Now the head of British Bomber Command for most of the war was a certain Air Marshal Sir Arthur Harris. Despite the fact that area bombing was attributable to decisions taken by Churchill and others at the top level of the British government, post-war British officials, and the British people more generally, evidently decided that this particular moral query had to be recognized—and perhaps atoned for—by some form of punishment for those involved. It was the veterans of Bomber Command, and Sir Arthur Harris in particular, who became the special targets of social retribution: the former failed to receive certain elementary military honors that were extended to other branches of the British armed services, and the latter was not only denied elevation to a Peerage, such as was given to other prominent British wartime commanders, but was effectively dismissed from the Royal Air Force in the bargain. No matter what one may feel about the injustice—or the hypocrisy—of such behavior, it is the fact that it took place at all that is suggestive, at least in terms of the evident feeling that an ethically dubious policy could only be (partially) redeemed if some sort of sanction was applied to certain of those involved.[32]

In enumerating the possible forms of punishment for dirty hands, it is well to return for a moment to the thinking of Max Weber. It may be that many, if not most, leaders can make use of the conceit of the "suffering servant," and even turn it to their own advantage. But there are sufficient examples of genuinely suffering servants that it would be idle to suggest that this is never a legitimate factor in the settling of moral accounts. Indeed one of the most powerful "sanctions" that may be identified for the dirty hands politician is his or her own self-condemnation. One example that might be cited is the case of former Secretary of Defense Robert McNamara, a major player in the escalation of the Vietnam War. The evidence suggests that McNamara was haunted for a number of years after leaving the Pentagon about his responsibility for the conflict in Vietnam. He was so emotionally distraught on this score that he refused to even discuss his role in the Vietnam War for a long period of time. As partial penance for his earlier activities, he not only devoted himself to Third World development as head of the World Bank, but later became associated with the movement to stop the nuclear arms race. Even some twenty years after his service as Secretary of Defense, it was said, he would break out in tears when the subject of Vietnam came up.[33] Eventually, of course, McNamara did put pen to paper in an attempt to explain what he called the "tragedy" and "lessons" of Vietnam. The writing of this book presumably was designed by the author as a kind of catharsis, and indeed he admits as much in the introduction. Even at this late date, however, the former defense secretary largely eschewed any direct examination of the moral questions raised by the Vietnam War, choosing instead to focus mostly on the mistakes in judgment and analysis that characterized Johnson administration policy. Perhaps such an examination, particularly as it involved his own actions, still remained too painful a topic for him to broach.[34]

One of the more interesting variations of the "self-punishment" theme on the part of the dirty-handed politician is resignation from office. The level or degree of punishment that such a step represents of course depends on a number of circumstances. For someone whose basic aspirations are directed toward the achievement of even higher office (assuming that to be available), or for whom official employment is a regular and expected source of income, to step down from one's position is an especially weighty statement. Thus Joseph Chamberlain resigned from the British government in 1886 because he disagreed as a matter of principle with his party's position on Home Rule in Ireland. The evidence suggests that in so doing he threw away a strong chance at becoming the next British prime minister.[35]

Whatever one may think of Chamberlain's substantive views on the Irish question, it is hard to deny that he was prepared to pay a very high price in order to assert his position. Sometimes official resignations can be offered at somewhat less cost, however. There is, for example, the interesting case of Cyrus Vance, who left the Carter administration in the Spring of 1980 in protest against the use of military force to rescue the American hostages in Iran, and perhaps also because of his sense of guilt at having given American allies the (false) impression that such force would not be used in dealing with the hostage question.[36] Vance had a reputation as a public official of unusual probity, and his resignation, perhaps rightly, may be considered an affirmation of this reputation. Still, it was unmistakable that his leaving the Carter administration came at a time in which that administration's reputation was at low ebb, and that Vance's "sacrifice" in resigning basically amounted to his having to return to his very lucrative private law practice. This is not to say that his leaving office was not a reflection of personal principle; it is to say that his decision was made a lot easier by his personal circumstances.

It is sobering to consider in this connection that although a number of middle-level officials in the State and Defense Departments during the Vietnam War period evidently had grave moral doubts about what the United States was doing in Vietnam, and were exceedingly discomfited by their own participation in Vietnam policy, there were very few resignations as a consequence.[37] Career considerations seemed to loom larger than concerns about making a "statement" or the search for personal absolution. This doesn't necessarily open these individuals to our condemnation, especially when we consider the case of George Ball, Undersecretary of State until 1966. Ball was perhaps the best-known high official whose opposition to the war was known or assumed, at least within the Washington establishment. Indeed President Johnson actively encouraged Ball's dissent in order to present the impression that all available alternatives to the current policy were being given fair consideration. Ball eventually did resign from the State Department, at least in part because of his frustration at being unable to change administration policy, but he did so very quietly and never made a public break with Lyndon Johnson on the matter of Vietnam—certainly not on any of the moral questions having to do with the war.[38] George Ball (like Cyrus Vance) had a lot more in the way of personal resources to fall back on than his more junior colleagues, and thus one can hardly be surprised perhaps that the latter decided that discretion indeed was the better part of valor, given Ball's own reluctance to make a public issue of his resignation.

A more recent case involving some of the same generic issues present in the Vietnam situation was American policy toward Serbian atrocities in Bosnia. As a consequence of his outrage at what he saw as Washington's inaction in the face of such atrocities, George Kenney resigned his post in the State Department in August 1992 as Second Desk Officer for Yugoslavia. Some eight months later another twelve career foreign service officers sent an official letter of protest—which was quickly leaked to the press—concerning American policy toward Bosnia to Secretary of State Warren Christopher. Several among them followed Kenney in resigning from the Department, but most remained in government service. Their in-house protest resulted in a meeting with Christopher but no discernible change in Washington's approach to the Bosnian question. The actions of Kenney and the others did represent, however, a most unusual expression of internal dissent within the State Department concerning an important policy question facing the current administration, although there was a clear difference in how far the individuals involved were prepared to take this dissent.[39]

The above cases do raise the troubling question of whether resignation is always the most admirable course that officials can take when they are troubled by their role in a doubtful policy. It is at least theoretically possible that to remain in office would constitute the higher moral good. Resignation might be viewed as an essentially self-centered attempt to refurbish a reputation, to seize the moral high ground, to appeal to a benevolent verdict from history on one's special moral bona fides. Might it not be more morally relevant, and demanding of more moral courage, to remain in office in order to combat or mitigate the evils with which one is involved? This is indeed one of the perennial problems in the intersection between morality and statecraft.

If George Ball had remained at the State Department, perhaps he could have at least moderated some of the more egregious escalation of the Vietnam War. If Kenney and certain of his colleagues had remained in government and continued to urge humanitarian intervention in the Bosnian crisis, their voices might have had at least some effect. There are numerous other cases involving the same sort of moral conundrum. Some of the most notable had to do with the "respectable" career civil servants in the German governmental ministries during the Nazi era. Ernst von Weisacker, for example, was state secretary at the German foreign ministry from 1938 to 1943. Although he was Joachim von Ribbentrop's second-in-command, he was later found innocent (on appeal) of a charge of crimes against the peace because he had spoken out within the ministry against Nazi plans for aggression and had some contact with the anti-Hitler opposition, passing on to them information about Nazi strategy. At the same time, he was given a separate seven-year prison sentence for crimes against humanity, the basis of this being that he had not specifically spoken up against the proposed Final Solution or resigned in protest when he learned of its implementation. In this instance, his supposed sympathy for the Nazi resistance proved unavailing as a defense. Remaining in office on the premise that he might be able to somehow mitigate the program of Jewish extermination was specifically rejected as a shield for his actions, given the fact that he had not actively opposed it within the corridors of government.[40]

In concluding this discussion of punishment for the dirty-handed politician, it might be well to return for a moment to an issue that has previously been touched on, and that is the excessive use of secrecy, and especially deception, in the conduct of statecraft. As we have already observed, such practices present a special problem in considering the general issue of dirty hands. While almost universally condemned as being inappropriate in private life, they are sometimes condoned as legitimate and even necessary in the affairs of state. This *raison d'état* defense argues that only by using secrecy and deception can the political leader defend the integrity of the state, which in turn allows the private individual to pursue a more pristine standard.[41] Such an assertion, of course, cannot be totally set aside. The invocation of secrecy in governmental affairs may at times rightly be defended as allowing a full and frank range of options to be discussed within governmental circles; it may also be necessary in protecting the rights of individuals or groups whose fate is under discussion or sometimes in maintaining the element of surprise (especially relevant in wartime).

Nevertheless, the overuse of secrecy, and particularly the practice of deception, becomes problematical in terms of the principle of accountability for political leaders. How are we to judge their dirty hands, and the legitimacy of their reasons for their having them, if we have so little insight into the actual circumstances in which they made their decisions? As John Stuart Mill asserted, how, without publicity, can citizens either "check or encourage what they were not permitted to see?"[42] More than this, the vice of excessive secrecy is a special impulse toward corruption on the part of those partaking in it, particularly those in positions of enormous influence. Sissela Bok rightly argues that "the transformation and isolation that secrecy can lead to are strongest when linked with great power, actual or potential, over others."[43] She makes a convincing case that it was the hermetically sealed existence of the atomic scientists, such as Robert Oppenheimer and others, at Los Alamos during the Manhattan Project that made them blind or at least oblivious to the serious moral issues that attended their work on atomic fission.

It seems almost impossible, in sum, to expect that a genuine moral accountability can exist for statesman if their efforts are often shrouded in a self-protective cloud of secrecy and even deception. The famous British classicist Gilbert Murray put the point very effectively over seventy years ago:

> The world has not yet sounded or measured the immense power of mere publicity. I do not mean advertisements in newspapers; I mean the knowledge that your actions are to be known and discussed, and particularly that you will have to answer questions about them face to face with your questioner. . . . If properly used it [publicity] may well prove to be about the most powerful weapon that exists in human affairs.[44]

Obviously this "powerful weapon" has not been totally in force in the years since he wrote, but the essential point remains: without the threat—or the opportunity—of having to explain yourself to others, what impulse is there to having to explain yourself to yourself?

A SUMMING UP

A steady theme throughout the previous discussion has been how a great many people—including some with a strong interest in moral philosophy—remain unconvinced that it is really possible to define a "moral" leader. There is a tendency to give a wide benefit of the doubt to the actions of politicians so long as it can be shown that such actions were not in pursuit of their private interests (financial, political, etc.) but were at least ostensibly for public purposes. There is also the notion that a leader assuming obligation to a particular community cannot be judged on the basis of anything except his or her achievement of goods for this group. Finally, there is the argument that in complex modern political systems, responsibility for given decisions is fundamentally diffused. Under these circumstances, the understandable tendency is simply to emphasize the *consequences* of policies rather than their moral origins, since it may be quite difficult to identify the actor or actors with real moral responsibility.[45]

At a more theoretical level, there are those who question whether there is any real basis for a comparative weighing of the ethical standards of one statesman as opposed to another, except insofar as their basic *goals* may be described as good or evil, such as the objectives of Churchill and Roosevelt in World War II compared to those of Adolf Hitler. Three assertions are advanced in support of this reluctance to judge. The first argues moral relativism, that is to say, there are no firm moral rules that stand independently of different cultures, different times, or different situations. The second assertion is that even if some such rules may be identified, they can only be regarded as general "guidelines" that the statesman may legitimately set aside in various circumstances and with no requirement for feeling guilty in so doing. Finally, it may be that some moral rules are indeed absolute, but if the statesman is only responding to necessity in breaking them (the Betthman-Hollweg principle) there can be no real argument that he or she is morally culpable, although some reflection of remorse in violating them may not only be laudable but perhaps even necessary.[46]

None of these arguments seems convincing on close analysis. At the same time, it does seem idle to suggest that statesmen can, should, or will conduct themselves with precisely the same rectitude in their public life as they may display in their private life. But the real issue for present purposes is this: under what circumstances can we say that the historical figure under study is a genuinely "wicked" individual, with dirty hands and more, is truly deserving of moral condemnation? In what cases does the dirty hands defense—that is, the notion that unpleasant choices are inherent to high politics—offer an inadequate rebuttal? The term "wicked" seems to be open to various interpretations and open to differing forms. The philosopher S. I. Benn, for example, offers an interesting discussion of "conscientious wickedness":

Conscientious wickedness is rarely a case of pursuing an end unaware of attendant consequences as evils; it is more often a case of a single-minded pursuit of an objective which . . . can reasonably be seen as good, but at the cost of a callous insensitivity to evil done by the way. It is not that the person believes the incidental evil to be itself good but rather that, having reason to think it evil, he nevertheless systematically disregards it.[47]

The mark of the "non-conscientious" wicked person, Benn continues, is "that such choices are for him neither difficult nor painful since the considerations that would make them so are systematically neutralized."[48] In these terms, perhaps a fair conclusion would be that many, if not most, important political leaders fall into the category of the "conscientiously wicked." They may regret the cruelties for which they are responsible in their political life, but nevertheless feel such are justified because they are in service to a higher good. The key factor here is, once again, what Benn calls their "single-minded pursuit" of their objectives.

Can we not, however, set out any general appeal to them as to the advantages of attending to moral thinking? To the politician, the pleasures of political life may seem at times to be pretty much an illusion and, in their more vexatious moments, almost an oxymoron. Yet those who aspire toward political power keep at it, and presumably for reasons other than pure altruism. Under the circumstances, it is the satisfaction and reward of power itself that would seem to motivate them to continue. How then can we persuade them to modify an unrestrained lust for such power, and in particular to be moderate in the sort of methods they choose to consolidate or express their power, especially since such moderation may actually seem to impede the attainment of their goals? How, in short, do we persuade them of the advantages of being moral?

Clearly one approach is to take the Kantian position that moral principles ought to be followed for their own sake, that "virtue is its own reward." Even given the cynicism that normally attends to the character of politicians, such a stance cannot or should not be dismissed out of hand. There is a variety of evidence that, given certain circumstances, the intuitive conscience of the decisionmaker may in fact be appealed to as a factor in policy. An interesting example of such a situation involved the Reagan administration's reaction to the Israeli invasion of Lebanon in 1982 and in particular the subsequent bombing of Beirut, the effects of which were shown in vivid detail on American television. One of Reagan's chief advisers, Michael Deaver, became particularly agitated at the images of civilian suffering in the city, and heatedly offered his resignation to the President. "I can't be part of this anymore," Deaver said, "the bombings, the killing of children. It's wrong. And you're the one person on the face of the earth right now who can stop it. All you have to do is tell Begin [the Israeli prime minister] you want it stopped." As it happens, Reagan seems to have shared Deaver's own outrage at the Israeli bombing, and he called Begin to demand that it be stopped, referring emotionally to the "holocaust" that Israeli air strikes were causing. "It has gone too far. You must stop it." The Israeli prime minister called back twenty minutes later and told the president that orders had indeed been issued to cease all bombing of Beirut.[49]

What is especially interesting about this particular episode was that it involved a close ally of the United States and that Reagan was normally reluctant to confront a friendly foreign leader on such a matter of principle. One recent study perhaps gives some insight into his behavior. It lays great stress on the findings of social learning and cognitive-development theory to suggest that even very powerful political figures do have a moral compass derived out of the basic social values of the society from which they emerge. This leads to a type of "self-regulation" in which individuals "punish" themselves for failing to follow such values and reward themselves for adherence to them. In more conventional language, leaders want to feel that what they are doing is right (or is generally considered right by others).[50] In such circumstances, adherence to principle is indeed its own reward.

Not surprisingly, however, it is well to reinforce this inherent appeal to virtue, and the somewhat amorphous gains from such an adherence, with an essentially pragmatic or utilitarian argument. Not only can leaders do good but they can also do well, that is to say, their evident moral probity can provide rather specific material returns. For one thing, the state they represent may acquire a reputation for honesty and fair-dealing in its affairs that will redound to its ultimate benefit because of the confidence and goodwill that it creates. In contrast, continuous use of deception and disinformation in a state's foreign policy, for example, threatens the basic comity of the international system, such as it exists, and thus the effective functioning of that system.[51] Even in its own terms, the good reputation of a state is not a value to be taken lightly. An appearance of fidelity to certain basic moral principles may also consolidate domestic support for the government's actions, particularly in democratic systems, and thus make them easier to carry out. There is also the element of national self-respect that Sissela Bok rather effectively describes:

> Even those who refuse to consider the effects of their actions on enemies,
> and take into account only the strictest national self-interest, would benefit

from weighing these differences [as to different methods]; for aggression and brutality abroad, whether openly or secretly carried out, have profound effects not only on the personnel asked to participate but on citizens at home. No nation can escape the burden of living with the results of clearly immoral or even questionable choices made in wartime.[52]

In all of these cases, the aura of *legitimacy* is enhanced by the individual leader's presenting a picture of sensitivity to principle as well as to power. All the same, there are limits to the degree to which we can appeal to decisionmakers' self-interest in behaving ethically. At the end of the day, they may be able to offer convincing arguments as to why their own interests may demand that they ignore certain moral imperatives. The most convincing position to adopt here, therefore, is (as usual) somewhere in the middle, embracing both utilitarian and intuitive reasons that we may present to the statesman for at least moderating his or her wickedness. A too blatant or casual acceptance of dirty hands on the politician's part can undermine popular support (at least in a democracy) and thus prove counterproductive to the leader's own political position, even if the populace accepts that politics can at times be a dirty business. Moreover, developing a reputation as someone who will stop at nothing to achieve various ends may lay oneself open to unwelcome pressure from all sorts of doubtful individuals or groups to adopt their special causes and without any special concern as to the means necessary to attain them. In this sense, the statesman can become a prisoner of his or her own reputation.

On the other hand, as I have attempted to argue earlier in this essay, the morally sensitive citizen has not only a right but even a duty to suggest that in terms of certain basic values the credo for the statesman should be "thus far and no farther." While they are difficult to identify in the abstract, there are moral principles that exist on their own merits and need rightful attention in developing policies. In this sense, we say to the statesman that we accept your doing things that would be abhorrent if done in private life, but that this grant of freedom to be sometimes wicked is not unbounded. Even here, moreover, there can be a utilitarian aspect in our message. Portia's comment in *The Merchant of Venice* conveys the idea. Speaking of the quality of mercy (surely one of the principal virtues that we may expect from the moral statesman), she proclaims that "it is twice blessed; it blesseth him that gives and him that takes." We must say to the politician: do this because it is inherently right but also be convinced of the practical returns from doing so. In this sense, a good conscience and self-interest mutually reinforce one another.

This previous point, as with most of the others in the first two chapters of this essay, is basically an abstraction and relatively disembodied argument for a certain standard of conduct. Any serious writing on applied ethics, however, must sooner or later descend from the level of generality to a consideration of specific cases in which the relevance of the ethical theory may be demonstrated. The remainder of our discussion here is thus taken up with two historical examples in which the problem of dirty hands presented itself with special force. The first of these has to do with what happened to the citizens of a place called Lidice during World War II, and what judgment may properly be rendered about their ultimate fate.

PART II

CASES

3

The Destruction of
Lidice: Background

On the evening of June 9, 1942, inhabitants of the small Central Bohemian village of Lidice in Czechoslovakia, approximately 12 miles west of Prague, were preparing to retire for the night. The town had a population of 400 men and women and around 100 children. At about 9:00 P.M. various German Gestapo units began forming a cordon around Lidice; they were soon joined by members of the *Schutzpolizei* (defense police) as well as regular Nazi army troops. Their orders were that Lidice be totally sealed off so that nobody could leave, although anyone who wanted to enter could do so. Soldiers awakened the sleeping citizens of the town by smashing in their windows. Dogs began running around the streets of Lidice in great excitement and were casually shot by the security police to quiet them.

At approximately 11:00 P.M., the head of the *Sicherheitsdienst* (security service) in Bohemia-Moravia, Horst Böhme, arrived in the village and immediately evicted the owners of a large house in the center of the village so that he could use it as a command post for the events that were shortly to transpire. The mayor of Lidice was summoned and ordered to produce all the documents and information that he had pertaining to the inhabitants of the town. Böhme had received instructions the previous day from Berlin on what he was to do next:

1. All men to be executed by shooting.
2. All women to be sent into concentration camps.

3. Children are to be concentrated, those capable of being Germanized, are to be sent to SS families in Germany and the rest elsewhere.
4. The commune is to be burnt down and leveled to the ground.[1]

During the remainder of the night every male of Lidice age 16 and over was methodically rounded up by the Germans, who then proceeded to collect a number of mattresses from the village that were placed against a stone wall of one of the barns outside the town. On the morning of June 10th, the men were led in groups of ten before an execution squad of 30 and shot without further formality. After 50 of the men had been dispatched, a pause was declared and schnapps was served to the firing squad in order to steady their nerves. By noon there were 17 rows of bloody corpses laid out, some 199 men in all. One miner from Lidice who was in the hospital with a broken leg at the time of the massacre was shot later in October after he had recovered. As a final touch, gold rings were removed from the fingers of the dead, and gold teeth were gouged out of their mouths.[2] The following day a work team of 30 Jewish prisoners from the concentration camp at Terezin nearby was deployed to Lidice in order to bury the bodies

Later that afternoon in the adjoining town of Kladno, the Gestapo assembled all the women and children of Lidice in the local grammar school in order to make a register of them. Virtually all the women were designated for immediate shipment to the concentration camp at Ravensbrück (four women who were pregnant at the time were allowed to deliver their babies at a Prague hospital and were then sent to join the others). After anguished goodbyes to their children, the women were taken away in 17 trucks covered with canvas. Then two large coaches pulled up to the grammar school and 94 children filed into them for shipment to the so-called "children's camp" at Gneisenau in German-occupied Poland. Of the 200 women, only 143 were eventually to return to Lidice after the war. The fate of the children was far sadder: a mere 16 were eventually traced and repatriated to Czechoslovakia. The vast majority were evidently gassed at the Chelmno extermination camp in Poland.

Meanwhile, the second part of Böhme's instructions was in the process of being carried out. Gestapo men systematically placed cans of gasoline in the homes and buildings of Lidice and set them ablaze. Within hours the village had been reduced to a smoking ruin. This was only the beginning, however. Workers from the *Reichsarbeitdienst* (Reich Labor Service) were dispatched to obliterate any trace of Lidice's existence. Explosives were used to level any buildings still left standing after the fire and machinery was used to remove the rubble. A brook running through the center of Lidice was diverted, new roads were constructed, and the place where the town had once existed was covered over with new soil and planted with grain. In a final measure to obliterate any trace of Lidice's former existence, the village's cemetery was uprooted, which involved the destruction of some 60 tombs, 140 family and 200 individual graves.[3]

The atrocity at Lidice stands as one of the most horrific examples in World War II of the Nazi capacity for brutality and almost mindless inhumanity. Even to a world benumbed by the cruelties of the Third Reich, news of the destruction of Lidice aroused special emotions. An American town and a Mexican village both changed their names to Lidice in recognition of this event. A number of Allied tanks went into action with the name of Lidice painted on their turrets. Some of the bombs dropped by the British Royal Air Force had Lidice painted on their side.[4] To know what happened at Lidice—and to remember what happened at Lidice—is indeed a responsibility in itself. But there is something more here as well: whom to blame for this outrage? At first glance the question seems a simple one, even an offensive one. Need we search farther than the Nazi machinery of oppression itself? The evidence is that Lidice was destroyed on the personal instructions of Adolf Hitler, who was in turned directed to the village's existence and suitability for elimination by SS Brigadeführer Karl Hermann Frank, state secretary of the Protectorate of Bohemia and Moravia, as the Nazis styled their regime in occupied Czechoslovakia. The loathsome Karl Böhme for his part was the one who brought Lidice to the attention of Frank. Finally, there were the men who carried out the actual executions. All were volunteers, and as it happened, after the first 50 executions, three of them refused to continue with their shooting of the men of Lidice (they were promptly replaced by three reservists). Those who actually pulled the triggers thus bear their own ineluctable share of responsibility. German dirty hands, indeed, from the highest to the lowest in the chain of command.

Yet it is vital to understand *why* Lidice became a particular target for extermination. Much if not most of the Nazi killing in World War II, aside from that on the battlefield, might properly be described as essentially psychotic, a consequence of the Nazis' absurd fixation on the "Jewish problem" and the "inferiority" of other races, or in many instances simply a glorification of destruction for its own sake. Not for nothing did one of Hitler's early associates describe the essence of Naziism as the "revolution of nihilism".[5] In the case of Lidice, however, there was at least some "rational" connection between the act itself and broader, essentially pragmatic, German interests. To understand this connection, it is necessary to summarize German policy toward Czechoslovakia prior to the fateful evening of June 9, 1942.

The Protectorate of Bohemia and Moravia

In some sense, the fate of Lidice may be tied to the agreement reached at the Munich Conference in September 1938 by the leaders of Great Britain, France, Italy, and Germany. Under the Munich accords, the Sudetenland area of Czechoslovakia (which formed the most heavily-fortified border regions of the country) was handed over to Germany because of Hitler's insistence on going to the "rescue" of the large German minority in this territory who were, he claimed, suffering unbearable oppression from the Czech authorities in Prague. In reality, Hitler's interest in the Sudetenland was only a forerunner to his broader goal of bringing the Czech lands totally under German domination. In March 1939, he ordered his troops to occupy the rump of what was left of Czechoslovakia, specifically the western regions of Bohemia and Moravia. The eastern part of the country, Slovakia, was allowed to establish itself as an "independent" state subject to the close tutelage of Berlin.[6]

Even after the Germans had established what they called the Protectorate of Bohemia-Moravia, the Czech authorities were allowed to retain a certain degree of governmental autonomy. They were denied any say in defense or foreign affairs, but were able to carry out many functions in the domestic sphere under the loose supervision of a Reichsprotektor appointed by Berlin. The new Czech regime, under the leadership of Emil Hácha as President and General Alois Eliáš as Prime Minister, made a conscious decision to cooperate as much as possible with the occupying power and not to lead or countenance any overt political or military resistance to the Germans, at least for the time being. This seems to have some desirable effects: the wages of Czech workers increased by 50 percent from March 1939 to April 1941, whereas the increase in living expenses was rather less. Even when a rationing system was introduced, it was no more severe than for the Germans in the Reich itself. The Czechs were also spared from forced service in the German armed forces.

As one of the leading authorities on this period comments, "the extent to which the Nazis allowed Czech officials to govern—under strict supervision, to be sure—was unparalleled in other countries [save for Denmark]."[7] The reason for this unexpected benevolence was not hard to find: the Nazis viewed the Protectorate as an area inherently unlikely to present any violent resistance, and one which had a high economic and military potential. As one testament to the latter, when the Germans occupied Bohemia and Moravia in March 1939, they captured some 1,500 aircraft, 2,200 pieces of field artillery, over 500 tanks, 500 anti-aircraft guns, a million rifles and 43,000 machine guns, most of these being products of the Skoda armaments works.[8]

Under the circumstances, it made sense for the Germans to treat the Czechs with relative leniency so as to maintain quiet and stability in the Protectorate. The first man chosen as Reichsprotektor was the career diplomat and former German foreign minister Konstantin von Neurath. Both the naming of Neurath and the tolerance of some continuing independent government for the Czechs had the added advantage for Hitler of muting international outrage at his blatant violation of the Munich accords of the previous September. That the Czechs were likely to enjoy only a relative freedom from Nazi terror was reflected, however, in the appointment of SS Brigadeführer Karl Hermann Frank as state secretary of the new protectorate. As part of his responsibilities, Frank was given control of the police and reported directly to the head of the SS, Heinrich Himmler. Frank was notorious for his hatred of the Czechs and Czech culture, and, as already discussed, he was to be directly involved in the massacre at Lidice.[9]

The outbreak of World War II on September 1, 1939 forced Hitler to reconsider what the role of the Protectorate should now be. His basic decision was to accelerate the economic exploitation of the Czech lands in service to the Nazi war effort, and once again to leave a final "settling of accounts" with the Czech people until the end of the war. At the same time, Karl Frank and his minions did embark on a gradually stiffening policy of repression and violence against any perceived Czech opposition to the German occupation, which in a self-fulfilling prophecy served to increase organized Czech resistance to the Nazi presence.

As it happens, despite Neurath's relatively benevolent policies, a nascent Czech resistance movement had in fact already developed in the country. A Home Army styled as the *Obrana Naroda* (Defense of the Nation), its founders mostly senior officers in Prague and Brno, managed to establish some thirteen divisions in all parts of the country by the end of the summer of 1939. Former political supporters of the prewar Czech regime organized themselves into the *Politicke ustredi* (the Political Center, or PU) and became the focus of communications with Czech exiles in London. Still another group represented the democratic left in Czech politics, and, finally, there was a partisan movement dominated by the Czech communist party. The non-communist opposition united in early 1940 and formed the Central Committee of the Home Resistance, or

UVOD, and was recognized by Eduard Beneš, the president of the Czech government-in-exile in London, as the directing authority of the home resistance.[10] One aspect of the UVOD's activities was the formation of the National Defense Organization, which was designed to coordinate all internal resistance to the Germans, including that of the Czech communists, and to establish contact with important Czech representatives abroad as well as the governments of Britain and France.

Signs that with the outbreak of the war there would now be a steadily increasing program of Nazi oppression in Czechoslovakia was suggested by the arrest in the fall of 1939 of almost 10,000 Czech army officers, intellectuals, and students suspected of contacts with foreign powers. On October 28 (the anniversary of Czech independence), there were a series of strikes and demonstrations throughout the Protectorate. As a reaction to further protests during the funeral of a student from Prague University slain during the earlier demonstrations, Frank ordered that all Czech universities be closed for a period of three years. A number of additional students and intellectuals were arrested and sent to concentration camps, and martial law was temporarily declared in Prague and surrounding districts. Overall, some 200,000 German army and security forces came to be concentrated in the Protectorate in order to deal with the increasingly recalcitrant Czechs.[11]

Despite this fact, over the next 18 months a low-level campaign of strikes, work stoppages, and boycotts (for example, of the official press) continued to exist. By the fall of 1941, Hitler decided that the relatively moderate Konstantin von Neurath had to be replaced by someone more severe in his views and actions. He had at hand a promising candidate: the head of the *Reichssichereitsamt* (RHSA), Reinhard Heydrich, who was in due course to be styled by the Czechs as the "butcher of Prague." Heydrich was named the Acting Reichsprotektor of Bohemia and Moravia on September 27, 1941, and on his arrival in Prague immediately indicated his intentions for the territory now under his control:

> For the protection of German interests I hereby proclaim martial law in the territories of Bohemia and Moravia which takes effect from 28th September, 1941. All acts against public order, economic life as well as labour peace together with the unlawful possession of firearms, explosives or ammunition, will be judged under this law. All assemblies in private rooms or public highways are forbidden. There will be no appeal against the sentences of these court martials. Sentences will be carried out immediately by shooting or hanging.[12]

One of Heydrich's first actions was to order the execution of some 142 Czech resisters and the dispatch of another 584 to concentration camps. A month later, these figures had almost doubled. Heydrich summarized his policy by saying that "my task is to teach the Czech people that they cannot deny the reality of their relationship with the Reich, nor avoid the obedience which the Reich demands."[13]

Reinhard Heydrich was perhaps the purest example of the Nazi ideal: a "Blond Beast" who was once described as a "young evil god of death."[14] He was a fanatical anti-Semite with no moral scruples about the most extreme brutality against the enemies of the Reich, and he had an almost obsessive taste for the accumulation of power for its own sake. His nominal chief, Heinrich Himmler, Reichsführer of the SS, described him with unconscious irony in the following terms: "In all his actions he was motivated by the fact that he was a national socialist and a member of the SS. From the depth of his heart and his blood, he realized the meaning of Adolph Hitler's philosophy of life (*Weltanschauung*)."[15] Hitler himself referred to Heydrich (with apparent accuracy) as "the man with the iron heart." His life before assuming the post of Reichsprotektor of Bohemia-Moravia was almost a model for the sadists and misfits who were drawn to the Nazi cause. At the age of 16 he had joined one of the reactionary paramilitary groups that blossomed in Germany after the defeat of 1918. Shortly after he decided to pursue a more respectable career by becoming an officer in the Germany navy. His rapid rise in the navy was short-circuited in 1931 when a court of honor cashiered him for a sexual escapade involving the daughter of the superintendent of the Kiel naval dockyard and a personal friend of Admiral Erich Raeder.[16]

Such a dubious history was no bar to—indeed in its own way was a recommendation for—service to the Nazi movement, and after early membership in an SS group in Hamburg, Heydrich was promoted to Himmler's deputy shortly after the Nazi seizure of power. By 1936, at the age of 32, he had become head of the SD, a counterespionage and domestic security organization and one of the principal components of the SS empire. By the outbreak of war, his responsibilities had expanded to include direction of the Gestapo as well as the Criminal Police. As a special testament to the high regard in which he was held within Nazi circles, he was placed in charge of the "final solution of the Jewish question" by Hermann Göring himself. His assignment in Prague was to develop the Protectorate as a model example of the New Order throughout German-occupied Europe, in which the Germans would be the acknowledged master race while those under their control would be subject to forced assimilation or, in the case of "undesirable" racial elements, physical destruction.[17]

What made Heydrich an especially formidable figure was the way in which he combined a total absence of moral scruple with considerable intellectual gifts (he played the violin well and enjoyed evenings of chamber music). As one writer puts it, "he was that rarity: the killer, possessing intelligence and lacking a conscience. He was, moreover, a killer who enjoyed his work and had administrative ability."[18] As a reflection of the latter, he reinforced an earlier theme in German governance in the Protectorate by presenting a clever "carrot-and-stick" policy to the Czechs. Special food rations were declared for those workers with a high record of productivity, especially in war industries, and the citizens of Prague were given some 116,000 free cinema tickets as well as 18,000 free passes to the theater. Some of the Czech workers, as part of Heydrich's *Peitsche und Zucker* ("whip and sugar") policy, were also sent to pleasant countryside holidays. He adopted as a credo the admonition from Edmund Burke (that was for some reason brought to his attention) to the effect that "force may subdue for a moment; but it does not remove the necessity of subduing again; and a nation is not governed, which is perpetually to be conquered."[19] As Heydrich himself said, his basic strategy was to avoid pushing the Czechs "to the point of explosion and self-destruction," a factor of special importance given the importance of the Czechoslovak armaments works to the German war effort. A further goal was the effective depolitization of the Czech population, whereby the individual would be forced or persuaded to concentrate simply on his or her material needs and economic welfare. The acting Reichsprotektor seems to have been largely successful in this effort. One of his biographers comments that "there is no doubt that to a considerable extent, Heydrich had taken the steam out of the Czech resistance movement by presenting himself as a public benefactor."[20] Yet another scholar agrees that after Heydrich's arrival, "more and more Czechs refused to support the resistance, even passively, and did all they could to remain absolutely neutral."[21]

Despite his occasional public demonstrations of benevolence toward the Czech people, Heydrich had a secret and far more drastic agenda, which involved a program for the permanent "Germanization" of the Czech lands. After final German victory, it was expected that Bohemia-Moravia would be directly incorporated into the Reich. Those who did not accept or adapt to this imperative were to be considered candidates for extermination or removal. Perhaps two-thirds of the Czech nation was destined either for execution or shipment to conquered territory in Russia in the Arctic regions. Heydrich was nothing if not blunt about his ultimate aims: "This entire area will one day be definitely German, and the Czechs have nothing to expect here. . . . The area is the heart of the Reich. We will *try* to Germanize these

Czech vermin."[22] Czech Jewry became an immediate target of this policy, and a concentration camp at Terezín (Theresienstadt) was established as a way station for Jews eventually destined for Auschwitz and other killing fields in Poland.

The continuing decimation of the Czech resistance movement received a great deal of attention from Heydrich as well. Some 4,000 to 5,000 people were arrested as part of that effort in the months after his arrival in Prague, and the main organization of the opposition, the UVOD, saw most of its links with the outside world severed. By the end of 1941, it had in fact almost ceased to exist.[23] According to the Nazi's own figures, there were 246 acts of sabotage in October 1941, 157 in November, but only 34 in April 1942, and some 51 the following month. It was against this background that a plan was developed by Czech exiles in London, under the leadership of Eduard Beneš, for the assassination of Reinhard Heydrich. This operation, code-named ANTHROPOID, was, as it turned out, effectively a death warrant for the villagers of Lidice.

Beneš and the Czech Government-In-Exile

Eduard Beneš might fairly be described as the "grand old man" of Czech politics in the interwar period. Even before World War I, he had been active in the Czech independence movement against the Hapsburg Empire. Once war broke out, he remained in Prague to coordinate activities between the home resistance and the Czech émigré community abroad. In 1915 he was forced to flee because of police harassment, and he spent the remainder of the war years lobbying for support for Czech freedom. In part because of his efforts, the Allies at the Versailles Peace Conference did give their imprimatur to the creation of an independent Czechoslovakia. In the postwar period, Bene served as Czech foreign minister from 1918 to 1935, at which point he succeeded Tomás Masaryk as president of the Republic. Throughout this time he was well-known for his strong pro-Western policy, which translated into a steady attempt to forge strong ties with Britain and France in order to protect the fragile independence of the new Czechoslovakia (although this strategy was also supplemented by a security treaty signed with the Soviet Union in 1935).[24]

The disaster of the Munich accords put paid to all these efforts, and Bene resigned the Czech presidency on October 5, 1938, refusing to accept the implied surrender of his country to German domination. He soon left for London, where he occupied his time preparing a course of lectures for the University of Chicago and writing his memoirs. Shortly after the German occupation of Bohemia-Moravia in March, 1939, Beneš returned from Chicago to London in order to take over the leadership of the Czechoslovak anti-German resistance movement abroad. He observed with his typical self-confidence that "I could think of nobody else who in this moment should and could raise his voice in protest and act freely in the name of the Nation except the second President of the Republic who from this moment was truly in exile and who, through what had just happened at home, was again quite free to speak and act."[25]

His assumption of such responsibility was not immediately accepted by all in the Czech émigré community, with particular opposition being expressed by Czech émigrés in France.[26] Nor did the British government seem to be overly impressed by Beneš's claims to authority. When he first arrived back in London from Chicago, he was greeted at Victoria Station by a low-ranking Foreign Office official who informed him that he would be granted asylum on the condition that he engage in no political activity.[27] Beneš's basic goals at this point were (despite the Foreign Office's admonitions) to organize and obtain recognition for a formal Czech government-in-exile, to secure an official British and French repudiation of the Munich agreement, to "solve" the problem of the large Sudeten-German population in Czechoslovakia, and to develop a close working relationship with the exiled Polish government as well as with the Soviet Union and the Czech communist movement concerning the future of the homeland.[28]

The Shadow of Munich

Perhaps the single greatest concern, amounting almost to an obsession, that moved Eduard Beneš following his return to London was to obtain the setting-aside of the Munich agreement and all its political and legal consequences. As Beneš himself says, "From September, 1938, sleeping and waking, I was continuously thinking of this objective [annulling Munich]— living for it, suffering on its account and working for it in every one of my political actions. In fact, it was already my only aim in life." He recalled his feeling that should Munich be allowed to stand, the Czech nation would suffer "an alarming retrogression politically, economically, socially and morally and its injuries would remain for decades, if not for centuries."[29]

Beneš found the British government's equivocation in formally repudiating Munich both exasperating and insulting. He laid the blame for their slowness in acting on the legal quibblings of the Foreign Office as well as on the fact that there were some in the Churchill government who had themselves been involved in the original Munich negotiations. In his private ruminations, he sometimes allowed his bitterness at the original British connivance in the Munich accords to emerge: "What reflections, what moral essays and ironical comments on political morality, on the march of events and on historic justice could be added!"[30] In pressuring London publicly to repudiate Munich, however, he not surprisingly stressed a more pragmatic line. "My point was that the complete liquidation of Munich would have a most important influence on the morale of the Czechoslovaks at home in their struggle against Germany, and, indeed, it dealt a powerful blow against Nazi rule in Czechoslovakia."[31]

That Beneš was so set on overturning the Munich agreement is hardly surprising. Any leader of the Czech government-in-exile in World War II would likely have had a similar commitment, especially given that Munich sanctioned the surrender of one of the most important areas of Czechoslovakia (the Sudetenland) to Germany. But in Beneš's case there seems to have been something more as well. According to František Moravec, the head of intelligence for the Czech government-in exile, Beneš indeed had almost a "Munich complex." Moravec recalled that Beneš was "ever conscious of this black spot on his political career, caused by over-dependence on the West as represented by France, [and] he bent every effort to erase it."[32] Not only did Beneš perhaps have a guilty conscience about the failure of his strategy in this regard, but there is also the fact that when pressed by a number of his military men (including Moravec) to order the Czech armed forces to fight rather than surrender to the Munich sellout, he ordered them not to resist. In this sense, he may have been doubly culpable (or felt himself to be so) for the German oppression that was visited on his native land.[33] Under these circumstances, anything that could be done to persuade the British and French to overturn Munich—such as a dramatic assassination of a German official in Prague—had an unusual and uniquely personal importance for Beneš himself.

The Development and Execution of ANTHROPOID

In service to his goals, Beneš announced in October 1939 the formation of the Czechoslovak National Committee, which was designed to be the equivalent of a Czech government-in-exile for the duration of the war. At first the Committee received only a polite response to its requests for official sanction by the Allies (in particular the British). In July 1940, however, Lord Halifax, at the time Winston Churchill's foreign secretary, extended formal recognition to the National Committee as the Provisional Czechoslovak government and assumed financial responsibility for it as well. Beneš from this point

onward considered himself effectively the reconstituted president of Czechoslovakia and the tender of British support as a de facto repudiation of the
Munich agreement (although it was not until August 1942 that Anthony
Eden, the successor to Halifax as foreign secretary, officially told Beneš that
the British government did explicitly repudiate the Munich accords).[34]

Beneš immediately proceeded to organize at least the general structure of a fully functioning government, including a quasi-Parliament in the
form of the State Council. Monseigneur Jan Šrámek, a venerable relic of
many venerable prewar coalition cabinets, was named as prime minister,
with Jan Masaryk, son of the first president of Czechoslovakia, appointed
as foreign minister. As Minister of War there was a tough professional
soldier, General Sergej Ingr, who set up a small intelligence unit as well
as a general staff and war office that could draw on the resources of various
Czech infantry and air force units that were then present on British soil. In
the aftermath of these developments, Beneš broadcast to his native land on
July 24, 1940 to the effect that an independent Czech regime existed once
again and that he (not incidentally) was prepared to reassume leadership
of the nation once the war was over.[35]

Shortly after the outbreak of World War II, the British established the
Special Operations Executive (SOE) as a way to gather intelligence on
German-occupied Europe and to conduct covert military operations against
the Nazi presence there. The Czechs soon became heavily involved in SOE
activities targeted toward their homeland, both in terms of intelligence-gath-
ering and with respect to more active resistance measures. At the same time
the newly founded Czech government-in-exile established contact with its
supporters in Czechoslovakia through both courier and radio. It was shortly
after this that Beneš's government, together with SOE, began a program of
infiltrating special agents into the country, mostly by way of parachute, in
order to gather intelligence and to stiffen the resistance movement. The latter
consideration was driven in particular by the growing evidence that
Heydrich's policies were bearing fruit. As various reports from the homeland
suggested, there was every indication that the new Reichsprotektor was
"corrupting the working class by means of ostentatious social reforms,
bestowed with dramatic gestures." Beneš's head of Chancery, Jaromir
Smutný, allowed as how "there are a lot of collaborators at home, and our
industry is today the greatest and keenest supplier of arms to Germany."[36]

Between May 1941 and April 1942, some 27 men were dropped into
Czechoslovakia to stimulate opposition to the German occupation. Among
these 27 were two individuals chosen to carry out Operation ANTHROPOID:
the assassination of Reinhard Heydrich. The origins of the plan to kill

Heydrich have been the subject of considerable controversy, but the evidence suggests that Beneš was both instigator and prime supporter of the idea. According to František Moravec, Beneš wanted

> a spectacular action against the Nazis—an assassination carried out in complete secrecy by our trained paratroop commandos. The purpose of this action would be twofold. First, a powerful manifestation of resistance which would wipe out the stigma of passivity and help Czechoslovakia internationally. Second, a renaissance of the resistance movement by providing a spark which would activate the mass of the people.[37]

The plan was originally formulated in October 1941 and held in the strictest secrecy. None of Beneš's Cabinet colleagues were advised of his intentions, nor was anything put into writing on the matter.

Throughout that month a number of Czech soldiers underwent training under the auspices of the SOE for the forthcoming mission.[38] The date for the attempt on Heydrich was originally set for October 28, Czech Independence Day, but various difficulties prevented the two men chosen for the actual assassination, Josef Gabčík and Jan Kubiš, from landing in the Protectorate until December 28, 1941 (even so, Beneš was so intent on the carrying out of ANTHROPOID that he insisted on shortening the already very concentrated course of training for the two assassins). Gabčík and Kubiš kept the real purpose of their mission hidden from their underground contacts in Czechoslovakia until the following May. On the 27th of that month, they intercepted Heydrich's open car on its way from his country estate to his headquarters in Prague and severely wounded him with a bomb. He lingered on in a hospital for several days but then died of his wounds on June 4. He was the highest-ranking Nazi official to be assassinated during the entire war.

Hitler's reaction to the May 27 assault on Heydrich was immediate and drastic: his first response was to order the arrest or execution of 10,000 Czech citizens suspected of disloyalty to the Reich. One hundred Czech intellectuals were to be shot that very night. A million marks were offered by the German government for information leading to the arrests of the assassins, and this figure was matched by the Czech Protectorate government.[39] Despite these inducements, the imposition of martial law, and the widescale efforts of the Gestapo, the Security Police, and other German officials in arresting and interrogating possible suspects, the perpetrators of Heydrich's death remained at large. Finally, on June 16, a certain Karel Čurda, an agent parachuted into Czechoslovakia after Gabčík and Kubiš, cracked under the pressure and turned himself into the Gestapo. His information allowed the police to track down the assassins to an Orthodox Church in Prague, where they eventually committed suicide (along with five others) in order to avoid capture.

Why the selection of Lidice as a reprisal for the assassination of Heydrich?[40] The village's fate was sealed by a bizarre combination of circumstances. A factory owner in the nearby town of Slany intercepted a letter to one of his employees and reported its contents to the local Gestapo. The Germans arrested a number of people as a result, including several from Lidice, one of whose native sons was known to be serving in the Czech army in Britain. Subsequent investigations failed to turn up anything incriminating in Lidice, but at this point the German authorities were desperate for success in their search for Heydrich's assassins, and the name of Lidice had entered their horizon. Quite aside from whether destroying the village might be of any use in finding the killers of the Reichsprotektor, there was at this point a necessity, in the German view, for a dramatic act that would discourage any further attempts to challenge their control of the Protectorate. The maintenance of such control was important not only in terms of the geopolitical significance of Bohemia and Moravia—the former was the main marshaling yard for German transportation throughout the Reich—but also in terms of the contribution these areas were making (as already noted) to the German war effort, especially the arms production coming from the famed Skoda works at Pilsen in western Bohemia.

An ironic detail is that it was only after the destruction of Lidice that the Gestapo learned that some of the Czech parachutists had in fact been given addresses in the village to contact. All the same, there is no evidence that Lidice played any real role, direct or indirect, in the death of Heydrich. Given this fact, determining the real responsibility for its devastation, for this slaughter of the innocents, becomes even more compelling. In any such calculation, the trail inevitably leads back to the man who was primarily responsible for ANTHROPOID, Eduard Beneš.

4

The Destruction of
Lidice: Evaluation

In an interview given in 1944 to his admiring, even adoring, biographer, Compton MacKenzie, Eduard Beneš expressed little if any doubt about his past actions or basic philosophy of life. He described himself in the following manner:

> Throughout I have tried to settle my human problems logically and with restraint, until finally I think I have acquired a harmonious conception of life. . . . Through the study of modern philosophy I have attained an internal harmony. I have lived in such a way as to avoid having anything on my conscience with which I could reproach myself. I have no guilty regrets, and, although I have had very strong opponents, I have never been spiritually worried by them because I have always dealt straight-forwardly with them. . . . If I retired I shall be quite content, and that contentment will be due to my philosophic and moral conception of this earthly existence."[1]

As a general matter, these words suggest a person of genuine balance and internal peace of mind that invites admiration. In the context of the destruction of Lidice, however, they may be open to a somewhat different interpretation, particularly Beneš's assertion that he had nothing on his conscience with which he could reproach himself. On June 17, 1942, shortly after the obliteration of Lidice, the Czech government in London passed the following resolution: "For all the German crimes committed on Czechoslovak territory or against Czechoslovak citizens there are personally answerable all those who have committed, instigated, helped, shared in, or supported them."[2] For purposes of this essay, that is, the assessment of dirty hands in political decision-making, the question here becomes whether Beneš himself was not indictable in these terms. The resolution was directed against the Nazis; may it not (ironically) have had an application somewhat broader than that? In arriving at a judgment on the matter, the following discussion will employ criteria set out in an earlier chapter in weighing the existence of, but even more important the defensibility of, dirty hands. The first of these has to do with what we have called the "intuitive values" of the leader in question.

BENEŠ THE MAN

Eduard Beneš was an ascetic figure who disdained smoking or drinking (he claimed to have decided at age 14 never to touch alcohol) and who had few if any close friends and loathed all idle social gatherings. In this respect he bore a close resemblance to Charles de Gaulle, another leader of a government-in-exile who was often an uncomfortable spur in the side of British authorities. According to one British intelligence agent, Beneš was "a difficult man to know well [with a mind] machine-like in its compact tidiness and in his reserve." His conversation was "factual and entirely unemotional. Each point was marshalled in its proper place and, when dealt with, was marked off on his fingers."[3] František Moravec, Beneš's chief of intelligence, noted the differences between his boss and Jan Masaryk, son of Thomas Masaryk and later Czech foreign minister: "Beneš always correct, weighing every word, dry, scholastic, without any emotion, rarely smiling and never joking; Masaryk emotional, fond of contact with common people, good-hearted, resentful of bureaucratic procedures, completely informal and never fussy about a salty word if it expressed his point."[4]

Despite this rather offputting personality, Beneš generally displayed a Micawber-like confidence that things would eventually turn out all right. As he himself said, "In the most difficult position I have never despaired. In politics I always behave as though I were playing tennis. When my opponent is 'forty' and I am 'love' and the next ball may be the last, I am still convinced I can win the game." As the last comment suggests, Beneš was not without self-confidence. Indeed, his ego reached heights unusual for even the most self-centered of politicians, and at times he almost became a caricature of the great leader infused with a sense of his own infallibility.[5] Thus he commented at one point, "I am considered in Central Europe almost a human symbol of that democracy which Hitler loathes." With his flair for the dramatic, he even suggested that he had once contemplated doing in the Führer with his own hand. Pressed by his aides to consider a meeting with the German leader before the war, Beneš recalled that he had agreed to do so, but only with a hand grenade in one pocket and a revolver in the other. "If he shouts at me as he has shouted at Schuschnigg [the Austrian leader] I shall throw the grenade and there will be a European scandal. Do you [still] want me to go?" Evidently his aides became quite alarmed at this potential scenario, and Beneš never did meet personally with Hitler.[6]

As president of Czechoslovakia from 1935 to 1938, Beneš had been a respected but hardly beloved head of his country. His reaction to the demands by the Sudeten Germans and the Slovaks for greater autonomy was routine liberal sympathy for the needs of minority populations, but he felt even more strongly the necessity of maintaining the unitary Czech state lest separatist pressures tear it apart. Partly because of the stress he was subject to at the time, and even more because of his inherent personality traits, Beneš grew increasingly impatient with any criticism of his ideas or policies. He remarked at one point that "there is nothing worse than when the press and public opinion criticizes foreign matters which it does not know and understand."[7]

These characteristics were to grow even more pronounced during his period as head of the Czech government-in-exile and were to figure in their own way in the fate of Lidice. We have spoken earlier of the problem of "multiple dirty hands," that is, the difficulty of assigning direct responsibility for a controversial decision to a specific individual. In the case of ANTHRO-POID, however, Beneš's leadership style was such that the operation can reasonably be considered his initiative alone. Even his (mostly) admiring personal secretary, Edward Táborský, admits that in London Beneš's "position became virtually that of a benevolent absolutist ruler, for he was not accountable to any other organ. . . . Actual decision-making in all major policy matters, and even some minor ones, remained in Beneš's hands." These included, inter alia, relations with the Hácha regime, the domestic Czech resistance, and general issues of foreign policy.[8]

The impression that one gains of Beneš, based in particular on the reminiscences of those who worked closely with him, was that he was the sort of person who loved humankind in the abstract but despised or at least was cold to it in the particular. From his earliest days of political activity, he displayed a strong commitment to social egalitarianism and progressive, even radical, political and economic change. At the same time, he seemed to have a penchant for intrigue and secrecy in service to these goals, accompanied, not incidentally, by a conviction that only strong leadership rather than spontaneous mass action could bring about real progress. It is perhaps not too much to say that he came to regard individual human beings as the objects rather than the subjects of politics. One of his closest aides and supporters, Jaromir Smutný, himself wondered at "the absence of everything human in his character. He is a machine for thinking and working, without human feelings, though with human weaknesses. . . . He has lost contact with people. Therefore he often misjudges them if their motives are other than political."[9]

Beneš may have lost contact with people, but it would be unfair to claim that he was totally indifferent to the effect that his decisions were likely to have on his followers. Indeed, before the development of ANTHROPOID, he had taken a fairly cautious approach to stirring up active resistance to the Nazis in Czechoslovakia, lest this lead to drastic reprisals against the Czechs by the occupation authorities. His support for—indeed his initiation of—the scheme for the assassination of Heydrich, however, can be attributed at least in part to a concern with his own personal political position that seems to have mitigated any qualms he may have felt about the potential effect of ANTHROPOID on his fellow citizens in Czechoslovakia.

He was facing increasing pressure from the Allies to demonstrate that under his leadership the Czechs were prepared to do or were capable of doing real damage to the Nazi war effort. He commented to his intelligence chief about their "humiliating insistence" on this point. Under the circumstances, it was Beneš's very credibility as a political figure that was now at stake. His concern on this score also extended to his reputation in Czechoslovakia itself, particularly in terms of his anticipated role in the country's politics after the war. Given Heydrich's drastic crackdown on the Beneš-led resistance forces in Czechoslovakia, Beneš was fearful that the Communist-led resistance, taking its orders from Moscow, would come to dominate the scene, and that in the postwar period Stalin would consider them the only legitimate authority in the country. In order to consolidate his position as the principal and undisputed commander of the Czechoslovak opposition to the Nazis, it was necessary that some drastic action be undertaken that would reaffirm his role.

Some of this, to be sure, can be interpreted simply in terms of Beneš's objective analysis of what was necessary for the future independence of his own people as well as for continuing Allied support for their cause. At the same time, Beneš's personal ego and self-image loom very large here as well. He had styled himself as the unquestioned leader of Czech aspirations, and it was not a role that he was disposed to relinquish. If it became necessary to undertake some radical step, with unforeseen but possibly draconian consequences, in order to maintain his position, then the Czech people would be asked to pay the price of his own ambition. In a somewhat bizarre comment on how he saw himself, he insisted at one point, "I abhor personal egoism, whether it reveals itself in an individual or in the collective will of a nation to dominate other nations."[10] The latter principle was an impeccable one, and there is no doubt that it did inform Beneš's thinking very heavily. The first part of the statement, however, can only be regarded as an act of self-illusion. As is usual in these situations, however, it is likely that Beneš saw his own personal political interests as being compatible with—indeed, almost equivalent to—those of the nation as a whole. Major political leaders rarely make a distinction between what is good for themselves and what is good for the collectives they represent. They typically feel that they can do good and do well at the same time.

In assessing Beneš's intuitive values, there is a final point that needs mentioning. We have earlier discussed the existence of "deontological ethics," in which certain virtuous acts are to be adopted regardless of their consequentialist results. Beneš seemed to be sympathetic to this credo. "There are matters of law, and principles of political morality, which must not be *sacrificed at any price, not even for the sake of any supposed or real opportunistic political advantages whatsoever, nor under the most cruel threats and pressure.*"[11] On another occasion, he argued, in his typically elegant language, that there was "an Absolute Truth with a universal value. We must return to the Absolute. The present war was largely due to the ignoring of the Absolute and the worship of the Relative. Man, in losing his belief in God, has lost belief in himself."[12] Whether or not immutable standards of conduct may be attributed to a belief in a Supreme Being, it seems that Beneš did feel that such standards existed.

The enduring puzzle is how he squared this conception with his orders for ANTHROPOID, how he balanced the likely suffering of his Czech compatriots against the "political advantages" that were anticipated from the assassination of Heydrich. What *were* the commanding principles to which he felt he had to adhere, particularly insofar as they affected other human beings? František Moravec offers a very revealing comment on this matter. He recalls that "in private, Beneš felt bitter about the fact that the Czech people were unable to create a strong fighting underground, like the French. He was particularly jealous of France, failing to appreciate her far more advantageous position, her relatively easy communications with England, from which the Maquis were being supplied with arms and other necessities."[13] The words "bitter" and "jealous" are what leap out from this statement. "Bitter" at his countrymen because they were unable to resist Nazi oppression (even while Beneš himself resided in London)? "Jealous" of the French because of their relatively greater success in the matter? Such attitudes (or emotions) raise very troubling questions as to those "Absolute Truths" that Beneš claimed to be required guides to action. Surely, respect for the circumstances—and the fate—of individual human beings should rank very high among these Truths. We have already conceded that Beneš was not totally indifferent to such an imperative. At the same time, this particular principle may have ranked relatively low in the pantheon of virtues to which he felt the moral leader must adhere.

THE RESULTS OF ANTHROPOID

A second test of the morality of political leaders has to do not with their inherent principles of conduct but with the actual consequences of their actions—not in terms of their own personal interests but in terms of the achievement of an acknowledged good end. As earlier stated, the consequentialist standard requires that politicians give due and careful attention to all the ramifications of their decisions, and make a careful assessment of the positive and negative effects likely to ensue from individual decisions. What to make of Beneš's commitment to ANTHROPOID in these terms?

Certainly anything that led to a weakening of the Nazi challenge, not just in Czechoslovakia itself but in Europe as a whole, had to be considered a good and legitimate end. At the same time, when Beneš ordered the assassination of Reinhard Heydrich, he could hardly have been unaware that drastic results were likely to follow for his fellow Czechs from such an act. The Nazis had developed a well-deserved reputation not just for taking an eye for an eye, a tooth for a tooth, but for making their reprisals out of all proportion to the original offense. In responding to the activities of partisans in the East, the standard formula was 100 local nationals to be shot for each German death. Even in Western Europe, however, the policy was grim enough. In October 1941, for example, 50 French hostages were executed in retaliation for an attack on the military commandant of Nantes. The ultimate sacrifice of Czech lives in the aftermath of ANTHROPOID has been variously estimated as being between 1,300 and 5,000. Under these circumstances, it is only fair to ask what positive consequences for the war effort, and in particular for the Czech cause, did Beneš anticipate from the killing of Heydrich. In order to view his actions in a positive moral light, we have to establish that he believed very substantial results would ensue from Heydrich's death, that he had given careful thought to the matter, and, finally, that his analysis was reasonably taken.

One impulse that seems to have been present in the development of ANTHROPOID is very hard to defend from any reasonable consequentialist perspective: a simple desire for revenge on the part of Beneš and his followers. After assuming the position of Reichsprotektor in late September 1941, Heydrich, as already detailed, had steadily undermined the power of the fledgling Czech home army and the Czech resistance. Prime Minister Eliáš had been arrested and scheduled for execution. The government of President Hácha seemed to be drifting ever more steadily into open collaboration with the Nazi occupation regime. All these developments seemed to mock Beneš's claims to be an effective leader of the Czech opposition and of an active government-in-exile. The death of Heydrich would demonstrate that the Czech forces in London still had the capacity to do damage to the German cause, thus bolstering their self-confidence and self-image, and, just as important, would show that Heydrich as well as other top Nazis were hardly impervious to retaliation for their activities. One curious piece of evidence testifying to the essentially symbolic importance attached to Heydrich's assassination was the fact that he was actually about to step down as acting Reichsprotektor in Czechoslovakia in order to assume new duties in France, and indeed was scheduled to fly to Berlin on May 27 (the day of the attack) in order to receive instructions on his new assignment.

It may be argued, of course, that ANTHROPOID could hardly have been designed as revenge for Heydrich's successful oppression of the Czech resistance since discussion concerning an assassination of a high German official in Czechoslovakia was first considered by Beneš and his advisers only five days after Heydrich's arrival in Prague.[14] Yet the actual assassination of Heydrich was carried out in late May 1942, and it seems fair to assume that a rather different constellation of reasons for ANTHROPOID may have emerged by that point. Assuming that a sheer desire for retaliation against Heydrich was one of these factors, the question becomes how much sacrifice could be expected of the Czech people in order to slake this thirst for revenge, even given that many living in Czechoslovakia would themselves take satisfaction in the demise of their oppressor.

Not surprisingly, Beneš disguised any revenge motive in his defense of ANTHROPOID, presumably because this would have appeared to be a pretty thin reed on which to undertake such a momentous enterprise. Instead, he spoke of overriding political imperatives that demanded some dramatic step against the German occupation of Czechoslovakia. These imperatives actually divided into several parts, one of which we have already briefly examined. Given that part of the Czech resistance was Communist-led, Beneš seems to have feared that if the non-Communist resistance did not demonstrate its mettle more clearly, Stalin would decide to cut off relations with them and instead throw his full support behind the Czech Communist underground. This in turn would greatly undermine Czechoslovakia's prospects for regaining its independence after the war under a democratic regime not dominated by Stalin's writ—and one led, not incidentally, by Beneš himself. It was certainly true that once the German invasion of Russia was underway, the Soviets became increasingly desperate for the Czech underground to do anything it could to undermine the German war effort.

The postwar fate of Czechoslovakia supposedly figured in another way as well in the development of ANTHROPOID. For some reason, in the spring of 1942 Beneš became convinced that a compromise peace between the Axis and the Allies was a distinct possibility. His assumption was that after further German advances in Russia, Hitler would propose a settlement in which Britain and France would retain (or regain) their independence in return for a free German hand in central and eastern Europe. Beneš thought that such an offer would prove highly tempting to powerful elements in the British government, especially since at the Munich Conference Britain had shown a willingness to sacrifice a small central European state in order to avoid a conflict with the Germans. Munich also suggested to Beneš that many in Britain regarded the Nazis as a useful bulwark against Soviet designs on Europe. Under these circumstances, some dramatic step by the Czech resistance would demonstrate its continued commitment to the defeat of the Germans and, most important, re-establish the bona fides of the Czech people as a nation worthy of support rather than betrayal.

On May 15, 1942, in a message broadcast from London, Beneš summarized his thinking:

> I expect that in a forthcoming offensive the Germans will push with all their forces. They are sure to have some success. . . . In such a case I would expect German proposals for an inconclusive peace. The crisis would be a serious one and it would shake some people even here among the Allies. . . . In such a situation, an act of violence such as disturbances, direct subversion, sabotage, or demonstrations, might be imperative or even necessary in our country. This would save the nation internationally, and even great sacrifice would be worth it.[15]

Heydrich's death, in short, would give the Czechs a "seat at the table" should serious negotiations begin about a compromise end to the war. Closely related to the above considerations was the expressed belief by Beneš and others that the assassination of Heydrich would spur a general uprising of the Czech people against their German oppressors, which in itself would act as an impressive testament to Allied leaders concerning the legitimate claims of the Czechs to favored consideration. As Beneš's intelligence chief put it, ANTHROPOID would provide "a spark which would activate the mass of the people," since the anticipated German reprisals would force the Czechs to "react to . . . German pressure with counter-pressure."[16]

Illusion and Reality

What to make of all these arguments? Nobody could deny, of course, that Munich *had* happened and that it set an ominous precedent for the willingness of others to sacrifice Czechoslovakia for their own interests. The spectre of Stalin's attempting to dominate Czechoslovakia after the war was also hardly an idle one, as postwar events were grimly to demonstrate. Nevertheless, a close examination of the rationale for ANTHROPOID reveals it to be an essentially flimsy collection of dubious propositions that hardly stood up to careful or reasonable analysis. It is not enough simply to say that Beneš proved to be wrong about the effects of ANTHROPOID. The real point is that his reasoning on the matter was suspect—even superficial—from the beginning and can hardly be considered a serious basis for an operation that was likely to have such drastic consequences for the Czech people.

Consider for a moment the proposition that ANTHROPOID was likely to spark the mass of the Czech people into revolt. Such a belief had to be regarded more as an article of faith, or willful hope, than a result of rigorous examination. The Czech resistance had always faced virtually insuperable obstacles in converting itself into a genuinely active and broad-based movement. Geography certainly played a role here, particularly the remoteness of the country from Allied sources of supply as well as the relative absence of forest and mountain areas as places of sanctuary. The concentration of the Czech people in urban areas also greatly facilitated Nazi security measures, and there was, finally, the generally willing collaboration of the Sudeten German population in the German occupation.

The Hácha regime in Prague went out of its way to stress these facts of life following the attack on Heydrich. President Hácha warned that "whoever works against the Reich in the slightest way will be destroyed." His head of propaganda, Emmanuel Moravec, referred to the Nazi taste for reprisals, and warned his listeners: "Just think a little bit, what would await the Czech people if the culprits were not found." Perhaps partly in response to such warnings, the Gestapo received over 500 tips from Czech citizens as to the possible identity of the attackers. So many of these came in that the Gestapo had to ask that only "serious" leads be reported.[17]

In sum, it is not to disparage the Czech people's capacity for courage or sacrifice to say that by the spring of 1942 all the evidence suggested that they had generally decided to make the best of their circumstances under the Nazi Protectorate and to await the larger outcome of the war to (hopefully) regain their freedom. The best description of the prevailing public attitude was that it was sullen but not mutinous. Interestingly, Karl Frank himself was at pains to convince Hitler that the assassination of Heydrich did not reflect any general rebelliousness among the Czechs. He called the attack on Heydrich "an isolated act engineered by the enemy abroad, rather than the result of a strong revolutionary or resistance movement of the Czech people."[18] Frank was hardly noted for his tender feelings toward the Czechs, and that he would offer such an argument thus seems rather significant.

Czech behavior under duress has frequently been seen as epitomized by the character of the "Good Soldier Schweik" from the famous novel of World War I by Jaroslav Hasek. "Schweikism" means that one ostensibly is loyal to prevailing authority while actually defying it in small ways—it is the contrast between the public and private personas that is typical of those living under oppression, and perhaps especially so in the case of the Czechs, who certainly had a long historical experience in having to deal with such oppression. In any case, it might be fairly said that by 1942 the Czechs as a whole had adopted "Schweikism" as their prevailing mode of operation. This meant that they might deny their cooperation to the Germans in various marginal ways, but essentially would tend to their private affairs and await the outcome of events. This was hardly an ignoble or difficult stance to understand. As one very perceptive study of the period suggests,

> In view of the overwhelmingly superior German forces and the lack of hope for quick help from the outside, the only chance for the Czech people in the Protectorate lay in refraining from an unequal struggle that would have cost rivers of blood, to preserve or even strengthen their national position, and collaborating just enough to give the Germans no cause for harsh repression and compulsory measures, while providing the lowest possible degree of effective aid to the German war machine.[19]

That the assassination of Heydrich would cause a fundamental transformation in this attitude was hardly more than a will o' the wisp; indeed, the assassination was far more likely to increase the caution of the Czech people, particularly given the fears about German brutality when challenged.

Ironically, Beneš seems to have implicitly accepted the basic point in this passage from his memoirs:

> I am a real democrat. I know that in the development of Nations and States there are periods when violent revolutions are necessary. But I also know that at certain moments of national history, attempts to stage a violent revolution may actually amount to a thoroughly bad attempt on the part of reaction. . . . Slow progress may be sometimes more revolutionary than unreasonable pressure and violence.[20]

The ultimate irony was that what came to be called the *Heydrichiáda,* the period of terror after the death of Heydrich, actually served to complete the German plan for the pacification of Bohemia-Moravia, although there was at the very end of the war a brief pitched battle between Czechs and Germans in Prague in which about 2,000 Czechs were killed. In the immediate aftermath of ANTHROPOID, however, the last remaining members of UVOD were arrested. By the end of 1942, of 26 parachutists dropped into Czechoslovakia at the direction of the Czech government-in-exile, 14 were dead, 3 were in jail, 2 had changed sides, and only 7 were still operating. By March 1943, all of the latter were either dead or collaborating. London at this point had totally lost contact with any remnants of the home resistance. Even the May 1945 uprising in Prague was basically a spontaneous action, and not one planned by London. As a consequence of ANTHROPOID, in sum, "the émigré movement lost not only its grip on the resistance movement but also lost control in general. After three years of more or less peaceful coexistence, the assassination of Heydrich was a great divide for Czechoslovakia."[21]

Given the sobering example of the *Heydrichiáda,* the general public itself basically retreated from all political or oppositional activity. As a British SOE report concluded, in the aftermath of the Heydrich assassination, "the spirit of open resistance" in the Protectorate had been broken. One symbol of the prevailing Czech passivity or fatalism in the face of German might was the fact that by the end of 1942, over 350,000 Czech administrative employees quietly worked away under the supervision of only 738 Germans at the Office of the Protector and another 1,146 in various other Czech agencies (before the arrival of Heydrich, the number of German officials in supervisory roles had been 9,300 and 4,700 respectively).[22]

After Heydrich's death, there were to be no more major acts of sabotage or assassination in the Protectorate. Heydrich's successor, Kurt Daluege, basically continued Heydrich's policy of "whip and sugar" and boasted of its great success: "The development of the current political line [brutal suppression of dissent but buying off of the workers] has proved correct."[23] From a strictly material point of view, the phenomenon of Czech "Schweikism" seems, incidentally, to have had rather desirable results. The overall population in Bohemia-Moravia actually increased by 236,000 during the years of the war, due largely to a rising birth rate. The number of non-Jewish Czech citizens executed by the Germans amounted to between 35,000 and 50,000, a tragic number by any reckoning but distinctly modest compared to other occupied countries.[24]

In suggesting that from a consequentialist perspective the assassination of Heydrich was, to paraphrase the American general Omar Bradley, "the wrong action, in the wrong place, at the wrong time," we need to consider another supposed rationale for ANTHROPOID: the necessity of demonstrating to the Allies that the Czechs deserved a serious hearing at the impending "peace negotiations" leading to a compromise settlement of the war. In response to the destruction of Lidice, Beneš offered the following clinical observation: "What the Germans are doing is horrible, but from the political point of view they gave us one certainty: under no circumstances can doubts be cast any more upon Czechoslovakia's national integrity and her right to independence."[25] The fact is that by the time of the carrying out of ANTHROPOID, the chances of a negotiation leading to a compromise peace were virtually nonexistent.

Britain had survived a real threat of Nazi invasion in the summer of 1940, not least because of her victory in the Battle of Britain, and was now waging an increasingly aggressive strategic bombing campaign against the German homeland. The United States had become a formal belligerent in the war in December 1941, and the Soviets had thrown the Germans back from the gates of Moscow in the same month, which put paid to the Nazi hopes of a decisive victory over the Soviet Union in the initial phase of Barbarossa. To be sure it was reasonable to expect (as Beneš himself argued) that the Germans would continue to conquer additional Soviet territory in the summer campaign of 1942, but any reasonable balancing of the forces arrayed against Hitler at this point compared with those he had at his disposal would have suggested that Berlin's ultimate defeat was almost a foregone conclusion. Under these circumstances, the motivation for the Allies to enter into a compromise peace with the Nazi regime was minimal.

Finally, the notion that the non-Communist resistance in Czechoslovakia had to undertake a spectacular action in order to demonstrate their *bona fides* when compared with their Communist rivals hardly stands up to serious analysis. Stalin was notorious for regarding the Communist partisans in Eastern Europe as essentially minor, although occasionally useful, adjuncts to the more fundamental power and geopolitical factors in place as he attempted to extend his sway over the region. The idea that he would surrender any of his long-term designs for bringing Czechoslovakia under his control because of his putative admiration for the courage of the Czech resistance was seriously to misinterpret his approach to politics. As it turned out, Moscow did allow a brief period of independence for Czechoslovakia in the postwar years, but not because of any close assessment of the behavior of the two Czech resistance movements. When Stalin did move to subjugate the Czechs in February 1948, it was because his analysis made such a move seem almost risk-free, given the overwhelming preponderance of Soviet strength in the area and thus the unlikelihood that the West would oppose his actions by force. Beneš could have ordered the assassination of a hundred Heydrichs without affecting the Soviet dictator's basic calculations in this regard.

In sum, the main defense that can be offered for Operation ANTHROPOID in terms of its practical consequences was that it managed to rid the world of a truly loathsome individual. Yet the German occupation of Czechoslovakia involved a whole host of loathsome individuals, as indeed did the Nazi movement as a whole. To kill one of them regardless of the effects of such a step on the welfare of the Czech people as a whole seems to have been a basically futile exercise. Hitler himself was curiously persuasive on this point. After the death of Heydrich, one of the Führer's immediate reactions was to consider the appointment of a certain SS general named Erich von dem Bach-Zelewski to succeed Heydrich, since he "saw in him evidence that he would act even more severely and brutally than Heydrich and have no scruples about wading through a sea of blood." Bach-Zelewski was indeed a "promising" candidate to be Heydrich's successor: it was he who employed the most repulsive tactics in putting down the Warsaw uprising of 1944 (and for which he was hanged as a war criminal after the war). The point was that the Czechs would discover, as Hitler put it, that "when they shoot down one, then someone else much worse will follow."[26]

This is not to argue that the Czech people should have simply accepted their lot under the German occupation without complaint; some tangible resistance to that occupation was necessary in both moral and practical terms and was to some degree even feasible. The point is that a less spectacular but more measured long-term resistance strategy would have likely paid far higher dividends in all respects than the one dramatic step of eliminating a single Reichsprotektor, who after all could be replaced (as Hitler said) by someone even worse. Ultimately the advisable course for the Czechs would have been to maintain a low-scale opposition at home while depending on the fortunes of war to transform their prospects for regaining their freedom. The assassination of Heydrich may have been satisfying to Beneš as an example of what his leadership could produce, and may even today appeal to those who have a taste for the dramatic in the defiance of tyranny. From the viewpoint of those most likely to be directly affected by such dramatic gestures, however, the final verdict on such matters is likely to be considerably different—and not without reason.

The Willing Suspension of Disbelief

In offering a critique of ANTHROPOID from a consequentialist perspective, it is important to weigh what those in London knew about conditions in Czechoslovakia. A moral defense of their actions might be tendered on the basis that given the information available to them, it was reasonable for them to conclude that ANTHROPOID would have important results, so important indeed that they would overshadow the inevitable suffering that Heydrich's assassination would bring to the Czech people. That they may have been mistaken in this estimation does not in itself make them morally culpable. After all, statesmen often (perhaps normally) have to make a best-guess analysis of the outcomes of their actions based on only partial or even flawed data. The consequentialist standard simply requires that they carefully consider all possible outcomes based on the available information and arrive at appropriate decisions ("appropriate" in terms of their anticipated proportionality) as a result. Political leaders *can* be accused of moral dereliction, however, if their policies lead to disproportionately evil results and they had adequate information at the time of decision to suggest that this would be so. The sins involved here may be either ones of omission or commission, that is, simply ignoring certain relevant facts on the one hand, or, on the other, twisting the available information around so that it conforms with certain preconceived ideas.

As it happens, we have a good deal of evidence on the quantity and quality of information available to the Czech government-in-exile concerning conditions in Czechoslovakia prior to the development of ANTHROPOID. František Moravec, the prewar head of Czech intelligence, had managed to escape from Prague in March 1939 with 11 of his top aides. Before leaving, he had established a network of agents in the Protectorate and in Germany itself numbering around 30, who in turn recruited others to work for Moravec's intelligence operation in London. Moravec's most important operative, however, was not a Czech at all but an officer in the German Abwehr named Paul Thümmel, who had been providing highly classified information to the Czechs as far back as 1937. Thümmel (code-named A54) was posted to Prague after the establishment of the Protectorate, and because of his anti-Nazi convictions proved to be an immensely valuable source of insight as to German policy both in Bohemia-Moravia and in a wider context as well (for example, he gave the London Czechs the exact date of the planned German offensive against the West in the spring of 1940).

The fact seems to be, then, that Beneš and his government-in-exile had a great deal of relevant information at their disposal as they contemplated ANTHROPOID. Beneš himself testified to this welcome situation:

> Our intelligence service . . . was quite first-class during the first period of the war. . . . It had, both in the Republic and in Germany, a magnificent net of intelligent agents among the German soldiers themselves, and especially among anti-Nazi Germans. In this way, until 1942 (up to the time of the purge after the shooting of R. Heydrich) we received from Germany . . . reports which were a source of great astonishment to the British and which were of immense usefulness in the guidance of our liberation movement abroad.[27]

As to his knowledge about the specific situation in the Protectorate itself, Beneš recalled that he received "very detailed reports about how matters were developing at home in the 'Protectorate' including . . . how our people were being treated, our politicians, our common people, our political parties, our clubs, our whole cultural life, how many of our people were already in concentration camps, etc., etc."[28]

The scope and sophistication of this intelligence effort suggests one of the more ironic (and presumably unintended) effects of the assassination of Heydrich. On balance, one of the key functions—perhaps the key function—of the Czech home resistance was in the gathering of intelligence to be sent abroad. Their success in this regard was perhaps the main marker that Beneš had to present to the Allies in gaining their support for the Czech government-in-exile and for full Czech independence after the war. As Moravec himself says, "The successful accomplishment of our Operation Transfer [Moravec's moving of his intelligence team to London] provided a pillar on which our liberation movement abroad could lean. It was our most positive contribution to the allied war effort."[29] In the aftermath of ANTHROPOID, however, the assets of Czech intelligence in the Protectorate were devastated, and thus the one contribution to the Allies that the government-in-exile was particularly proud of was effectively eliminated, or at least greatly diminished.

There is a curious story in this context that deserves at least brief mention. It has sometimes been suggested that the real goal of ANTHROPOID was to protect the operations of Paul Thümmel, who was under increasing suspicion by Heydrich's security apparatus after the acting Reichsprotektor established himself in Prague. The logic of this assertion evidently is that with Heydrich's death the pressure on Thümmel would subside. On balance, however, this rationale for ANTHROPOID seems to have been something only thought of ex post facto in order to render the terrible suffering of the Czechs after Heydrich's assassination more acceptable. The fact is that Thümmel was arrested by the Gestapo in March 1942, and shortly thereafter dispatched to the concentration camp at Terezín, some two months *prior* to the assassination of Heydrich (Thümmel was eventually executed on April 20, 1945.) It is rather striking under these circumstances that František Moravec, in his memoirs published some years after the war, claims that Thümmel contacted Czech intelligence *after* Heydrich's death and continued to work for them, even meeting with Czech agents in Istanbul, and that he cooperated with the Czech underground as well. It was only later, Moravec claims, that Thümmel was arrested.

The head of Czech intelligence defended ANTHROPOID to the last as a good and reasonable decision even though it admittedly did lead to some brutal consequences for his Czech compatriots. His "confusion" concerning Thümmel can only be interpreted from this perspective as an attempt to offer an important justification for the suffering caused by his (and Beneš's) actions. To return to the larger point here, however, it seems that *prior* to ANTHROPOIDs being carried out, the Czech government-in-exile had ample information on actual conditions in the Protectorate that made it highly unlikely that so dramatic a step as the killing of Heydrich would produce benefits proportionate to the reprisals that the Germans were likely to take. The fact that Thümmel would not be around to benefit from Heydrich's death was only one of these pieces of information. There was a lot more that suggested that the German grip on the Protectorate was so firm that simply removing Heydrich was hardly likely to improve the situation in any material way. Moreover, the history of German retaliation for assaults on their personnel (let alone someone as important as Heydrich) should have been ample evidence that the consequences of ANTHROPOID were likely to be especially terrible. Beneš and others in London chose either to ignore these indicators or to rearrange them to accord with their preferred vision of how they could influence events in the Protectorate. Either way, they hardly met the consequentialist imperative in the making of important political decisions.

5

THE WELFARE OF ALL

The final imperative in the making of those decisions is due attention to what we have called the "universalization" principle. This requires that careful consideration be given to how a particular action will affect the interests of *all* concerned parties. The concept of universalization inherently places demands on decisionmakers to consider their policies in the broadest possible context, and to give appropriate weight to the needs and concerns of those who may not have been involved in the making of a decision but who will nevertheless feel its impact. This does not mean that there cannot be some legitimate ranking of the interests involved and, in the final analysis, an emphasis on some at the expense of others. The basic requirement simply is that political leaders demonstrate an awareness of the full range of interests likely to be affected by their actions, and to make at least a good faith effort to reconcile these as much as possible.

In the case of Eduard Beneš and the assassination of Reinhard Heydrich, the dictates of universalization essentially had to do with the likely impact of ANTHROPOID on various of his own compatriots. The question was to what degree was it fair and just for Beneš (safely situated in London) to expose his fellow Czechs to the wrath of the Nazis that was sure to follow the demise of Heydrich. Beneš, of course, had many awesome responsibilities, not the least of which was to maintain Allied support for Czech concerns and independence after the Germans were defeated and, perhaps more indefinable, to sustain a sense of national pride and self-worth among the Czech people that would be vital in restoring their image as a nation after the war. It was precisely the latter function that De Gaulle saw as one of his most important tasks in leading the Free French resistance to the Nazis. To serve such a goal, sacrifices could and perhaps legitimately should be demanded in the interests of the nation as a whole.

But this does not mean that they could be insisted on routinely or without careful thought as to their proportionality. Attention had to be given to the *level* of sacrifice likely to be involved in any particular action and to what degree that action was likely to be important in the achievement of a good cause—in the first instance, the defeat of the Germans themselves, but also in support of the postwar status of the country and the maintenance (or recovery) of the national morale and spirit. Barring a clear and explicit connection between the given sacrifice demanded and an outcome (or outcomes) reasonably to be expected from the event, neither Beneš nor De Gaulle nor any other wartime leader had the right simply to ask as a rote matter that their compatriots "suffer" for the cause, no matter how vague the utility of their suffering might be. In a sense the application of Kant's Categorical Imperative to the planning of ANTHROPOID raises the following scenario: suppose that the tables were reversed, and Beneš was a member of the underground living in Czechoslovakia rather than a luminary living in London. Would he in these circumstances have been content with or at least accepting of an order to kill Heydrich that was likely to mean his—and a great many others—demise?

In announcing his resignation as president of Czechoslovakia follow-ing the Munich agreement (to be followed shortly by his departure for England), Beneš offered the following pious sentiments to his fellow Czechs: "I do not leave the ship because the sea is stormy, but because it is a political necessity. I remain conscious of my duties as a citizen. For all our citizens I wish better times in the future, both for them and for our beautiful country. Good-bye to you. Remain united, brave, and faithful."[30] This somewhat treacly farewell message raises the question of how closely attuned Beneš actually was to "better times" for his fellow Czechs in his capacity as head of the government-in-exile. More specifically, did he give reasonable atten-tion to and due care for the likely effect of his decisions on those who would feel their impact? Did he go beyond his personal political calculations and interests in weighing the interests and rights of all others? In developing answers to these questions, we need to break down the discussion by considering in turn differing groups of individuals with differing roles and stakes in the carrying out of ANTHROPOID.

The Foot Soldiers of ANTHROPOID

The first of these were the actual men chosen to kill Reinhard Heydrich. It is important to recognize that Josef Gabčík and Jan Kubiš were uniformed members of the Czech armed forces stationed in Great Britain and that they had, moreover, volunteered for ANTHROPOID. Under these circumstances they had to accept the possibility of their lives becoming forfeit at the discretion or orders of higher authority. The fact that they were volunteers seems especially germane here: by offering their services in an obviously dangerous mission, they presumably gave at least an implicit nod to the necessity and rationale of their task. Whatever later complaints they might raise about their mission would seem, in these terms, open to discount.

Even so, a commander-in-chief has a responsibility to see that the fighting men under his command are not simply idly sacrificed in ill-planned or fruitless assignments. He may rightly order them to do danger-ous things, even to the extent of knowing that they will likely die in the course of carrying them out. But he must always value their individual right to life and accept as a primary obligation that this right will not be abridged carelessly. What to say about Beneš's treatment of Gabčík and Kubiš in these terms? František Moravec recalls that "the day before they left the two men were received by President Beneš. He stressed the historical importance of what they were about to do. He knew this was a do-or-die mission and I could see that—like me—he was affected by the moving simplicity with which they accepted their lot. When he said goodbye to them, there were tears in his eyes."[31]

As it turns out, the tears in Beneš's eyes could not disguise the fact that his supposed analysis of the situation in the homeland—which had led to the development of ANTHROPOID—left something to be desired, as Gabčík and Kubiš soon discovered after being parachuted into Czechoslovakia. In postwar testimony by one of the survivors of the Czech resistance, Vaclav Krupka recalls the parachutists telling him when they first landed of their confidence that the war would soon be over and that the Allies were sure to invade the Continent in 1942—all this based on what they had been told in London. The evident reality that the Germans were far from beaten, and that in fact their hold over the Protectorate was stronger than ever, was a cruel blow to their optimism. "For them," Krupka recalled, "this was like being awakened from a delightful dream." At first, they had anticipated that after killing Heydrich they would only have to hold out a short time before Allied victory assured their survival. Now this seemed to be a forlorn possibility. "They were young and they loved life. Certainly, they had volunteered; but not for a hopeless mission. . . . But in fact they had been told in London that the end was near. The wholly different reality that confronted them must have weighed heavily on their spirits."[32]

This weight evidently had to do not only with their own slim chances of survival, but even more with the realization that the terrible reprisals the Nazis were likely to take (and then did take) after Heydrich's death would be all out of proportion to what had been achieved. Shortly before they undertook the actual assassination of Heydrich, Gabčík and Kubiš seemed to hesitate at actually going ahead, but after all they were soldiers and accustomed to obeying orders. Their commitment to military discipline, however, did not prevent their having genuine pangs of anguish at the scope of the reprisals that followed Heydrich's demise. Particularly after the destruction of Lidice, their despair became complete. They even considered turning themselves into the Gestapo in order to save lives, or, more dramatically, placing themselves on a park bench in Prague with cardboard placards around their necks announcing that they were Heydrich's assassins. At the

moment the police arrived, they would swallow the poison pills they had
with them in order to avoid torture and interrogation.[33]

Their colleagues in the resistance talked them out of taking such steps,
but of course Gabčík and Kubiš did eventually meet their almost preordained
fate in the crypts of the Karl Boromejsky church. Their torment over what they
had wrought seems to have carried to the very end. In a conversation with a
certain Dr. Petrek, one of the priests at the church who was later executed by
the Germans, Kubiš seemed almost to want absolution from Petrek for his
having thrown the bomb that killed Heydrich. Hundreds had died as a result
of his actions, Kubiš mused, and he rather imploringly assured the priest that
"We [he and Gabčík] are not heartless."[34] This evidence of personal anguish
on the part of those who actually carried out ANTHROPOID inevitably raises
questions about the conduct of those who laid these wreaths of guilt about the
shoulders of two young men who began by thinking they would be doing good
and then wound up feeling they had unleashed far greater evil.[35]

The Czech Resistance

In considering the impact of ANTHROPOID on various groups, one likely to be
particularly affected was the Czech resistance itself, of which Gabčík and
Kubiš were only temporary—and imported—representatives. The lot of the
resistance was obviously a parlous one (as we have already discussed), and,
especially after the arrival of Heydrich, an increasingly problematical one.
Their situation was shot through with ambiguities and dilemmas. On the one
hand, the whole point of their existence was to continue to harass the
occupiers and to contribute, even if only in a small way, to the discomfiture
of the Nazi war effort. In this enterprise there is no question but that Beneš's
government-in-exile in London was regarded as the legitimate and overall
guiding political force behind the resistance. At the same time, those who
were fighting the Nazis within Czechoslovakia itself had to attend to their
own perceptions of local conditions and to the most effective strategy for
carrying out their activities. The latter factors were almost inevitably bound
to conflict with the former, and indeed the story of ANTHROPOID was the
epitome of this tension in operation.

As far back as the fall of 1939, the Czech underground had warned
against demands for "unnecessary sacrifices" in the homeland—partly for
reasons of humanity but even more because they were seen as pragmatically
counterproductive. At this point Beneš was in concurrence, especially since
he expected the war to be a short one. Once Heydrich arrived in Prague, the
local resistance had even more reason to be cautious, particularly given his

efficiency in shattering the infrastructure of UVOD and enforcing a sullen calm on the Czech scene. Beneš was anxious about what he saw as this increasing conservatism on the part of the underground, and he took pains to disabuse those at home about London's willingness to tolerate any lessening of fervor on the part of the resistance. In a somewhat peremptory message on February 11, 1942 to Josef Bartoš, for example (one of the leading resistance figures), the following sentiments were offered:

> If our view of the organization of the home resistance is correct, it is vitally necessary to stimulate it from abroad by all valid means. It was with this intention that we have sent and that *we shall continue to send* groups of parachutists into the different regions of the country.[36]

Once the reality of what ANTHROPOID involved began to sink in, the alarm of the local Czech resistance reached full bore, and there seems to have been virtually unanimous doubt as to the wisdom of such an undertaking. Perhaps the most important single leader of the underground was a certain Ladislav Vaněk, code named "Jindra," a former chemistry teacher from Moravia who left his family in order to go to Prague to help in coordinating the opposition to the Nazis. Vaněk's view was that "the political situation in the Protectorate was wholly unfavourable for action of that kind" (the killing of Heydrich), and that ANTHROPOID would be a "very perilous undertaking" because of the likely Nazi retaliation.[37] If it was absolutely necessary to kill some prominent personality in the Protectorate, Vaněk said, it should be someone like the hated collaborator Emmanuel Moravec rather than the acting Reichsprotektor himself. He and Josef Bartoš sent the following urgent message to London on May 9 and again on May 12, demanding that the attempt to assassinate Heydrich himself be canceled:

> An attempt against Heydrich's life . . . would be of no use for the Allies, and its consequences for our people would be immeasurable. Not only would it put our hostages and political prisoners into jeopardy, but it would also cost thousands of additional lives and expose the nation to unprecedented suppression. At the same time it would sweep away the last remains of [our] organization, thus preventing any further action here which would be of use to the Allies. We beg you therefore to see that the attack is not carried out. To delay is dangerous. Give the order immediately.[38]

What is especially striking about this communication is the way in which it blended arguments of both a practical and a humane character. Not only would the assassination have no tangible benefit for the Allied cause and certainly none for the Czech underground, but the loss in Czech lives because of Nazi reprisals would be enormous as well.

Beneš gave no direct reply to these messages, but a communication of his own back to Czechoslovakia on May 15 indicates his indifference to it and his stubborn insistence on the execution of ANTHROPOID. His familiar argument was that the Czechs needed to show some "spine" if they were to be treated favorably as part of a compromise peace. There is some evidence that certain members of the Czech government-in-exile community in London wanted to reconsider ANTHROPOID in view of the alarming message from the homeland, but their views obviously did not prevail. Vanék himself had felt sure that London "would understand our position," but after they had in fact brushed it aside, he tried to play the good soldier, saying that after all Beneš's government "was dealing with matters and events far more important than ours. What weight could a request or a warning from a resistance movement in the Protectorate have in London's eyes?"[39] The answer is that "London" could have given due attention to the views and concerns of those who were most intimately acquainted with circumstances in the home country, and whose interests were very much at stake in the proposal to kill Heydrich. In particular, they could have weighed the argument that the Czech people were *less* likely rather than more likely to support the resistance in the aftermath of the inevitable reprisals following on Heydrich's death. In the final analysis, London could have *abandoned* ANTHROPOID because of the home underground's opposition.

The Czech People

In considering the effects of ANTHROPOID, the largest group that deserves attention is, of course, the Czech population generally. After the assassination had been carried out, Vanék seems to have reassessed his "good soldier" response to Beneš's insistence on going ahead with ANTHROPOID. He plaintively remarked, "What I had feared so much—and that is also why I asked London to call off the assassination—came true."[40] Not only was the resistance itself virtually destroyed, but there were all the other sacrifices as well. In a 1965 interview, Vanék summarized the enduring effects for him personally of what had been undertaken in late May 1942.

> Today there is an emptiness around me. My friends, those who worked with me, are all dead. Or nearly all of them. My hair is gray, once again I teach chemistry and walk between the school benches. The Heydrich

assassination has become history. For us, who by chance escaped with our lives, that time is the most terrible chapter of our lives. . . . The Heydrich period is not only a sad memory, it is something we have to learn from for the future.[41]

One of the things to be "learned from for the future" clearly has to do with the relationship between leader and led in times of crisis—and the ultimate responsibility of the former to have due regard for the safety and welfare of the latter. Perhaps the ultimate indictment of ANTHROPOID involves the dolorous effects of that operation on the average Czech citizen who was in no way directly involved either in the scheme itself or in the resistance more generally. We have already detailed the executions, arrests, transportation to concentration camps, and of course the destruction of Lidice that were a consequence of the killing of Heydrich. As already mentioned, a prime factor in Vaněk's opposition to ANTHROPOID was its likely effects on the individual Czech. In attempting to persuade Gabčík and Kubiš not to carry out the assassination, he offered this grim prediction, "Just picture to yourself what will happen afterwards: the Germans will arrest our people, torture them, kill them."[42]

The Czech people were prepared to accept some sacrifice in the effort to regain their independence and national pride—and to deal a blow to Nazi tyranny. Yet there seems to have been a prevailing indifference among Beneš and others in the government-in-exile as to a more measured and practical action that would have in its own way proclaimed the continuing defiance of the Czechs under occupation and yet have avoided the terrible reprisals attendant on the death of Heydrich. After the war the long-serving editor of the Prague newspaper *Der Neue Tag* offered the following germane observation:

If the Czechs had been asked whom they would like to see killed, they would pretty certainly not have said Heydrich, but Frank, for if they detested anyone it was their Sudeten-German enemy Frank. To them he appeared to represent the epitome of their loss of national greatness, the epitome of the slave-master. From a Czech nationalist point of view Frank was the obvious target for assassination. From the standpoint of Allied strategic interests it had to be Heydrich.[43]

No matter whether Karl Frank, or possibly Emmanuel Moravec, could be suggested as a more suitable target for ANTHROPOID, the impression remains that Heydrich was chosen simply because—it was hoped—his death would somehow *force* the "passive Czechs" to rise up against the Nazi occupation of their country. The British Labour MP Ronald Paget wrote after the war that among the tactics to encourage the resistance in Europe was the "provocation of reprisals in order to stoke up hatred against the occupying force and attract more recruits into the Resistance! That was the reason why we flew a squad into Czechoslovakia to murder Heydrich."[44] What this comment suggests is that ultimately the Czech people were only the objects of policy rather than its subjects—abstractions that could legitimately be manipulated in order to secure larger geopolitical and strategic concerns. There is an old saying that in the final analysis, there are no ends in politics, only means. The end of defeating the Nazi indifference to human life and liberty was certainly an admirable and necessary one; the means chosen in this particular case hardly seem to have been consistent with the values inherent in that end.

BENEŠ'S CONDUCT SUMMARIZED

One of the prime indicators in judging the defensibility of political leaders' dirty hands in particular situations is their frank willingness to *accept* that they had to do something very unpleasant indeed even though (they argue) it was necessary. This doesn't mean that we have to accept their reasoning, but it does mean that they should perhaps receive at least a certain benefit of the doubt. In the case of ANTHROPOID, however, what we see is a systematic attempt to blur personal responsibility for the decision to assassinate Heydrich. This was especially apparent in Eduard Beneš's statements on the matter after the war. He denied that he had been the prime mover behind ANTHROPOID and in fact took considerable pains to draw a veil over his participation in the operation, even going so far as to refuse to discuss the subject. His memoirs, basically a dry and impersonal recitation of documents and formal policy papers, character- ized by a sea of references to himself in either the first or third person, do not even mention Lidice or ANTHROPOID, although there is a passing reference to Reinhard Heydrich.

     Beneš's disinclination to be associated with ANTHROPOID was hardly his alone. This escape from responsibility characterized virtually everyone else involved in the plan as well. As one writer says, after the war "there was not a single person who would stand up and say with pride, I am the one who ordered the assassination or, at least, organized it."[45] This effort at forgetting extended even to the memory (or rather lack of memory) of those who had sacrificed themselves in eliminating Heydrich. There was almost no formal recognition of the efforts of the parachutists, especially Kubiš and Gabčík, not even some kind of memorial at the Karl Boromejsky church where they had made their last stand.

The disguising of Beneš's role and that of others in the development of ANTHROPOID actually dated back to the very moment of Heydrich's assassination. Thus public statements emanating out of London from Czech spokesmen referred to Heydrich's death as a "spontaneous" act by the local Czech resistance, those "freedom-loving peoples of the Czechoslovakian Republic [who] are in the vanguard of the fight."[46] That ANTHROPOID had been entirely the creature of the government-in-exile was systematically denied or at least obscured. No mention was made, for example, of the training of Czech parachutists under the aegis of the SOE that had gone on over the last year, notably that given to Jozef Gabčík and Jan Kubiš, Heydrich's actual killers. Even a year after his demise, the Czech government-in-exile continued to proclaim that "no order for Heydrich's murder was ever issued from [us]. In fact the whole Nazi theory about a fight for freedom being conducted and ordered from London is false, as all acts of resistance in the homeland are directed and decided by its own headquarters there."[47] Needless to say, this was a highly creative rendering of the actual circumstances behind the killing of Reinhard Heydrich.

Not surprisingly, the Germans took considerable pains after the death of Heydrich to suggest that the calamity visited on Lidice as well as other reprisals were indeed directly attributable to Beneš's government-in-exile. One typical propaganda statement piously invoked "the curse of Czech mothers on the heads of the cowardly criminals who had fled the country and now, from safe armchairs in England, are bringing destruction on their countrymen."[48] Ironically, the brutal but in some ways pragmatic Karl Frank actually used this line of argument as a reason for not undertaking even *more* drastic mass reprisals for the death of Heydrich, "since they would play into the hands of our enemies, who wish to prove that killings and sabotage arise from the will of the entire Czech nation and that the nation as a whole supports them. World opinion must totally lose the impression that any national uprising is concerned: we must say that it is merely a question of individual actions."[49]

The logic of Frank's argument is in its own way at least a partial explanation and perhaps exculpation for the Beneš's government's initial denial of any responsibility for ANTHROPOID. In order for Heydrich's death to have maximum political effect, not only in Czechoslovakia but especially outside the country, it was indeed understandable that London should try to paint the event as a spontaneous reflection of the power of the Czech home resistance. But what of the hypocrisy inherent in Beneš's and others' refusal even long after the event to accept direct responsibility for the operation? We have already argued that such hypocrisy is in itself an important piece of evidence in arriving at a moral judgment on the conduct of leaders. There are situations to be sure in which statesmen may feel an action is legitimate and necessary, but in preserving their own personal political position they disguise the reality of what has been done (and what perhaps *had* to be done). This should not always be an occasion for condemnation: public opinion after all is not invariably right as to the possibilities for moral conduct, and politicians may often be granted some sympathy at feeling that they have been—or will be—unjustly denounced for an action that was necessary but ill-understood by those insufficiently versed in the dilemmas of their position.

Even so, the existence of political hypocrisy always raises troubling questions for those attempting to arrive at a reasonable moral assessment. The very fact of such hypocrisy presents at least a prima facie assumption that the decision arrived at was from its inception a doubtful one, and the decisionmaker realized this. That the plan to assassinate Heydrich may have fallen into this category receives support when we examine Beneš's procedures at the time of the drawing up of ANTHROPOID. As already noted, he kept the scheme a closely guarded secret even from his own ministers and declined to put anything on paper about what was being contemplated. His head of intelligence, František Moravec, was given only oral instructions. Moravec later reflected on these procedures and the rationale for them: "The first essential of my task was secrecy. The few persons involved the better, if the attempt was to be regarded as a spontaneous act of national desperation. We hoped that the spontaneity would become genuine when Heydrich was dead and the nation closed ranks and struck back against the Nazi terror."[50]

Given the sensitivity of the scheme to assassinate Heydrich, and the normal necessity in covert operations of preventing information from leaking out about the intended action, this virtual obsession with secrecy was perhaps only to be expected. Yet it seems unmistakable that Beneš was also anxious not to leave a paper trail that would later reveal his direct connection to ANTHROPOID should it turn out badly. The absence of such documentation would also make it possible to assign blame for the affair to Moravec, a game of "deniability" that has long been standard in the secret world of intelligence. Even if it is standard procedure, however, it hardly stands as a defense against the behavior of those with real responsibility for the decision.

The Test of Proportionality

When all is said and done, how do we defend that behavior? The destruction of Lidice, as well as all the other effects of ANTHROPOID, can ultimately only be assessed, once again, in terms of the perennial principle of proportionality: did this particular act produce more good than evil? We have already offered a fairly detailed consequentialist analysis of the morality of Beneš's ordering the assassination of Heydrich. It might be appropriate at this point to offer some summary reflections on the basic issue.

An indirect indication that Beneš himself was troubled about the issue of proportionality could be seen in his 1943 rejection of suggestions that Karl Frank or Kurt Daluege (Heydrich's successor and a particularly unattractive Nazi thug in his own right) should be accorded the same treatment as Heydrich. While prepared to contemplate attacks on Czech collaborators, Beneš turned aside any idea of repeating ANTHROPOID since "the death of a German national would mean great reprisals."[51] František Moravec seems to have taken a similar line. Some months after Heydrich's death, Soviet representatives pressured the Czech government-in-exile to organize a massive sabotage of the Skoda armaments works at Pilsen in order to put it out of operation or at least deny its output to the Germans for a period of time. Moravec told his Soviet counterpart, a certain Cicajev, that "as a small nation we could not afford such an action. The German reprisals would far surpass the sacrifice extorted as the price of Heydrich's life."

Cicajev's response was that millions had died in the Soviet Union during collectivization and the war, and that even 20,000 dead would be a small price to pay for sabotaging the Skoda works, but Moravec would have none of it. "In vain I explained that such losses would be unbearable for our nation, that the Germans intentionally chose our best people for execution." The Soviets remained unconvinced by this argument, and Moravec remembers their accusing him later of intentionally holding back on organizing partisan activity in Czechoslovakia for "political" reasons, which he was willing to concede to since "I had no wish to encourage underground activities which had no military importance whatsoever."[52] These comments seem to admit of only one interpretation, which is that the shadow of Lidice and other German reprisals after ANTHROPOID had so affected Beneš, Moravec, and those around them that they could not stomach the idea of some sort of reprise.

Even so, it is striking how various writers of Czech background have attempted to defend the morality of ANTHROPOID even some years after the event. Given the impact of this operation on their own campatriots, their views are of special interest. Consider, for example, the following comment from John Bradley:

> President Beneš and the Czech émigrés did not expect such a terrible response from the Germans. They obviously miscalculated the importance of the Protector, and had to pay dearly for it. But the assassination achieved the original aim: it confirmed President Beneš's leadership of the Czechs in Allied eyes, and the destruction of Lidice made the Czechoslovak cause for independence extremely plausible to Allied politicians and public opinion all over the world.[53]

There is also this from the Czech journalist Miroslav Ivanov:

> From the international point of view, the attempt on Heydrich's life formed invaluable moral capital for Dr. Beneš, the President of the Czechoslovak republic in exile, maintaining the prestige of the Czechoslovak government in London and allowing it to develop its policies.[54]

With all due respect to the integrity and seriousness of these two individuals, such comments raise a number of questions: *Why* was there such a "miscalculation" as to the effects of Heydrich's assassination? Was the confirmation of Beneš's leadership really such an overriding requirement? In what way did the destruction of Lidice make the idea of Czech independence plausible?

Bradley admits that "practically the entire resistance movement was destroyed in the terror," but he goes on to argue that the German reprisals were self-defeating, since they finally brought home to the Czechs that the Germans were bent on their destruction and would have to be resisted violently. Under these circumstances the Czech émigré movement in London was the principal organization offering leadership and support for such a struggle. Such a view would have been congenial, of course, to representatives of the government-in-exile at the time of ANTHROPOID. The only difficulty with it is that it is based on a false premise. Well before the assassination of Heydrich, the Czech people were quite aware that the Germans were hardly a benevolent occupier, given the arrests, executions, and transports to concentration camps of Czech citizens that had already taken place. Moreover, the lesson drawn from Lidice was not that the Nazis had to be resisted violently but that, on the contrary, such tactics only backfired in the most drastic fashion. Beneš's intelligence chief, František Moravec, was forced to admit as much: "Our hope that the Czech people would react to the German pressure with counter-pressure did not materialize. Indeed that had been our problem throughout the war and we were never able to solve it. The causes were beyond our influence."[55]

Was the carrying out of ANTHROPOID, with the resultant massacre at Lidice, crucial in establishing Czechoslovakia's right to reemerge as an independent state after the war? This rationale for killing Heydrich was, of course, a standard theme in Beneš's defense of his actions, and has already been addressed. After news of what had happened at Lidice emerged, Beneš commented to his colleague, Jaromir Smutný,

> it is terrible what the Nazis do but from the political point of view these events brought one surety to us: the situation now cannot develop in which Czechoslovakia would not be recognized as an independent state. All the time I feared a negotiated peace. Negotiated peace is still the only hope for Germany, but now I feel secure. . . . I was afraid that they [the Allies] would leave us in one way or another integrated with Germany. . . . The executions . . . consolidated our state of affairs. This is the great political consequence of these events.[56]

If the above analysis is accepted, perhaps the sacrifice of Lidice could be considered a painful but necessary (and justifiable) service to the cause of the Czech people generally. Yet once again there seems to be little if any connection between the premise and the reality.

To reiterate our earlier argument: by late May 1942, the chances of a "negotiated peace" with Germany were by any reasonable calculation either slim or none. If Churchill had failed to respond to Hitler's offer of a negotiated peace in June 1940, when Britain's fortunes were at their lowest ebb after the defeat of France, what motivation would he have for accepting such a negotiation two years later, when both the Soviet Union and the United States had entered the war as Britain's allies? Given the devastation that the Nazis had wreaked on the Soviet Union, and just as important the German defeat at the gates of Moscow the previous December, what serious reason could Stalin have for treating with Hitler concerning a "compromise" settlement? Nor was there the slightest indication that President Roosevelt was interested in discussing such a compromise himself. Some nine months later, in fact, Roosevelt insisted on adopting unconditional surrender as the only basis for ending the war. The reality in the spring of 1942 was that the future independence of the Czech people, as well as all the others in Europe subject to the Nazi yoke, depended primarily on the defeat of the German war machine. Such an outcome was hardly likely to be decisively affected by what the small Czech nation did or did not do in resisting the German occupation.

Some of the more interesting commentary on the morality of ANTHRO-POID came from František Moravec, interesting because he tended to stress some rather more amorphous benefits of the operation in terms of the honor of the Czech people. Moravec recalled warning Beneš that the costs of assassinating Heydrich would be high, and to this extent he cannot be accused of wishful thinking concerning the consequences of ANTHROPOID. Moreover, he admitted in his memoirs, "It is not easy to analyze the results of this operation, which represented the greatest problem of my long Intelligence career. The cost and the worth of killing of Heydrich has been the subject of much controversy." This suggests that he (unlike Beneš) was able at least to recognize that there was a moral question involved, and that it needed to be addressed. In defending ANTHROPOID, Moravec based his case partly on relatively pragmatic arguments, for example, that Heydrich's death did damage the German war effort since no worthy successor to him arose, that German oppression of the Czechs would have continued even if ANTHROPOID had not been undertaken, and, perhaps most striking, that Heydrich's demise was a blow to Nazi morale in that it demonstrated that no top Nazi leader was now safe from Allied assassination.

The real thrust of Moravec's comments on the proportionality of ANTHRO-POID, however, has to do with things less definable. As a Czech patriot, his position was that the killing of Heydrich was necessary and appropriate as a way to demonstrate that the spirit of the Czech people was still alive, that they "were continuing the fight for their independence, that they had not resigned themselves to occupation and collaboration with the Nazis." As to the sacrifices incurred by the citizens of Lidice and other places following Heydrich's death, Moravec offers the following: "In my opinion, the problem of cost can be reduced to a simple principle . . . freedom, and, above all, liberation from slavery, have to be fought for, and this means losses in human lives."[57]

As it happens, Moravec had been one of those who had urged the Czech government to resist by force of arms the Munich *diktat,* even if it had to stand alone in doing so. That advice had been rejected, but in pondering the execution of ANTHROPOID, Moravec drew a comparison between that opera-tion and the earlier Czech passivity, and offered a ringing summary of his views on the proportionality question:

If in 1939 [*sic*] Czechoslovakia, instead of yielding to the Munich decision, had fought Germany, as I am convinced it should have done, it would have suffered much greater losses than it did after Heydrich's death, but it would also have earned a worthier place in history. Operation Heydrich might never have occurred. Given the circumstances in which we were placed at the time, it was a good try. It was the largest resistance operation in the country and it is a good page in the history of Czechoslovakia in the Second World War. The Czech people should be proud of it. I am.[58]

Moravec's emphasis on the notion of death before dishonor cannot be lightly set aside. There may indeed be situations in which the self-respect of a nation requires actions that go against impossible odds but are necessary just the same. This may be particularly the case when, as in this instance, it is a matter of a humane and democratic society opposing the darkest forces of twentieth-century barbarism. At the same time, to argue that the preeminent goal of the Czech people should have been to demonstrate that they would "not go gently into that good night" has troublesome implications. It is not a sign of cowardice or surrender for a society to attempt to do what it can in the face of overwhelming oppression and hope for better days. We have already argued that a type of "Schweikian" resistance on the part of the Czechs seems not only to have been the preferred course in practical terms but was also in accord with the special qualities of the Czech people, and was not in itself dishonorable. As the novelist Kurt Vonnegut once put it, there has to be more to love than death, even when it is love of country. Operation ANTHROPOID seems to have ignored this basic principle.

The Sudeten Germans

In offering a final evaluation of ANTHROPOID, we might give at least brief mention to another issue that was to be strongly influenced by the killing of Heydrich and its bloody aftermath. This had to do with the German minority population living in the Sudetenland area of Czechoslovakia. The question of the Sudeten Germans is actually significant in two ways: it reveals a lot about Beneš's own intuitive values, and it was yet another demonstration of his attitude concerning the impact of ANTHROPOID on a segment of the Czech population.

Before the war, the ethnic German community in Czechoslovakia numbered around three million, which constituted about 23 precent of the country's population. Their roots could be traced back as far as the tenth century, and they had become influential factors in the mining and industrial activity of the Sudetenland region. The prewar Czech Constitution guaranteed the "protection of national, religious, and racial minorities," and in fact the ethnic German population attained a high degree of autonomy in such areas as education and cultural activity. They also enjoyed full political rights, and under Czechoslovakia's system of proportional representation, sent over 60 members to the Chamber of Deputies. From this perspective, there was no question but that Prague's treatment of this minority set a high standard of democratic principle.[59]

Prior to the 1930s, the Social Democrats had been the prevailing political force among the Sudeten Germans, but with the depression, and especially after Hitler's coming to power, there was a decided turn to the right. Particularly prominent in this process was Konrad Henlein's Sudeten German Party, which became effectively a mouthpiece of Berlin in demanding a virtual state within a state for the Sudeten Germans. It was the agitation of Henlein's forces just prior to Munich that set the stage for that lamentable agreement. Under the circumstances, it was not surprising that many Czechs viewed with bitterness the evident collusion of the German minority in the dismemberment of the Czech state. At the same time, there remained a large anti-Nazi element among the Sudeten Germans who were loyal to their Social Democratic traditions and who accepted Hitler's occupation of their country with as little enthusiasm as their Czech brethren. The question was how to make a reasonable distinction between those who had remained loyal to Czech democracy (Beneš himself estimated their number at between 600,000 and 1,000,000) and those who might reasonably be considered targets for retaliation because of their connivance with Hitler's plan for the destruction of the Czech state.

Beneš's basic decision was to lump virtually all of the Sudeten Germans together in arriving at what he called a "radical" and "definitive" solution to the problem of the German minority within Czechoslovakia. Both those tarred with the collaborationist brush and others who were basically guiltless of such betrayal were to be subject to removal from the postwar Czechoslovak state. As Beneš rather dramatically put it, "The small Czechoslovak Nation cannot live with a German revolver permanently against its breast."[60] In the event, some 1,800,000 Germans were expelled from Czechoslovakia at the end of the war amid scenes of considerable brutality and violence (about 165,000 managed to remain). This was an event that remains sensitive to the conscience of Czechoslovakia even today, so much so that the current Czech president, Vaclav Havel, felt compelled to issue a formal public apology for the lack of discrimination in the treatment of the Sudeten Germans.

The mass expulsion of the Sudeten German population was justified by Beneš, however, as a *"just retribution for all direct and indirect, active and passive war criminals [and] as a lesson for the future."*[61] To be fair, Beneš did hold conversations in London with the leader of the Sudeten German Social Democrats, Wenzel Jaksch, about separating out his followers from those of Henlein in what was to come. No agreement could be reached on the details of such an arrangement, however, and Beneš decided to move ahead with a "maximal" solution to the problem of the Germans living in Czechoslovakia. In doing so, he had to meet the concerns of his Allied sponsors, especially the British, who seemed to feel that the indiscriminate expulsion of a whole minority population was hardly in accord with the goals of the democratic nations in fighting Hitler, as reflected, for example, in the Atlantic Charter. In order to mollify uneasy Western opinion, Beneš did speak of allowing some small territorial cessions to Germany after the war of those Sudeten districts where the population was overwhelmingly German.

The point for present purposes is that ANTHROPOID proved to be very effective in swaying the Allies to support the expulsion of the Sudeten Germans. According to one of Beneš's closest associates, Prokop Drtina, this was indeed one of the most important outcomes of the operation from their point of view. "The response to the assassination and Lidice in Allied opinion was so enormous that it equalled for us a victorious battle. . . . Without Gabčík, Valčik, Kubiš and other fighters determined unto death, we would never have achieved the purification of the Czech lands from the German settlements."[62] The concept of "purification" bears a certain resemblance to the notion of "ethnic cleansing" that has been associated with the disintegration of the former Yugoslavia, and is subject to the same query: can such a goal ever be defended in terms of basic democratic values and principles of reasonable discrimination in the treatment of large groups of human beings? Perhaps it was reasonable to target certain pro-Nazi elements among the Sudeten German population for punishment. But should all of those who merely gave their votes to Henlein's party be equally subject to such a drastic fate as expulsion? And what about those who did *not* support Henlein: did they not have certain enduring rights that required appropriate attention? What is particularly disturbing about Drtina's statement above is the notion that the destruction of Lidice somehow made it "feasible" for the Czech government-in-exile to plan a palpable injustice.

The Hácha Conundrum

There is a final issue that deserves attention in any overall assessment of ANTHROPOID. To criticize the Czech government-in-exile under Eduard Beneš for the plan to kill Reinhard Heydrich requires at least some comment about the conduct of the Czech government that attempted to function under the Germans in the homeland itself. Collaborationist regimes such as those that existed under Emil Hácha in Czechoslovakia and Marshal Pétain in France are usually the subject of derision in accounts of the period, and in most instances such scorn seems amply justified. These were indeed "governments" open not to all the talents but to all the opportunists, and in the case of the Vichy regime, French authorities even anticipated German demands for the arrest and transport of French Jews to the concentration camps by enacting various pieces of anti-Semitic legislation that paved the way for the implementation of the Holocaust in France.[63]

As far as the Protectorate government of Emil Hácha is concerned, the verdict can hardly be much more approving. While the Czech authorities can perhaps be excused from the sort of overt cooperation in persecution of Jews that was to be found in France, the general pattern was one of ever-increasing subservience to the Germans as the occupation unfolded. Hácha himself became an increasingly pathetic figure, subject to bouts of senility, and surrounded by sycophants, the most notable of which was Emmanuel Moravec, the Minister for Education and Propaganda. In the aftermath of Heydrich's assassination, Moravec offered the following observation: "The terrible murder committed by agents has put the question of our national existence upon a knife edge; it is quite right that seven thousand traitors should perish in order to save seven million people."[64]

However repulsive Moravec's casual reference to 7,000 "traitors" being a suitable sacrifice following the death of the Butcher of Prague, there was at the same time a certain perverted logic to his statement, at least in terms of the Czech people's welfare being placed on a "knife's edge" as a consequence of ANTHROPOID. This was indeed the central dilemma faced by the Czech authorities under the Protectorate during the entire period of the German occupation: what were the practical *and* the moral requirements of their position? It is not to offer a defense of their collaboration to suggest that this dilemma was one that deserves at least some sympathetic reflection.

In response to statements out of London that he was a traitor to the Czech cause, Hácha made a not totally unreasonable response:

> Mr. Beneš . . . does not see, as I do, the tears of mothers and wives who address their desperate pleas to me because their sons and husbands fell into disaster having been seduced by deceptive radio broadcasts. He is in a position to permit himself illusions, to build castles in the air, and to paint alluring pictures of the future. . . . For us, there is no way but to face reality with resolution and to soberly act in accordance with bare facts.[65]

The Czech president considered resigning his office in November 1939, after the German crushing of the Czech student demonstrations, but decided against it because he felt such a step would only bring worse oppression to his fellow citizens. At this point in time, Beneš expressed his understanding of Hácha's cautious policy and presented no objections. After the German victory over France in late spring, 1940, Hácha seems to have concluded that the Nazis would definitely win the war, and he embraced a policy of more or less active collaboration with the occupiers. Beneš attempted to stiffen his resolve by assuring him that the Germans were bound to be defeated, and perhaps fairly soon, and added a warning that the London government-in-exile would suspend all relations with the Hácha regime if it continued with its present policies.

As it happened, physical exhaustion and a general psychological malaise caused Hácha to prepare another letter of resignation on September 27, 1941, by which time Heydrich had arrived in Prague. The new acting Reichsprotektor managed to persuade him to stay by offering promises of renewed autonomy for the Czech people, which Hácha, balancing hope against experience, accepted. By November 1941, Hácha seemed to cave in completely to German pressure. He urged the Czechs to "fulfill [their] obligations to the Reich completely and sincerely in a manly and determined manner." He went on to warn his compatriots about listening "to the heckling talk of the exiles . . . who by asking us to follow their radio allurements can only bring us great catastrophes. . . . At stake is not merely the fate of individuals but the fate of your children and of the whole nation." From this point onward, Beneš cut off all relations with the Hácha regime and openly denounced the Czech president as a hopeless collaborator.[66]

In retrospect, the saga of Emile Hácha's attempting to maintain a vestige of Czech governmental independence—and Czech self-respect— under the Nazi yoke seems to have been self-defeating, an increasing exercise in illusion manipulated by those who were past masters at fostering such illusions in the occupied countries. In a presumed tribute to his (erstwhile) Czech "co-workers," Karl Frank commented after the war that the attitude of the Hácha government was that of "realistic politicians who firmly stuck to their national existence." The practice of "realism" can, of course, often be no more than a disguise for a surrender to evil, and it is against this charge that Hácha and his cohorts must stand permanently accused. Yet the question remains whether he had any other morally attractive course open to him. In the immediate aftermath of the assassination of Heydrich, the Hácha regime condemned the Czech government-in-exile as the "Enemy No. 1 of the Czech nation." It argued that as a result of its own policy, "many Czechs had been saved, sentences reduced, trials deferred. What the exiles had destroyed for us, we would attempt to reconstruct. At that very moment a heinous crime was jeopardizing all that had been achieved so far."[67] Operation ANTHROPOID undeniably cost thousands of lives. Hácha's policies may have saved only a few. The question, as always, remains: To what purpose the sacrifice of the thousands, how much credit for the saving of the few?

The Nazi attempt to erase all memory of the village of Lidice was ultimately defeated. After the war, the Czech authorities constructed a new Lidice immediately adjacent to the old one, with some 150 houses and about 500 people. It presents an immaculate appearance, with well-maintained homes, a community center, and wide streets shaded by birch trees. An advertisement at the local bus stop advertises a "video discoteck" to be held that Saturday in the cultural center for the young people of the town (admission fee 20 *korunas*). The only remnant of the old Lidice is the excavated stone cellar of the Horák farm, where the men of the village were shot on the morning of May 11, 1942. The rest of the area where the town once stood is a gently rolling meadow of grassy mounds, cherry trees, and fields of poppies. Distant wheat fields lie gleaming in the sun.

A monument to the dead of Lidice in the shape of a granite semicircle stands on a small rise overlooking the lush green countryside. A series of plaques lists other atrocities of World War II, including Oradour and Dresden, as if to place the victims of Lidice within a fellowship of suffering. Around the semicircle are numerous vases of red roses, the symbolic flower of Lidice. The flowers tremble slightly in the gentle breeze. A small museum stands to the left of this monument. Its most notable exhibit is a photo montage of all of the inhabitants of Lidice as of June 10, 1942. Among the faces staring back at the visitor, the most poignant are those of the children. Shortly after they were shipped to the camp at Gneisenau, these children were allowed (or ordered) by their Nazi captors to write postcards to their families in Lidice describing their good treatment. They could hardly know that their Lidice no longer existed. These postcards survive today and are on display in the museum. The following was written by one Marie Šrouboková:

> Dear Uncle and Auntie, we have been here for two weeks now and have not had a change of clothes. Please send some underwear and thread, needles, spoons and some money—German coins. Send us bread, if only the crusts that you feed to rabbits at home. Also, tell us what happened to Ma and Pa![68]

Shortly after this, Marie and the other children were sent on to the extermination camp at Chelmno for "final disposal."

The fate of Marie and all the rest of those from Lidice cries out for some explanation. Some meaning has to be given to their tragedy. An analysis of the moral dilemmas facing statesmen, and not only Beneš, runs the risk of becoming so abstract that we lose sight of what is really at stake in human terms. What was at stake in this case was the life of Marie Šrouboková and all her dreams and ambitions for the future, a future that she was never to see. One wonders whether Beneš might have acted any differently if he had had a picture of the young Marie on his desk as he was deciding on ANTHROPOID. Perhaps it would be a good idea if all political leaders had pictures of the Maries of the world in front of them before they made their decisions.

5

The Darlan Deal: Background

On the morning of July 16, 1942, there began a series of events in Paris that were later to cause that day to be described as *jeudi noir* (black Thursday). Commencing at around 4:00 A.M., some 4,500 French police began a systematic round-up of Jews without French citizenship. The police had with them over 27,000 index cards listing foreign Jews who were then living in Paris and its surrounding suburbs. Those arrested were divided into two groups: men and women with children under 16 were taken to the Vélodrome d'Hiver, a glass-covered sports stadium in Paris, and those without young children were dispatched to the French concentration camp at Drancy outside the city. By the end of the following day, close to 13,000 people had been taken by the police, including 3,000 men, over 5,000 women, and some 4,000 children.[1] An eyewitness described what she saw of the events of July 16: "I heard screams rising to the heavens: not cries and squawks such as you hear in noisy and excited crowds, but screams like you used to hear in hospital delivery rooms. All the human pain that both life and death provide." A number of people attempted suicide, including one woman who threw her two children from a fifth-floor apartment and then jumped herself.[2]

By the end of July, the 5,000 people sent to the camp at Drancy had all been sent on to the killing ground at Auschwitz in Poland. Only 47 people are known to have survived from among this group. This left approximately 8,000 Jews interned at the Vélodrome d'Hiver. Conditions there could only be described as catastrophic. A Red Cross nurse recalled "the nervous breakdowns, shouting, weeping of children and even of adults who were at the end of their tether. Several deranged individuals spread panic. All was helter-skelter, it was impossible to sleep, there were no mattresses, people were piled one on top of the other."[3] Within a few days, about 4,000 adults and older children were transferred to other holding centers around Paris and from there sent on to Auschwitz (19 survived). There now remained 4,000 youngsters under 14 at the Vélodrome d'Hiver who had to fend for themselves—but not for long. By early August they too had been dispersed to other camps and from there to Auschwitz. Not a single one of these children is know to have survived the war. Yet another eyewitness described their state just before deportation to the East:

> I will never forget the faces of those children; endlessly they parade before
> my eyes. They are serious, profound, and, what is extraordinary: in these
> little faces, the horror of the days which they are living is branded. They
> have understood everything, like adults. Some of them are accompanied
> by their little brothers and sisters, and take admirably good care of them.
> They have understood their responsibilities.[4]

This reference to the "responsibilities" the children took upon themselves leads to a consideration of the responsibility for the events of July 16, 1942. At one level, they can simply be regarded as a reflection of the Nazi obsession with dealing with the "Jewish problem," and certainly the overall directives on this occasion emanated from Berlin. At the same time, the *implementation* of these directives bore the imprint not of the German authorities but of the French. The Germans had too few Gestapo or SS personnel in Paris at the time to carry out the round-up of the Jews efficiently, which meant that they had to rely on the cooperation of the French police. This in turn required that the wartime French government at Vichy issue the appropriate instructions to French police to cooperate with the persecution of the Jews. That they would not shrink from doing so was suggested by the fact that the operation of July 16, 1942 was only a continuation of earlier round-ups of Jews in France that had taken place in May, August, and December of the previous year through the authorization of the Vichy regime. Some of the Vichy police involved in these persecutions seemed to go out of their way to exceed even the zeal of their German counterparts. They "searched the bundles of children as young as two or three, seizing bracelets and earrings from little girls. In one case when an earring did not open easily, a French inspector simply tore it from the ear of a terrified ten-year old."[5]

The events described above serve as an introduction to our second case study on dirty hands. As noted, the French government at Vichy cooperated in the atrocity visited on the Jews in mid-July 1942, and earlier ones as well. However, this record did not deter the United States from maintaining diplomatic relations with Vichy, and indeed during the preceding two years Washington had attempted to establish a reasonably cordial working relationship with the French authorities. More than this, American officials were eventually to agree to an arrangement by which one of Vichy's most notorious figures, Admiral Jean François Darlan, would be granted an American imprimatur for continuing Vichy governance in French North Africa. Both the overall policy, and the specific agreement with Darlan, represent perhaps a classic case in which the dictates of morality and pragmatism collided and reached an uneasy compromise. In considering that case, it is necessary to consider the roots of the Vichy regime, and the controversy surrounding its character that has continued even down to the present day.

THE ORIGINS AND CHARACTER OF VICHY

In the early hours of May 10, 1940, some 144 German divisions, together with 2,800 tanks and over 3,000 aircraft, began a massive assault against Allied positions in the Low Countries and northern France. Within three days, the Germans had broken through the supposedly impregnable Ardennes forest region, and in the process made useless the Maginot line of French defenses into which so much effort had gone before the war. In World War I, the French (and her allies) had fought the Germans to a bloody standstill over four long years. In this instance, after only a hundred hours of combat, French Premier Paul Reynaud felt compelled to telephone the new British prime minister in London, Winston Churchill, with the plaintive report that "we are beaten; we have lost the battle."[6] Churchill later recalled that this was perhaps the single most astonishing message he was to receive during the entire Second World War, and he found it hard to credit, given his knowledge of the French army's valiant efforts in the first war.

Unfortunately, Reynaud proved to be all too accurate in his assessment. By May 20, German armored units had reached the English channel, after which they soon enveloped the large Allied forces trapped in the area around Dunkirk. As it turned out, in a miracle of military improvisation, over 300,000 Allied troops—mostly British but including French and Belgian forces as well—were evacuated to Britain to fight another day. This episode represented only a brief stay, however, in the German plan for the subjugation of the French armed forces and the French nation. On June 5, Nazi troops turned south to finish the job they had started, and by June 14 they had entered Paris and were spreading rapidly into the farthest corners of France.

Just before the capture of Paris, the Reynaud government had moved to Bordeaux and there engaged in a furious debate as to whether to decamp to French-controlled North Africa in order to constitute itself a government-in-exile and to continue the struggle against the Germans. The level of defeatism within his cabinet was such, however, that Reynaud felt compelled to resign on June 16, to be replaced by the octogenarian military hero of the First World War, Marshal Philippe Pétain. The latter proceeded to sue for peace with the Germans, and on June 22 an armistice was signed at Compiégne, the very site where Germany had been forced to sign an armistice of its own with the French at the conclusion of World War I.

Under the terms of the Compiégne agreement, France was divided into two parts, an Occupied Zone including all of the northern half of France plus the Atlantic coast stretching down to the Spanish border, and an Unoccupied Zone, consisting of the southeastern third of France. The reorganized French government, soon to establish itself at the small resort town of Vichy, was theoretically to govern both parts, but its role in the Occupied Zone was directly subordinate to the dictates of the German authorities there (although the Vichy administrative apparatus did provide the main means for maintaining order and conducting day-to-day affairs). Under the circumstances, these could not be considered totally punitive peace terms, but they reflected two very practical considerations on the part of Hitler: his reluctance to commit the level of military resources necessary to control the entire country, and his confidence that the new French Vichy government would do his bidding on all points of major concern to him.[7] It was the latter premise that is central to the controversy that arose at the time and later concerning the character of Vichy as a regime, not only in terms of how it represented the interests of the French nation itself, but also in terms of its attitude toward some of the more brutal aspects of Nazi doctrine.

At the outset of any evaluation of Vichy, it must be admitted that the regime found itself in an extremely difficult, perhaps even impossible, situation. As a consequence of the catastrophic defeat at the hands of the Germans—and in particular because this defeat was seen as the result of gross incompetence and even betrayal on the part of French political and military figures—there was a deep-seated psychological malaise among Frenchmen of all stripes. Not only had their country been humiliated by a traditional enemy, but it looked very much as if Nazi control of the Continent would stretch on into the distant future. At this point only Britain remained in the war, and the conventional wisdom was that it would be quickly brought to heel by the Germans as well. Given the situation, then, one can have at least some sympathy with the apologists for Vichy who argued that the best and really the only legitimate goal for any French government of the time was to retain as much independence for the French people as was possible under very dire circumstances. This meant in particular preventing the Germans from physically occupying the remainder of France and from imposing total control over the daily lives of the French population. According to this argument, a continuation of the resistance to the Nazis would have been a romantic but essentially futile gesture, especially since there was so little will among the French people for such a course of action. At his trial for treason after the war, Marshal Pétain piously proclaimed that "while General De Gaulle, outside our frontiers, continued the struggle, I prepared the ground for liberation, by keeping France alive, though in pain. What good would it have been to liberate ruins and cemeteries?"[8]

All this has a certain logic to it, but it leaves a lot unsaid and unexamined as well. Obviously France was in a very difficult situation following the German victory in 1940, but it is in the nature of such a crisis that none of the options available are particularly easy or attractive. At the time of the Munich agreement in 1938, Winston Churchill assessed his own country's policy by saying that the British government had a choice between dishonor and war. "She has chosen the former," Churchill said, "and she will receive the latter." French political leadership, and indeed the French nation as a whole, had in the summer of 1940 a roughly similar dilemma between Scylla and Charybdis. They chose a policy of appeasement, but eventually were to suffer most of the tribulations that policy was designed to avoid. The Nazis did occupy the rest of France following the Anglo-American invasion of North Africa in November 1942, and Vichy increasingly did become effectively a puppet of its German masters, carrying out orders that represented a virtual surrender of the interests, and the honor, of the French people.

It is important to recognize that there *was* an alternative (or alternatives) to the establishment of the Vichy regime and to its policies. One would have been for the government to remove itself to French North Africa in June 1940, as was actually debated at Bordeaux, and to continue the fight against the Nazis from there. This would have denied the Germans the convenience of being able to call on a "friendly" French government in the homeland to do its bidding and would have had some considerable military effect as well, given the large French naval and ground forces based in North Africa (and those that could be moved there, particularly the units of the French fleet based at Toulon). It was precisely his conviction that the war was *not* over, and that France still had a considerable role to play in defeating the Nazis, that moved General Charles De Gaulle to issue his famous proclamation from London on June 18, 1940, to the effect that "France has lost a battle, she has not lost the war," and to form the Free French overseas resistance movement. There was also the alternative of resistance within France itself. There were Frenchmen (admittedly in the minority) who refused to accept the finality of the French defeat and carried out continued operations against the German occupying forces. The success of this *maquis* may not have been decisive in the eventual defeat of the Germans, but their efforts nevertheless represented a morally far more attractive response by the French people to occupation than the defeatism of Vichy.[9]

An indictment of Vichy, however, rests on more than the fact that there were other choices to collaboration available at the time. Perhaps even more telling is the way in which Vichy, far from attempting to combat the worst excesses of Nazi doctrine, went out of its way on occasion to emulate such doctrine, even in the absence of formal German pressure to do so. It is true that the Vichy regime was hardly homogeneous, and that there was some variety of viewpoint as to the relationship with the Germans and the course of domestic policy. On balance, however, the circle immediately around Pétain was of an extreme reactionary nature, and thus found a good deal to admire in the practices of the Third Reich. A prime piece of evidence in this regard concerns Vichy's treatment of Jews.

The round-up at the Vélodrome d'Hiver was only an early instance of the prevailing anti-Semitism that characterized the officialdom of Vichy, a stance that went beyond the historical prejudice toward Jews found in French history (as represented, for example, by the Dreyfus affair) and was eventually converted into a willingness to assist the Nazis in sending many Jews to the death camps. As early as August 27, 1940, the Vichy government revoked a decree of April 21, 1939 that punished slander and libel "toward a group of people who belong by origin to a particular race or a particular religion." Two months later, the "Statute of Jews" excluded French Jews from the civil service, the media, education, and elective office.[10] Vichy did tend to make a distinction between Jews with French nationality and so-called "alien Jews" who had fled from other European countries and had assumed exile status in France. The latter were subject to far more draconian measures than the former and, beginning in the spring of 1942, were regularly taken by the police and handed over to the Germans for shipment to Auschwitz and other places. Nazi SS leader Heinrich Himmler issued a demand to the Vichy government in June 1942 that a total of 100,000 Jews be made available for "transport" from both the Occupied and Unoccupied Zones, and Pierre Laval, at the time the Vichy prime minister, accepted on condition that the burden fall basically on Jews without French citizenship.

The only thing that can be said for Vichy's policies toward the Jews is that they had the effect of sparing a relatively higher percentage of Jews in France from the gas chambers than in other European countries. Thus "only" 26 percent of French Jews—native and foreign—were slaughtered during World War II compared with 55 percent in Belgium and 86 percent in Holland. Even so, some 80,000 (both foreign and native) were sent to their deaths, and it is highly unlikely that the figure would have been even this high if the French security forces had not connived to the extent they did in the Nazi Final Solution—and indeed provided the basic administrative apparatus for the oppression of French Jewry, even in the Occupied Zone.[11] It is well to remember in this regard that the Germans had only about 10,000 police of all types in France and thus had to rely on the 100,000 men of the French security forces to "assist" them in their various activities.

Above and beyond its policy toward the Jews, Vichy seemed intent on convincing Berlin of its credentials as an acceptable member of the Nazi New Order in Europe. Many of the political and ideological themes that had been introduced by Hitler himself into Germany following his accession to power in 1933 were now adopted, at least in modified form, by the French authorities. Under the rubric of the so-called "National Revolution," there was a systematic effort to diminish or even eliminate some of the basic principles of republicanism in France as they had existed for almost 150 years. The famous Declaration of the Rights of Man, for example, dating from the French revolution, was formally repudiated. On July 10, 1940, a cowed National Assembly in effect established the legal basis for dictatorship by granting Pétain full powers to promulgate a new French Constitution by decree. The slogan of the new regime was "work, family, and country," replacing the traditional "liberty, equality, fraternity." Political party and labor union activity was severely constrained, and in several instances totally banned, and there was a systematic crackdown on the heretofore fractious and diverse French press. In order to demonstrate its bona fides as a member of the New Order, Vichy authorities forcibly rounded up French workers for transport to Germany. Over 650,000 French men and women were eventually involved in such forced labor.[12]

A final indictment of the Vichy regime rests on the fact that it agreed to continue its operations even after the Germans moved into the Unoccupied Zone of France after the Anglo-American invasion of North Africa. From this point onward, it increasingly became simply an indigenous agency of enforcement for Nazi policy throughout France, represented, for example, by the creation of the *Milice* under Joseph Darnand in January, 1943. Darnand was a true *eminence grise* of the Vichy government, having earlier established the elitist Service d'Ordre Légionnaire (SOL), an anti-Semitic, anti-Gaullist, and antidemocratic political police force that was officially recognized by Pétain in January 1942. The *Milice* was a follow-on to this organization and consisted of some 45,000 thugs and fascists who willingly participated in German repression of the resistance and other "undesirable" elements.[13]

All of the above seems to lead to only one conclusion. There are reasons that can be advanced for Vichy policies, and for the whole concept of a separate French Vichy regime. But at the end of the day the apologists for Vichy, who included some of France's most distinguished intellectual figures, such as Charles Maurras, had an extremely difficult, and, on balance, unconvincing brief to offer. This was indeed a repugnant, and ultimately fraudulent, expression of the French nation. No casuistic rationales for its behavior can disguise the fact that Vichy was an embarrassment to the French tradition of devotion to liberty and humanity, and deserves to be judged in these terms. Given this conclusion, it is a matter of some interest to examine the policy that the United States adopted toward the Vichy regime, and more than this, toward one of its principal figures, Admiral Jean François Darlan. In undertaking such an examination, we are presented with a particularly compelling example of the problem of dirty hands.

THE AMERICAN RELATIONSHIP WITH VICHY

Among the various controversies that still linger concerning American diplomacy in World War II, one that continues to be the subject of heated debate concerns the position taken by Washington with respect to the French Vichy regime in the period from July 1940 to the Allied invasion of North Africa in November 1942 (at which point Vichy broke off diplomatic relations with the United States). Given the character of the Vichy government, not only its domestic policies but especially its open collaboration with the Germans, there were many at the time who questioned—and many who continue to question—whether the United States ought to have had *any* association with such a regime.

In the event, Washington did decide to establish and maintain an ongoing relationship with the Vichy regime following its establishment in July 1940. Secretary of State Cordell Hull laid out some of the general considerations for doing so:

The President and I had no hesitation in continuing diplomatic relations with the Pétain Government, while waiting to see what its ultimate policy would be. . . . The Pétain Government was a legal Government. . . . Our only excuse for breaking off diplomatic ties with Vichy could have been the fact that the Pétain Cabinet was leaving the democratic traditions of France for a dictatorial form of government which smacked of fascism. But at that time we still maintained relations with such completely fascist governments as those of Germany, Italy and Spain. . . . It seemed to us to be the part of common sense to continue full contact with Vichy.[14]

A particularly important testament to the importance that the Roosevelt administration placed on continued dealings with Vichy was the appointment of Admiral William Leahy as American ambassador beginning in January 1941. Leahy was a former chief of naval operations, and President Roosevelt anticipated that his military background would give him the ability to talk to Pétain and others in the Vichy regime in language that they would understand. As Leahy recalled his conversations with Roosevelt before assuming his new duties, his basic marching orders were "to keep the French on our side in so far as possible."[15]

The primary theme—or justification—that underlay the American decision to deal with the Vichy regime was the conviction that maintaining a relationship with the Pétain government would assist in keeping the unoccupied area of France out of German control and, more than this, deter Vichy from becoming an open military ally of the Nazis. Of particular importance in this latter regard was the disposition of the French fleet based at Toulon, which comprised three battleships, eight cruisers, and a number of supporting vessels. The fear was that if Vichy were totally isolated, and saw itself surrounded by enemies, it might make common cause with the Germans by agreeing to joint naval operations with the Nazis. In that event, the balance of power in the Mediterranean would be irreparably altered, with quite disastrous consequences for Allied strategy in the region. Another factor of military significance was the disposition of the territories in the overseas French empire, particularly in North Africa and the Levant, together with the large French forces based there. As with the French navy, there was great concern that if these territories and troops were given over to German military exploitation, dire results might well follow for the Allied cause.[16]

All of these were important factors, and it has led some intimately associated with American policy toward Vichy, such as the American diplomat Robert Murphy, rather impatiently to dismiss quibbles about dealing with what seemed to be a rather dubious regime: "I cannot recall that it ever occurred to any of us that our government had any alternative other than to maintain relations with whatever French Government was established in France. . . . Our relations with Vichy, with which I was intimately associated from beginning to end, never were a 'gamble.' At all times we had much to win and we never risked a substantial loss."[17] This assumption that dealing with Vichy was the only logical course open to Washington was heavily influenced by the feeling that De Gaulle's Free French movement was hardly a viable alternative. Indeed, as will be discussed farther on, the United States, rightly or wrongly, saw De Gaulle as essentially a posturer with little real influence on the course of events. As one writer sympathetic to Roosevelt's policy says, "It must be perfectly obvious that our policy toward Vichy France was conditioned in part by our hope or lack of hope in the Free French."[18]

In any event, what developed was a situation in which American representatives at Vichy were authorized to offer the Pétain regime all support possible within the confines of the Neutrality Act, provided that Vichy refrained from signing a formal and final peace treaty with the Germans.[19] Perhaps the most notable example of such support came in the form of the so-called Murphy-Weygand agreement, first negotiated in late 1940. Under this arrangement, French authorities in North Africa were given leave to buy nonstrategic American goods, using French funds frozen in the United States after the German victory in June, and have them shipped through the British naval blockade then operating. A number of American "vice-consuls" (in reality American intelligence agents) were to be sent to North Africa to supervise the importation of these mostly consumer items in order to insure that they did not fall into the hands of the Germans. The Murphy-Weygand deal experienced a series of ups and downs from its inception until the Allied invasion of North Africa in November 1942, and only a small percentage of the anticipated items were ever delivered, partly because the British were strongly opposed to the arrangement. Nevertheless, it stands as an important piece of evidence concerning the basic thrust of American policy toward Vichy, with all of its ambiguities and (sometimes) contradictions.

There was from the outset, as we have already noted, considerable criticism of the American relationship with Vichy from a variety of sources in the United States. Such liberal journals as *The New Republic* opined that "it is certain that the policy [of dealing with Vichy] frittered away much good will on the part of the anti-Fascist French, and raised doubts all over the world about our war aims." The influential journalist Walter Lippmann summarized American policy toward Vichy as a case of the "tail wagging the dog."[20] Robert Murphy himself was aware that a great many of his own countrymen took a rather different view from his on the merits of dealing with Vichy. He admitted that to many Americans, Vichy carried "the connotation of Fascist, pro-Nazi, collaboration, anti-Semitism, totalitarian treachery." Indeed a public opinion poll taken in December 1941 revealed that fully 75 percent of those polled did not feel that Vichy represented the "real" France; 65 percent felt that Pétain took his orders directly from Berlin and the same percentage guessed that eventually he would hand over the French fleet and French bases in North Africa for Axis use.[21] A particularly telling criticism of American policy toward Vichy was the way in which it continued virtually unabated even after the Japanese attack on Pearl Harbor and the formal entrance of the United States into the war against the Axis. Perhaps a case could be made for Washington's dealing with Vichy before this event, but in its aftermath many found it hard to understand why the United States would treat with a regime that was effectively serving the purposes of the German government.

Under all of these circumstances, the Roosevelt administration went out of its way to conceal the full extent of its dealings with the Pétain government. As Murphy recalls, "Instructions to our embassy in Vichy were classified as top secret, not only to conceal Washington's plans from the Germans but also from the American public."[22] And perhaps from the United States's closest ally as well. Great Britain had from the beginning harshly questioned the idea of the democracies doing business with Vichy. Prime Minister Churchill, for example, in a speech to the Canadian parliament in 1940, proclaimed that "it was their duty [the French government] to go to North Africa, where they would have been at the head of the French Empire. In Africa, with our aid, they would have overwhelming sea power. They would have had the recognition of the United States, and the use of all the gold they had lodged beyond the seas. . . . But their generals misled them."[23]

The duplicity involved in the Roosevelt administration's dealings with Vichy might be considered in itself at least prima facie evidence that the policy being pursued was a doubtful one, although the strictures of wartime secrecy might be cited as an extenuating circumstance. In any case, the sensitivity of the American government to the questions raised about its relations with Vichy led the State Department, the War Department, and the Office of Strategic Services to authorize William Langer, a noted Harvard historian (and wartime official in OSS), to write a history of the relationship, based on secret documents normally closed to scholars for many years. In the preface to his book, Langer stressed that he accepted this assignment only on condition that he be allowed to let the facts lead him where they might, and that his account would thus not be an "official" one.[24] As it turned out, Langer's book produced some welcome (and presumably anticipated) conclusions for American officialdom arguing for the essential correctness of Washington's policy toward Vichy. Whatever view one takes of Langer's analysis, it is evident that what came to be called the "Darlan deal" was simply a logical extension, and in effect a summation, of the United States' general approach to dealing with the officials of the Vichy regime. The immediate background to the Darlan deal had to do with Allied preparations for, and the carrying out of, an invasion of North Africa, code named TORCH.

BRINGING THE WAR TO THE AXIS

In June 1942, President Franklin Roosevelt and Prime Minister Winston Churchill met in Washington to consider future operations in the war against the Axis. They agreed that a direct assault against Nazi-occupied Europe was out of the question for the time being, and in its stead they developed a tentative plan for an Allied move into North Africa. The controlling metaphor giving rise to this scheme had to do with the so-called "soft underbelly" of Europe. The notion was that the Mediterranean theater of war presented far greater opportunities for Allied forces at this point in the war than a heavily fortified western Europe and that success here could not only secure the Mediterranean sea lanes, an important objective in itself, but also be a prelude to subsequent operations in southern Europe. A month later, TORCH was definitely agreed upon, and General Dwight Eisenhower was appointed as overall commander of Allied forces landing in North Africa. This decision was partly dictated by the fact that the Vichy armed forces in the area—numbering around 120,000 men together with about 500 combat aircraft and powerful naval units at Dakar—were considered far less likely to resist an American-led military operation than a British one. So focused was President Roosevelt on this factor that he even asked Churchill to keep the British forces involved in TORCH out of action for at least a week.[25]

The plans for TORCH called for two separate movements of Allied troops. A large convoy of ships and men would sail directly from the United States directed toward the area around Casablanca in French Morocco, while at the same time two additional Anglo-American flotillas would leave British ports in order to come ashore in the environs of Oran and Algiers in French Algeria. The date of the initial TORCH landings was set for November 8, 1942, and the invasion forces included some 500 warships and 350 transport and cargo ships. Within the first three weeks, they were to land around 185,000 men, 20,000 vehicles, and 200,000 tons of supplies. The basic strategic design was that once the Allies were safely ashore, especially in Algeria, they would advance rapidly to occupy Tunisia and thus enclose German general Erwin Rommel's *Afrika Korps* in a pincer movement (Rommel's troops at this point already being in retreat from the assault of the British Eighth Army at El Alamein in Egypt).[26]

One of the key uncertainties with respect to the TORCH operation, as noted above, was the likely reaction of the large French military contingent in North Africa to the invasion. Theoretically subject to the orders of the Vichy regime, which had pledged to defend its overseas possessions against any and all intruders, these units could—in the worst case scenario—actively resist the Allied invasion and in so doing put it at considerable risk, or at least greatly increase the losses incurred by Allied forces. The basic dilemma facing the United States was summarized by the ubiquitous Robert Murphy:

> The President was keenly aware of the delicate situation which would be created by sending American troops into the territory of a professedly neutral government with which we had amicable relations. In view of our declared principles [sic], it would be difficult to establish a case for landings in French Africa without the formal consent of the Vichy Government. And, lacking such approval from Marshal Pétain's administration, we must anticipate that a military invasion would be forcibly resisted by some French commanders who had sworn allegiance to the marshal. There were only two possible ways to conquer this inevitable French resistance—by transporting overseas Allied troops and equipment vastly superior to the French fighting forces already stationed in Africa; or by diplomatic maneuvers to persuade the French commanders that victory over Germany would result from cooperating with the American expedition, and that allegiance to France was more important than allegiance to Pétain.[27]

As it was, TORCH hardly disposed of forces vastly superior to those of the French in North Africa. Under these circumstances, then, the thinking of Murphy and a number of others almost inevitably turned to the realm of "diplomatic maneuvers." The individual on whom these maneuvers would come to focus was a certain Admiral Darlan, who at the time was commander-in-chief of all Vichy armed forces. He also happened to be one of the most controversial—and, in many quarters, reviled—representatives of the Vichy regime. From this latter fact flowed much if not all of the subsequent controversy that was to attend the famous Darlan deal.

THE PERSONA OF ADMIRAL DARLAN

Jean François Darlan was born at Nérac in the Gascony region of France in 1881. His father was a local official and eventually became minister of justice in the French cabinet from 1896 to 1898. Despite coming from a strong Republican family, Darlan decided early on to pursue a career in the military, and he saw a great deal of service in World War I, participating in the battles of Salonica, Verdun, and Champagne. During the interwar years, Darlan carved out a reputation as being the preeminent "political sailor," staking his advancement more on his ties to prominent figures in government than to his military achievements. He served several terms as *chef de cabinet,* for example, to Georges Leygues, a fixture as the cabinet minister responsible for the French navy. By the outbreak of World War II, Darlan had become a full admiral in command of all French naval forces.

Following the catastrophic defeat of May-June 1940, Darlan for a brief period became minister of marine in the new Vichy government, with Pierre Laval as the premier. When Laval was ousted in December of that year, however, the French admiral assumed center stage in Vichy affairs. In February 1941, he was appointed vice president of the Council of State and foreign minister, and the next day, was officially designated as Pétain's successor. Several days later he added the portfolio of minister of the interior. In short order, he had become the second most powerful figure in Vichy. Darlan managed to maintain this position for 14 months until Laval returned to power in April 1942. Even then, he was named as commander in chief of all the Vichy armed forces and thus continued to play a key role in Vichy policy.[28]

Admiral Jean François Darlan was often described as an "enigma," as one wartime study of his career put it.[29] His supporters argued that he was always a French patriot and that, in his various posts under the Vichy regime, he dealt with the Germans only to the extent that it was necessary in order to protect fundamental French interests. His many opponents had a rather different image of the man as someone who had innately reactionary views, was more than willing to do the Germans' bidding even beyond what was asked, and above all was the supreme opportunist. Given the heated debate that took place at the time and later concerning the real persona of Admiral Darlan, it might seem difficult if not impossible to render a true verdict on his character and conduct. But the obstacles to doing so may actually be more apparent than real. In actuality the guiding principles that moved Darlan are not especially hard to decipher, and the argument concerning his true motivations can be resolved with reasonable confidence.

One key to his behavior was his almost obsessive dislike, even hatred, of the British. This attitude evidently was shaped as far back as the Washington Naval Conference of 1922, which established comparative naval force levels for the major European powers (Britain, France, Italy) as well as the United States and Japan. Darlan blamed London for what he regarded as the inferior status to which the French navy was consigned under this agreement. His detestation of Great Britain was only increased by the events at Dunkirk in May 1940. He was convinced that Churchill had been indifferent to the fate of French troops around Dunkirk so as long as his own men were safely evacuated, and Darlan offered scathing comment on the number of French soldiers left behind once the operation was concluded.

The final straw as far as Darlan was concerned took place on July 3, 1940. The Churchill government was highly anxious about the fate of the French fleet, fearing that if it should come under German control, it would irrevocably change the balance of power in the Mediterranean. Orders were thus given to take over French ships then in British ports, and to persuade the French naval commanders in North Africa either to sail their forces to Britain or at a minimum to some neutral country. The French naval units at Alexandria in Egypt conceded to the British ultimatum with only token resistance, but the outcome was far different at Mers el-Kebir outside Oran in French Algeria. The man in command there, Admiral Marcel-Bruno Gensoul, refused all the British demands, and as a consequence a large British fleet standing offshore opened fire on the French ships, sinking or disabling many of them and killing or wounding about 2,000 French sailors. The Vichy regime broke off diplomatic relations with Great Britain as a consequence, and there were even fears that Vichy would formally declare war on the British and thus become an active partner in the Axis war effort. Even though this failed to materialize, the shadow of Mers el-Kebir hung over Anglo-French relations for the remainder of the war, and at the very least confirmed Darlan in his belief that perfidious Albion was as loathsome as he had always felt it to be.[30]

His feelings were especially aroused because of his dogged devotion to the development and prestige of the French navy, in many ways his "first and only love." Darlan had repeatedly fought for increased appropriations for the navy through the spare years of the 1930s, and he was determined to see it emerge as a world-class maritime power. His efforts acquired for him unusually deep respect and devotion among French naval officers and even among the other services, particularly the air force, who saw him as the personification of French military pride. His reputation was consolidated by his success in persuading the Germans to release 60,000 French naval prisoners-of-war after the armistice. The attack at Mers el-Kebir thus struck Darlan at his most sensitive point, since it suggested to him that British policy was inherently designed to humiliate France and to reduce the country to second-class military status.

This stance goes some way toward explaining his attitude toward the Germans. Darlan *was* a French patriot in the sense that he was hardly anxious to substitute Nazi domination of France for that of the British. At the same time, he seems to have operated on the premise that "the enemy of my enemy is my friend" (or at least someone with whom one ought to do business). This led him in the early period of Vichy into pushing for a series of arrangements with Hitler that to an unbiased observer would seem to have represented full collaboration in all but name. One of his German negotiating partners offered the interesting observation that "when we ask Laval for a chicken, we get an egg; when we ask Darlan for an egg, we get a chicken." All accounts tend to agree that he was particularly flattered by being granted a personal audience with Hitler at which he sketched out his vision of future Franco-German cooperation.

The most notorious of Darlan's dealings with the Germans came in May 1941. In that month he was a prime figure behind a series of agreements with the Germans whereby Vichy France would provide materiel and facilities in the Middle East in support of the revolt by pro-German elements in Iraq led by Rashid Ali. Vichy would also give the Germans harbor and railway facilities in Tunisia, and allow both the harbor and airfield at Dakar in Senegal to become a German base. Given the fact that the French navy under this accord would now patrol the sea route between Bizerta (in Tunisia) and southern Europe to protect German shipping, Darlan was effectively aligning French resources to the Axis cause. Such an arrangement proved too much even for Pétain (and other figures in the regime as well, such as General Maxime Weygand, the top Vichy military figure in North Africa), and Darlan's deal with the Germans was never put into effect.[31]

This was not the only instance in which Darlan attempted to tie the French wagon to the German star. In July 1941, he proposed that a "provisional peace treaty" between Germany and France replace the armistice. Under this treaty France would formally commit herself to the New Order in Europe and join a Three-Power Pact to defend it. French naval forces would attempt to reconquer dissident colonial territories and would be used against any British attempt at "aggression." In return, Germany would accept Vichy's full sovereignty over all of France, return all French prisoners of war, and respect France's colonial empire in Africa. Hitler rejected this proposal with disdain, but Darlan seemed hardly discouraged. Later that year he arranged for information on British convoys in the North Atlantic to be given to the German navy, allowed for German torpedo boats to be transferred through Vichy France to the Mediterranean, and told Berlin that if Field Marshal Erwin Rommel's troops in Libya should be forced to retreat into Tunisia, they would be welcomed by French forces there, who themselves would join in resisting British attacks.[32]

Now a best case analysis can be made that Darlan was only dealing with the Germans in order to maximize the remaining independence of the Vichy regime and thus preserve some shred of continuing French self-respect. Nevertheless his conduct raised, at the very least, some very troubling questions. The first of these was his evident naiveté in assuming that the Nazis would maintain any sort of privileges for Vichy or for France once their tactical usefulness was exhausted. Hitler's record in other areas would have suggested that such a premise was quite beyond believing. Moreover, the Nazi regime *did* represent a fundamental assault on all basic human values of which the French people had been a proud (if sometimes inconsistent) champion. By agreeing to work with Berlin, Darlan was in effect conniving in the attempted destruction of these values.

The most serious charge that can be leveled against Darlan actually is that he may not have been all that concerned about the maintenance of such values. Much in the catechism of the New Order, it may be assumed, had an inherent appeal to him, and his own support of the so-called National Revolution during his term as Vichy prime minister represented at least an approximate commitment to such Nazi shibboleths as order, racial purity, and the elimination of "unhealthy elements" in the body politic. It is of interest in this connection that he referred to the growing French resistance movement as simply being the activity of "vulgar terrorists." He also was moved to suggest that "the entire system of parliamentary government in France [has] been rotten."[33] Finally, Darlan established the basis for the events of July 16, 1942 at the Vélodrome d'Hiver when he effectively removed legal protections for all Jews in France not carrying French citizenship. As Vichy minister of the interior a year earlier, he had sent the following circular to all prefects: "I have decided that no foreigner of the Israelite race will henceforth be freed from lodging or internment centers if he did not live in France before May 10, 1940."[34]

There was one other element in Darlan's character that needs emphasizing and one that his critics rightly stressed: his constant opportunism accompanied, not incidentally, by an overweening ambition. The lodestar of his existence, it might fairly be said, was first and foremost a devotion to his beloved French navy accompanied by, but not contradictory to, his belief that the more power given to him the better for all concerned, not just for the navy but for France more generally. The means adopted to this end were a matter of tactics rather than principle. Thus when it looked as if Nazi power would prevail in Europe for generations, Darlan ingratiated himself with his German "partners." When the military situation began to change, he moved to adopt a somewhat different strategy. Evidence of Darlan's essentially cynical approach to his relationship with the Germans, or for that matter with the Allies, can be seen in his comment to American ambassador William Leahy on August 1, 1941 (over a year before the TORCH operation) to the effect that "when you have 3,000 tanks, 6,000 planes and 500,000 men to bring to Marseilles, let me know. Then we shall welcome you."[35]

Any chance that the Allies would be able to land such a formidable force on the French mainland in 1941 was, of course, extremely dim and would remain so for a considerable period of time afterwards. Nevertheless, the possibility that Darlan might be persuaded to cooperate with the Allied war effort, or at least the American side of it, remained as a tantalizing prospect to various American officials and would eventually result in one of the most celebrated (or notorious) political-military arrangements of the war.

DEALING WITH DARLAN

The origins of what came to be called the Darlan deal supposedly rested in some measure on an accident of timing and place. The plans for the TORCH operation, that is, the Allied invasion of North Africa, had been finalized during the fall of 1942, and, on the morning of November 8, American and British troops began to come ashore in Morocco and Algeria. Admiral Darlan happened to be in Algiers on the day of the invasion in order to attend to his son, who, it was feared, was dying of infantile paralysis. The chief American diplomat in the city, Robert Murphy, woke Darlan in the early hours of November 8 and urged him to order the Vichy forces to agree to a cease fire in the area around Algiers. Darlan answered that he had to receive approval for such an order from Pétain himself, but later that day he did agree to issue the requested instructions even in the absence of Pétain's approval (whether such approval was ever provided remains one of the mysteries of the whole affair). Darlan also indicated a tentative willingness to extend this order to include all of French North Africa.

At this point General Dwight Eisenhower, supreme commander of TORCH, ordered his deputy, General Mark Clark, to fly to Algiers in order to negotiate a broader agreement with Darlan. Clark was fairly unsubtle in his dealings with Darlan. As he himself admitted, his reputation became that of a "big American who does nothing but shout and pound the table."[36] Eventually Clark and Darlan arrived at an accord along the following lines: in return for Darlan's ordering *all* Vichy forces to cease resistance to the Allied invasion—and, not incidentally, instructing the French fleet in Toulon to sail for African ports—the Americans would recognize Darlan as "high commissioner" of Algeria, Morocco, and French West Africa with full civil and political powers. General Henri Giraud (about whom more will be said later) was designated as commander in chief of French military forces in North Africa. Darlan was predisposed to accept the American offer for a variety of reasons, among them his own ambitions and the fact that the Germans had by then moved into the remainder of unoccupied France, which from his legalistic viewpoint removed a good deal of his obligation to the Pétain regime. More fundamental was his perception that by working with the Americans, he could sustain the general character of the Vichy regime in North Africa (which meant, among other things, keeping the top Vichy officials in place) and, not incidentally, thwart the British as well as De Gaulle's Free French movement.

In sum, the so-called Clark - Darlan agreement provided that in return for short-term military advantages to TORCH, Darlan would be legitimized as the supreme French authority in North Africa. An American historian summarized its essence with some asperity:

> The most important clause of the Clark - Darlan agreement was that which left the Vichy administration in North Africa intact. Nowhere in the agreement could be found a stipulation which in the least implied that the French would be required to expunge Fascist elements from the governmental structure. If the High Commissioner chose to maintain in office the Vichy-appointed governors—Noguès, Boisson, and Chatel; if he kept anti-semitic laws patterned on Hitler's Nuremberg decrees in effect; or if he took no steps to liquidate the Service d'Ordre Légionnaire (S.O.L.), the North African version of the Schutzstaffel [SS], there could be no justification for Allied interference unless it could be shown that such policies endangered military operations.[37]

A not unimportant aspect to the American negotiations with Darlan could be found in their broader background and reinforced the image of the French admiral as a consummate opportunist. As noted, the standard account has it that the deal with Darlan was struck only because he happened to be in Algiers visiting his sick son on the first day of TORCH. In fact, Robert Murphy recounts that Darlan had been making discreet overtures to the United States for some 13 months *before* the invasion to the effect that he would be willing to participate in a joint French–American military operation. These overtures were reported to Washington and London, were given close consideration in the months before the invasion, and on October 17, 1941, Murphy received a message from the White House authorizing him to initiate any deal with Darlan that might be helpful to military operations. Admiral Raymond Fenard, Darlan's chief representative in Algiers, had told the Americans that he was in favor of such cooperation as well if the French forces were given sufficient equipment to make resistance to the Germans feasible. Both Fenard and Darlan urged the United States to place the "minor concessions" that Vichy had to make to the Germans in context, and to accept that French North Africa had to be regarded as a totally separate entity from metropolitan France.[38]

It is hardly surprising that when news of the Darlan deal became public, the reaction in various circles was mixed, to say the least. General De Gaulle wrote to one of Roosevelt's representatives with his customary bluntness, "I understand that the United States buys the treachery of traitors, if this appears profitable, but payment must not be made against the honor of France."[39] The deal was denounced by others as a "sordid nullification of the principles for which the United Nations were supposed to be fighting." It was described as a "base and squalid" arrangement that led logically to the conclusion that "if we will make a deal with a Darlan in French territory, then presumably we will make one with a Goering in Germany or with a Matsuoka in Japan."[40] Churchill himself warned President Roosevelt on November 17 that the Darlan deal could "only be a temporary expedient justifiable solely by the stress of battle. We must not overlook the serious political injury which may be done to our cause, not only in France but throughout Europe, by the feeling that we are ready to make terms with the local quislings." He went on to add that "there is above all our own moral position. We are fighting for international decency and Darlan is the antithesis of this."[41] One of President Roosevelt's own advisers, Treasury Secretary Henry Morgenthau, summarized the feelings of many when he told his boss that the Darlan deal was "something that affects my soul."[42]

The moral outrage that greeted the Darlan deal was later reinforced when it appeared that it was to be only one of a series of agreements with unsavory Vichy officials. Marcel Peyrouton had been minister of the interior at Vichy for a period of time in 1940, which meant that he was in charge of the French police, and his instructions to them about dealing with dissident or "unreliable" elements were particularly harsh. During his short tenure in office, for example, the first anti-Jewish laws were promulgated. Peyrouton was later involved in a plot to remove Pierre Laval as prime minister, and as a consequence he was eventually forced to leave France by accepting appointment as Vichy ambassador to Argentina, where he was generally supportive of the pro-Axis views of the host government. Once Darlan had received the imprimatur of the Americans as high commissioner for French North Africa, he demanded that Peyrouton be appointed to his administration as governor general of Algeria (supposedly because of his knowledge of the region and his demonstrated "administrative" skills). On the recommendation of Robert Murphy, Peyrouton was subsequently flown in an American aircraft from Buenos Aires to Algiers to assume his new post. As Murphy typically says, "it never occurred" to him that Peytrouton's appointment would provoke controversy, even though, he admits, it soon assumed proportions almost equal to the Darlan deal itself.[43]

The naming of Peyrouton seemed to confirm the impression held by many critics that the United States was prepared to deal with any figure from the Vichy regime, no matter how disreputable, for short-term advantage. The reaction of De Gaulle's Free French movement need hardly be guessed at, and in fact was particularly virulent. Also significant was the stance taken by Wendell Willkie, Republican presidential candidate in 1940, and still a very prominent influence on American opinion. Willkie had agreed not to make a public issue of his dissatisfaction with the Darlan deal, but when news of Peyrouton's appointment was announced, this was for him at last a step too far, and he vigorously denounced it.[44] The Peyrouton affair only added to the travails that various American figures, such as General Dwight Eisenhower, had been experiencing in the aftermath of the Darlan accord. Eisenhower's main defense was that he had known nothing of Peyrouton's background when Murphy recommended his appointment, and that he assumed the State Department had approved the arrangement. The president himself was also feeling the heat, and he took pains to indicate that he had not approved of Peyrouton's appointment and in fact had not even known of it.[45]

The man who negotiated the deal with Darlan himself, General Mark Clark, seemed to be baffled by all the furor that his actions had aroused. "I was nothing less than amazed that our use of a man who had collaborated with the Nazis had resulted in such tremendous political pressure." He insisted that "military expediency dictated that we do business with Darlan. . . . If I had it to do over again, I would choose again to deal with the man who could do the job—whether it turned out to be Darlan or the Devil himself."[46] Roosevelt himself seemed to be taken by this line of argument. In attempting to deflect criticism of the Darlan deal, he quoted an old Balkan proverb of the Orthodox church to the effect that "you are permitted in times of great danger to walk with the Devil until you have crossed the bridge."[47]

This may have suggested a certain truth concerning the relationship between dirty hands and politicians with great responsibility, but it hardly addressed the full range of questions raised by the Darlan deal (and that with Peyrouton as well). Given the French admiral's predispositions and past record, what ethical judgment can legitimately be passed on the United States treating with such a man? Was this a betrayal of an essentially moral cause, the defeat of the Nazi threat to all civilized values (and all those who connived in the threat)? Or was it a legitimate arrangement in service to other moral goods, including the saving of the lives of the soldiers involved in TORCH and even the very goal of besting the Nazi menace itself? Such questions require close analysis if they are to be meaningfully answered. As with Beneš's role in the Lidice affair, it is necessary to subject the Darlan arrangement to a systematic moral enquiry and to parse out the ethical justifications for and objections to it in as rigorous a manner as possible.

6

The Darlan Deal: Evaluation

At the outset of any formal ethical critique of the Darlan deal, one very important distinction has to be made between this case and that of Lidice. In the latter instance, responsibility for the decision to assassinate Reinhard Heydrich could reasonably be assigned to one man only. It is true that President Beneš received support in the development of ANTHROPOID from others around him, notably his chief of intelligence, František Moravec. Yet the fact remains that Beneš's voice was always the decisive one in the Czech government-in-exile, and his style of decisionmaking was such that he arrogated all really important questions to his own judgment. Whatever one may think about his wisdom—or qualifications—in doing so, an inevitable result was that credit for the successes and blame for the failures of the London Czech government attached very strongly to him alone.

In the case of the Darlan deal, however, a rather different situation applied. This was indeed an example of what we have called multiple dirty hands, that is to say, the fingerprints of a variety of individuals could be found on the final decision. In offering a moral assessment of the arrangement with Darlan, therefore, it is necessary to cast our net rather wider than was done in the matter of ANTHROPOID, particularly in terms of the "intuitive values" that various policymakers brought to the decision. The following analysis thus focuses on six different individuals who played a more or less significant role in the Darlan affair: Robert Murphy, the chief American diplomatic representative in North Africa before and during TORCH; General Mark Clark, Eisenhower's deputy, who did the actual final negotiations with

Darlan; General Dwight Eisenhower himself, who was in overall command of TORCH and had to approve Clark's arrangement with Darlan; and, in Washington, three figures intimately involved in the Darlan controversy: the president, Secretary of State Cordell Hull, and the chief of staff of the army, General George C. Marshall. As we have already said, several of these men were not in the strict sense "political leaders," but they were all involved in one way or another in the making of political judgments within the context of the Darlan deal.

The main issue for examination here is how these individuals actually felt about the United States having dealings with a man such as Admiral Jean François Darlan, and, more broadly, what their ethical position was with respect to the Vichy regime itself of which Darlan was such a prominent member. How did they feel about Vichy's treatment of Jews, for example, or its other authoritarian policies that had done so much violence to the French parliamentary tradition as it had existed since 1870? What moral weight did they apply to Vichy's steadily deepening collaboration with the Nazis, a regime that represented a threat to all standards of civilized conduct? What, in short, were the basic attitudes that shaped their conduct and their analyses at the time of the arrangement with Darlan?

THE WORLD OF THE DECISIONMAKERS

Their value orientations actually seemed to extend across a surprisingly large spectrum involving a variety of different themes. There was, for example, the strictly pragmatic or utilitarian approach to working with Darlan and Vichy. From this perspective, the internal workings of Vichy were largely (or entirely) their affair, and in any case were so murky and confused that Americans were hardly likely to be able to understand them. The indicated course of action therefore was to use Vichy officials, including Darlan, strictly in terms of their practical contribution to American interests without any embarrassing (and irrelevant) queries about their past behavior. General Mark Clark was clearly the prime exemplar of this approach. His basic theory was summarized in the following comment:

> I was charged with fighting a war . . . and getting on as rapidly as humanly
> possible with the war against the Axis in Tunisia. That meant I was trying
> to save American, British and French lives—a great many of them. . . .
> To carry out this mission, I was ready to deal with anybody who could do
> the job. . . . I simply had to find a sound instrument through which we

could get the French to cooperate with us in Algiers and in Tunisia. . . . I didn't care much if that instrument were named Darlan, Giraud, or Pétain himself."[1]

Clark's knowledge of French politics and history was, to put it mildly, rather limited, and he was particularly impatient with what he considered abstract philosophical musings when there was a war to be fought. The only important variable to him was whether a particular course of action would advance the cause of Allied military victory. Everything else was subsidiary, even invisible, in his assessment of what to do. Perhaps Clark's philosophy was best caught in his perennial references to "YSOB's" in his secret cables to General Eisenhower and the Allied chiefs of staff. This colorful acronym stood for "yellow-bellied sons of bitches," and it referred to anyone who stood in the way of Allied military progress. Darlan was from this perspective *not* a YSOB, except to the extent that he created complications that impeded the goal of getting the Vichy forces in North Africa to lay down their arms. Darlan's past record, on the other hand, was essentially a tabula rasa to Clark, and a matter of almost total indifference to him.

Mark Clark stands out as almost a caricature of the pure warrior unencumbered by bothersome reflections on the broader implications of the war effort in which he was involved. The same could not be said for others, however: they *were* sensitive to some of the basic political and moral questions involved in dealing with Darlan and Vichy, but they arrived at rather different conclusions in this regard. Robert Murphy, for example, saw Darlan as an individual true to his French patriotism who was attempting— and had attempted—to make the best of a bad deal. Murphy recalled his contacts with the French admiral by saying that "probably I got to know him better than any other American ever did and, strangely, I grew to like him. I was particularly impressed by how cleverly Darlan safeguarded French national interests. . . . Whatever Darlan's apparent failings during his Vichy period [sic], he proved during his last weeks that he was a French patriot." He agreed with Mark Clark that Darlan had contributed as much as any Frenchman to the success of the TORCH operation, and for this reason, if for no other, he deserved American gratitude.[2]

As to the origins and character of the Vichy regime that Darlan so loyally served (at least prior to November 8, 1942), Murphy expressed his understanding of the supposed dilemmas of the Pétain government. "I felt a great deal of sympathy for the appalling predicament in which these French legislators found themselves." Part of this sympathy derived from Murphy's appreciation of the need to restore some measure of French pride after the devastating defeat in the spring of 1940, but a subsidiary (if often understated) theme behind Murphy's thinking was that Vichy had after all brought a degree of "order" to French life and that their seemingly more doubtful policies could be at least partially explained in terms of the burden of French history. Murphy's views were also shaped by his perception that Vichy was very much anti-Communist and that international communism had for a long time been the bugbear of French democracy and the democracies more generally. He argued, for example, that before the war "French and international Communists were much more responsible for defeatism [in France] than the relatively few so-called fascists. American Communists also were doing everything possible then to discourage our own military preparedness and to oppose any assistance to France and Britain." Murphy bewailed the extent to which the Communists had managed, so he claimed, to infiltrate the French government, including the French police.[3] Not incidentally, he went out of his way to befriend the representative to France of the new Franco regime in Spain, particularly since the French government of the day was effectively snubbing him because of its hostility to the regime that he was serving.

On Vichy's anti-Semitic policies, Murphy asserted that prejudice toward Jews had been prevalent in France long before the Vichy regime came to power and that even so various members of the regime continued to resist the imposition of anti-Jewish decrees. While not approving of Vichy anti-Semitism, Murphy also allowed as how it could be explained in terms of the fact that the prewar Popular Front government of Leon Blum (who was himself a Jew) had "neglected" French rearmament and thus embittered many members of the French military establishment as well as others. He also observed that the restoration of the special rights of French Jews in Algeria after the Allied conquest of that country "required extremely delicate handling, in view of the passions which had smoldered for generations among Algerian Christians as well as Moslems."

General Dwight D. Eisenhower's stance toward the Darlan deal was rather different from that of Murphy's and is of particular interest since it was he who dispatched Mark Clark to Algiers to undertake the negotiations with Darlan, and it was his career put at most immediate risk by the subsequent uproar. Indeed there was a point at which Eisenhower questioned whether he would be able to survive the controversy that had developed. His moment of peril was especially great during the additional furor surrounding the appointment of Marcel Peyrouton, which seemed to many to be only a further noxious example of the attitudes that had led to the original arrangement with Darlan. As his chief aide, Commander Harry

Butcher, recorded in his diary, "Eisenhower's neck is in a noose and he knows it."[4]

As it turned out, Eisenhower was able to extricate his neck from the noose, and he went on to even greater glory. Possibly because of the personal trauma that he experienced over the Darlan deal, however, his stated position on dealing with such a controversial Vichy figure did stand somewhat apart from the utilitarianism of Clark and the (sometimes) oblivious or apologetic attitude toward Vichy adopted by Murphy. Perhaps the most attractive aspect of Eisenhower's comments on the matter was his straightforward acceptance of responsibility for what had been done. "If resulting political repercussions [from the Darlan deal] became so serious as to call for a sacrifice," he said, "logic and tradition demanded that the man in the field should take complete responsibility for the matter, with his later relief from command becoming the symbol of correction."[5]

Beyond this, however, Eisenhower seemed to recognize that working with Darlan had a number of problematical aspects. He was insistent about the positive returns from the Darlan deal, but carefully avoided any expressions of pleasure in having to deal with such a man.

> My entire acquaintanceship with Darlan covered a period of six weeks. His reputation was that of a notorious collaborator with Hitler, but during the time that he served as the administrator of French North Africa he never once, to our knowledge, violated any commitment or promise. On the other hand, his mannerisms and personality did not inspire confidence and in view of his reputation we were always uneasy in dealing with him.[6]

It is evident as well that Eisenhower was sensitive to the accusation that his complicity in, and for that matter approval of, the deal with Darlan was evidence of his indifference to liberal values. At one point, he protested to British diplomat Harold Macmillan, "I can't understand why these long-haired, starry-eyed guys keep gunning for me. I'm no reactionary. Christ on the mountain! I'm as idealistic as hell."[7] Aside from his stereotypical (and somewhat contradictory) characterization of idealists as "long-haired, starry-eyed guys," there is evidence that Eisenhower was indeed uneasy about some of the longer-term implications of the Darlan deal. At one point, for example, he was blunt with Darlan about the character of his unfolding administration in North Africa: "Because of your former position in the Vichy government, you are, naturally, unpopular in the United States. Nevertheless, I have asked our government to let us alone. If you had an enlightened liberal government in action, the antipathy toward you would change." Eisenhower seemed to be particularly concerned about the continued existence of anti-Semitic decrees in French North Africa. He insisted that "the French authorities ameliorate anti-Jewish laws and practices."[8]

Even in this instance, however, a large dose of pragmatism informed Eisenhower's attitudes. He was persuaded that given the historical antagonism between Arab and Jew in North Africa, it would be a mistake to move too quickly in changing Vichy policies (which had basically catered to Arab prejudices), lest there be a violent Arab reaction that would complicate Allied military operations. "It is easy to understand," he said, "that the situation called more for caution and evolution than it did for precipitate action and possible revolution." On the more general matter of replacing Vichy officials in North Africa, he reflected (in particular connection with the Peyrouton case) that "it was difficult indeed to find men who had any experience in French colonial administration and at the same time bore no trace of the Vichy trademark."[9]

On balance, then, General Eisenhower emerges as a man who displayed a practical mind-set fairly typical of his profession—particularly in wartime—but who at the same time demonstrated a greater concern with issues of conscience and politics than was characteristic of other of his brethren such as Mark Clark. Perhaps this was one of the reasons (one might hope) that he went on to achieve ever more important military responsibility and eventually high political office.

The Men in Washington

Murphy, Clark, and Eisenhower might be considered together as the "men in the field," individuals whose total professional responsibility was tied up with the unfolding of TORCH and whose attentions were entirely concentrated on the operation's outcome. There were, on the other hand, three other men who had considerable involvement in North African affairs but had a whole raft of other responsibilities as well, and thus might perhaps be expected to view the Darlan deal from a somewhat different perspective than those concerned with the immediate day-to-day problems presented by TORCH.

General George C. Marshall, the chief of staff of the army, was one of the most revered officials in Washington during the war and not just by his comrades in uniform. He was universally regarded as a person with impeccable integrity who had an uncanny ability to cut to the nub of even the most complex issues. He was especially noted for his sensitivity to his subordinates, and for his insistence that personal self-interest and aggrandizement be set aside by one and all in deciding on broad questions of policy. He himself stood out as an exemplar of this credo: his deepest wish was to be named commander of OVERLORD, the code name for the Allied invasion of Europe, but when Eisenhower was chosen for this post instead, he accepted without complaint or demur. President Roosevelt summarized the esteem in which Marshall was held by saying that he "would not able to sleep at night" if his army chief-of-staff was out of the country.

Marshall was carefully attentive to the traditional civil–military tradition in the United States whereby career military men avoided injecting themselves directly into political questions. At the same time, he seems to have had doubts about the general course of American policy toward Vichy from its inception, particularly since he regarded Vichy officialdom as essentially a pack of opportunists and collaborators who had sullied their personal honor (a matter of great significance to Marshall) in their dealings with the Nazis. Darlan, of course, could be considered to rank very high on this list of undesirables. When he received the initial reports of the Clark–Darlan agreement, therefore, Marshall was uneasy about its implications and found it instinctively distasteful for his government to be dealing with such an individual. Early on, for example, Marshall cabled Eisenhower that there was "strong sentiment" in Washington for an early end to Vichy's anti-Semitic decrees in North Africa, especially those requiring Jews to wear yellow armbands.[10] He also instructed his chief of intelligence to develop closer ties with representatives of De Gaulle's Free French movement based in Washington.

Another of Marshall's most admirable traits, however, referred to above, was his loyalty to his subordinates and an appreciation of their difficulties. Throughout the rising furor over the Darlan deal, the chief-of-staff went out of his way to bolster Eisenhower's position and to assure him of his support. He was particularly intent on preventing Eisenhower's becoming a "sacrificial lamb" for his involvement in the Darlan negotiations. He wired the commander of TORCH that he should "leave the worries to us, and go ahead with your campaign" while he and Secretary of War Stimson attempted to put out the fires of protest at home.[11] That this would be no easy task was reflected in the comment of one reporter that he had "never seen [Marshall] so concerned as he was on this occasion."[12] But his support for Eisenhower never wavered. On December 8 he summarized his feelings in the following communication:

I want you to feel that you have not only my confidence but my deep sympathy in conducting a battle, organizing a fair slice of the continent, and at the same time being involved in probably the most complicated and highly supervised negotiations in history, considering the time element and other circumstances.[13]

Eisenhower certainly appreciated this support, and in communicating his feelings to Marshall, he expressed some of his own attitudes concerning the Darlan deal. "I know you understand that the necessity for dealing with turncoats and crooks is as distasteful to me as to anyone else, and I am grateful indeed that you have taken such an understanding attitude on the situation."[14]

Marshall's "understanding attitude" toward the Darlan deal derived basically out of his philosophy that he should give full support to his field commanders when they faced difficulties. This did not mean that he regarded the arrangements with Darlan as anything other than a temporary—and, as Eisenhower put it, distasteful—expedient tied to current military operations. For Secretary of State Cordell Hull, on the other hand, the Darlan deal was hardly anything to be ashamed of, and Hull's "understanding attitude" toward it was based on more than simply its short-term military utility.

The secretary of state had long been identified in Washington as perhaps the prime force behind the American policy of accommodation with Vichy and certainly its chief apologist. This stance was accompanied, not incidentally, by what can only be described as an unusually personal animus toward De Gaulle and his supporters. The disdain that he felt in this regard was best caught in a sneering reference he made at one point to the "so-called" Free French (a description that even Murphy found unfortunate). The secretary asserted that whereas 95 percent of the French people were basically anti-Nazi, "more than 95 percent of this latter number are not De Gaullists and would not follow him."[15] How he arrived at these statistics was left unexplained.

Hull's unabashed enthusiasm for the American policy toward Vichy subjected him over a period of many months to a drumbeat of criticism from those opposed to the policy in Washington and elsewhere. Indeed he became the chief lightening rod for denunciations of the Vichy–American relationship and, not surprisingly, became increasingly bitter and defensive at this failure to recognize his achievements as a foreign policymaker. He accused his critics of thinking "largely of ideologies, less of American interests" and insisted that "we fought Hitlerism at Vichy as strongly as we fought it anywhere.... Our policy toward Vichy involved no sacrifice of principle."[16]

Given these attitudes, when the Darlan deal came along, Hull was perhaps unique in the way in which he trumpeted it as a vindication of his past diplomacy. In the process, he shrugged off virtually all the doubts that others felt about Darlan, even those who were basically supportive of the

deal (such as Marshall). Once again, he accused critics of the arrangement of Darlan as being motivated basically by "ideology" rather than realism and summarized his own attitude toward the ideological question (for example, Darlan's dubious past) by saying that in his view "civil questions were subordinate except as they contributed to military effectiveness."[17] This comment suggests that in Hull's opinion concerns about the continuance of Vichy governance in North Africa were essentially an irrelevant intrusion into tactical military considerations.

Hull can hardly be accused of turning a blind eye to some of the doubtful features of the Vichy regime, notably its various forms of collaboration with the Nazis and its authoritarian domestic policies. Indeed he was willing to accept that some aspects of Vichy could legitimately be described as fascist. At the same time, the secretary of state was a man of unusual (some would say remarkable) confidence in his own judgment, and he was ill-disposed to engaging in any genuine dialogue with his critics about American dealings with Vichy generally or Darlan specifically. What strikes one about his behavior, then, is not that he was totally oblivious to the moral questions involved in policymaking, but that his arrogance and obsession with reputation moved him systematically to set aside any willingness to admit publicly to these moral questions, lest in doing so he provide ammunition to his many critics.

It remains now to consider the values of the person who had ultimate responsibility for the Darlan deal—and for the overall American policy toward Vichy itself. President Franklin D. Roosevelt's true attitudes toward the myriad foreign policy questions with which he had to deal during World War II were in some ways a reflection of Winston Churchill's famous description of Russia: "a riddle wrapped in a mystery inside an enigma." As a masterful politician, he often seemed to be all things to all people, with a knack for persuading first one and then another that he was (at least privately) in full agreement with their views, even if objective analysis showed that these views were contradictory. Under the circumstances, then, it is not easy to divine his exact thinking about the American relationship with Vichy, and, more particularly, the arrangement with Admiral Darlan.

Nevertheless, certain basic themes in Roosevelt's approach to these matters can be identified. Certainly he shared in good measure the essentially pragmatic attitude toward Vichy of Hull, Murphy, and others. He referred to the Vichy government as being "in a German cage" and argued that maintaining American relations with such a government provided at least some hope that it would not totally go over to Nazi control. At the same time, Roosevelt was careful to insist that this marriage of convenience

with Vichy implied no longer-term political commitment. Indeed he went out of his way on a number of occasions to emphasize that the United States had no intention of recognizing "any one person or group as the [future] Government of France until a liberated French population could freely choose their own government. . . . I will not help anyone impose a Government on the French people."[18]

His liberal supporters could (and perhaps did) interpret this to mean that Roosevelt's dealings with Marshal Pétain had no long term significance for the future of the French state—and take comfort from this. On the other hand, an equally valid interpretation was that Roosevelt had De Gaulle, not Pétain, in mind in adopting such a stance. As will be discussed farther on, Roosevelt, along with a number of other American officials, regarded De Gaulle as a poseur with a special talent for self-promotion, and with a whole range of irritating personal qualities in the bargain. At one point, the president caustically remarked, "we all have our crosses to bear, and mine is the Cross of Lorraine [De Gaulle's personal symbol]." It seems fair to suggest that Roosevelt's intense personal aversion to De Gaulle played at least some role in a greater willingness to deal with Vichy and especially with Darlan than otherwise would have been the case.

At the same time, it is evident that almost from the inception of the Darlan deal, the president was troubled by the implications of the United States dealing with such a well-known Vichy figure, one who in particular was identified with close collaboration with the Nazis. He sent a private communication to Eisenhower in which he assured him of his "complete support" but made the point that "we do not trust Darlan" and that it would be "impossible to keep a collaborator of Hitler and one whom we believe to be a fascist in civil power any longer than is absolutely necessary."[19] Roosevelt seems to have been greatly taken aback by the widespread domestic criticism of the arrangement with Darlan—especially since so much of it came from his usual liberal supporters—and he was hardly immune to the arguments of his critics. His sensitivity on the matter was testified to by one of his principal aides and speechwriters, Samuel Rosenman: "He showed more resentment and more impatience with his critics throughout this period than at any other time I know about. At times he refused to talk about the deals in North Africa at all; at times he bitterly read aloud what some columnist had written about them, and expressed his resentment."[20] In a meeting with two of De Gaulle's representatives at the White House, he angrily proclaimed, "Of course I'm dealing with Darlan, since Darlan's giving me Algiers! Tomorrow I'd deal with Laval, if Laval were to offer me Paris!"[21]

Roosevelt's sensitivities with respect to the Darlan deal were best reflected in a public statement that he issued on November 17, 1942. He indicated his acceptance of Eisenhower's arrangement with Darlan, but only as a temporary measure.

> We are opposed to Frenchmen who support Hitler and the Axis. No one in our Army has any authority to discuss the future government of France or the French Empire. The future French Government will be established not by any individual in metropolitan France or overseas, but by the French people themselves after they have been set free by the victory of the United Nations. The present temporary arrangement in North and West Africa is only a temporary expedient, justified solely by the stress of battle.[22]

Roosevelt went on to say that he had requested that all those who had been imprisoned in North Africa because of their anti-Nazi views should be immediately released, and that all laws and decrees "inspired by Nazi governments or Nazi ideologies" should be revoked without delay. Darlan, it might be added, was not exactly enthusiastic at Roosevelt's description of his status. He commented privately that the Americans evidently considered him "only a lemon which [they] will drop after they have squeezed it dry," and he went on to insist that he had indeed been given "the rights and responsibilities of a government . . . which would represent France in the world."[23]

One factor that seems to have influenced the president to look on the Darlan deal as at least a tolerable short-term arrangement was essentially idiosyncratic and personal. Darlan, as earlier noted, was in Algiers on the morning of November visiting his sick son, who was suffering from polio (infantile paralysis). Roosevelt, of course, had been crippled by this disease a number of years earlier, and there is some indication that Darlan's having to deal with such a tragedy predisposed the president to take a somewhat more tolerant view of the admiral's character than otherwise might have been the case. Admiral Leahy, his chief of staff at the time, records that when he told the president of the nature of Darlan's visit to Algiers, "the first thing that impressed Roosevelt was the nature of the boy's illness. Roosevelt remembered his own illness and proposed that we send a letter to Darlan [expressing sympathy]."[24] The president later arranged for Darlan's son to be sent to the polio treatment center at Warm Springs, Georgia, accompanied by his mother, and Darlan himself was holding discussions with American officials about joining them just before his assassination.

In assessing Franklin Roosevelt's values in the context of the Darlan deal, one item remains troubling. Despite his demand that Vichy decrees in North Africa "inspired by Nazi ideology" be revoked, the president's attitude toward Vichy anti-Semitism was a good deal more ambiguous than his general statement suggested. His stance was in fact quite similar to that taken by Robert Murphy. Roosevelt himself was certainly not anti-Semitic in the traditional sense but at the same time he thought it necessary to "understand" the reasons for French anti-Semitism—and even for the German variety as well. Thus at the Casablanca conference in January 1943, the following sentiments with respect to the status of Jews in French North Africa were reported:

> The President stated that he felt the whole Jewish problem [sic] should be studied very carefully and that progress should be definitely planned. In other words, the number of Jews engaged in the practice of the professions (law, medicine, etc.) should be definitely limited to the percentage that the Jewish population in North Africa bears to the whole of the North African population. Such a plan would therefore permit the Jews to engage in the professions, at the same time would not permit them to overcrowd the professions, and would present an unanswerable argument that they were being given their full rights.[25]

Whether Jews living in North Africa would regard Roosevelt's plan as an "unanswerable argument" that they were now enjoying complete liberty seems doubtful. Nor did the president address the question of how the Jewish proportion of those in the professions was to be regulated. Roosevelt in any case seemed to feel that his plan had a broader application. He went on to state that it "would further eliminate the specific and understandable [sic] complaints which the Germans bore towards the Jews in Germany, namely, that while they represented a small part of the population, over 50 percent of the lawyers, doctors, school teachers, college professors, etc., in Germany, were Jews."[26]

A fair summary of Roosevelt's intuitive values as they affected his attitudes toward Vichy and the Darlan deal itself thus remains a mixed picture. He emerges as someone who was more sensitive to the ethical implications of the arrangement with Darlan than others around him, but at the same time was capable of caricature and superficial treatment of some of the genuine moral issues presented by the Darlan deal. Perhaps this is inevitable in the instance of leaders with supreme political power—and supreme political responsibility. Yet troublesome questions about Roosevelt's stance on Vichy and Darlan remain despite this commonplace. In such a case, an attention to the practical consequences of a politician's actions becomes even more important in arriving at a final judgment on his ethical bona fides.

DOING GOOD AND DOING WELL

In the immediate aftermath of the Darlan deal, the hope in Washington was that the protest against it would quickly subside once news on the course of military operations in North Africa pushed it out of the headlines. In this, the Roosevelt administration was greatly disappointed. Far from subsiding, the anger and moral outrage at the Darlan deal seemed steadily to escalate. President Roosevelt was so shaken by this continued uproar that he felt compelled, as noted, to issue the statement of November 17, which (he hoped) would deflate the controversy. His arguments on this occasion serve as a convenient starting point for a consequentialist analysis of the Darlan deal: did it contribute to a just cause (the defeat of the Nazis) to such an extent that its negative side effects were more than counterbalanced? In short, was the arrangement with Darlan proportional in that the good it did outweighed the evil?

The president attempted to defend dealing with Darlan along the following lines:

> The present temporary arrangement [sic] has accomplished two military objectives. The first was to save American and British lives, and French lives on the other hand. The second was the vital factor of time. The temporary arrangement has made it possible to avoid a "mopping-up" period in Algiers and Morocco which might have taken a month or two to consummate. Such a period would have delayed the concentration for the attack from the West on Tunis, and we hope on Tripoli. Admiral Darlan's proclamation assisted in making a "mopping-up" period unnecessary.[27]

It is perhaps not surprising that, in attempting to put the best face on the Darlan deal, Roosevelt should have stressed certain favorable outcomes while fudging certain others. What is surprising is the way in which he omitted any reference to certain other goals that were originally posited as a reason for working with Darlan.

One positive result of the Darlan deal that the president did not mention, for example, had to do with French territories in West Africa. As a consequence of the Clark–Darlan negotiation, General Pierre Boisson agreed to concede to the Allies the entire region and in particular the important port of

Dakar, which included the battleship *Richelieu,* several cruisers, destroyers, and submarines, and 75,000 trained troops together with six air groups.[28] As to the matter of saving Allied lives as well as those of the French, which the president did mention, he had a relatively convincing argument to offer. Estimates of combat casualties avoided by Darlan's ordering a cease-fire are necessarily speculative, but General George Marshall, a man not normally given to hyperbole, made an effective case that the Darlan deal indeed had beneficent results. At a Washington press conference in late November, Marshall stressed that the American invasion force had suffered only 1,800 casualties (500 of these being killed in action). Preinvasion planners had estimated that there would have been 18,000 casualties as of this date. Marshall pointed to this difference in anticipated and actual losses as the main justification for the Darlan deal.[29]

Even in this instance, however, the help that Darlan provided in reducing Allied losses has to be carefully considered. TORCH began on the morning of November 8, and Darlan was not persuaded to issue an initial cease-fire order to Vichy forces around Algiers until late that afternoon. This had the effect of bringing the fighting there to a halt, but hostilities still continued at Oran and Casablanca. Darlan continued to dally 36 hours more about extending his cease-fire instructions to Auguste Noguès, Vichy resident-general in Morocco, since Darlan wanted to obtain Pétain's implicit agreement with such an action. Finally, on November 10, at the insistence of Mark Clark, he did issue an order for a cease-fire to all French forces in North Africa, although it would be two more days before all resistance actually ended. The record suggests, then, that although Darlan undoubtedly made a contribution in reducing Allied casualties, this contribution would have been even more substantial had he acted rather more swiftly and effectively than he actually did.

As far as the situation in Tunisia was concerned, the president proved unduly optimistic about the effect of Darlan's role in advancing Allied interests. The Vichy commander in Tunis, General Jean Estéva, effectively ignored Darlan's orders and indeed surrendered his command to a small force of Germans there without any meaningful resistance. This allowed Hitler to begin a massive reinforcement of Axis military strength in the country and to insure that the subsequent campaign to free all of North Africa from Axis forces—involving General Montgomery's 8th army advancing from the east and the troops of TORCH pushing from the west—would be a long and drawn-out affair. Tunis in fact was not finally liberated until May 1943. The avoidance of a "mopping-up" period in Algeria, which Roosevelt posited as a reason for the Darlan deal, thus was an illusory achievement at best.[30]

Then there was the question of the French fleet at Toulon. Keeping this force out of the hands of the Germans had, of course, been a steady theme in the earlier American willingness to treat with the Vichy regime. It was hoped that as part of the Darlan deal the French admiral would issue instructions to the commander of the French naval force at Toulon to sail his ships to some port in North Africa. Winston Churchill was exceedingly uneasy about the Darlan deal (at least in private), but he admitted that "if I could meet Darlan, much as I hate him, I would cheerfully crawl on my hands and knees for a mile if by doing so I could get him to bring that fleet of his into the circle of Allied Forces."[31] Doing so was a step of particular urgency at the time of the TORCH invasion given the expectation that the Nazis, in response to TORCH, would likely occupy the remainder of France (as in fact they did) and attempt to seize the French ships. In the event, Admiral de la Borde emulated his colleague in Tunis by refusing to follow Darlan's orders to remove the fleet from Toulon. To be sure, the Nazis were never able to use this formidable military asset, since de la Borde ordered the fleet to be scuttled as German forces approached the port. This was only a partially satisfactory outcome, however, as the addition of the French ships to Allied strength in the Mediterranean would have had significant effects.

In short, the immediate military benefits of the Darlan deal have to be considered rather mixed. Some of the rewards anticipated from working with Darlan did prove out—particularly in bringing a relatively early end to Vichy resistance against the Allied invasion force—but other positive consequences of the negotiation proved ephemeral or nonexistent. This does not in itself mean that the deal was without justification or should be condemned outright. In the fog of war, it is rare that all the anticipated good results of a particular action actually bear out. Nevertheless, a consequentialist analysis of the Darlan deal inevitably must remain ambivalent. This means that in arriving at a final moral verdict on this particular episode, it is necessary to consider still other evidence. An important piece of such evidence has to do with what we have called the principle of universalization.

INTERESTS NARROW AND BROAD

Important political decisions produce a series of ever-widening effects. The question for ethical judgment is whether the decisionmakers in a particular case have given due and appropriate attention to the full impact of their actions on concerned parties. It was suggested earlier that Eduard Beneš had been derelict in this regard in the planning and carrying out of ANTHROPOID.

What verdict can we offer concerning the Darlan deal in terms of the requirement of universalization?

It is necessary first of all to identify the main concerned parties. These included, inter alia, the Allied troops landing in North Africa as part of the TORCH invasion; the residents of the area whose safety and welfare would be directly affected by the course of operations; the French resistance movement; the French people more generally; and, finally, all of those in whatever country who were committed to the struggle against fascism and the defense of freedom and civilized values. The effects of the Darlan deal on these various constituencies were inevitably diverse, and it is important to attempt some sort of net assessment of these effects in arriving at a moral judgment concerning the deal itself.

We might take the most generally affected group first—that is, all those who saw the war as a struggle for certain basic principles. It is suggestive that Winston Churchill himself expressed considerable misgivings about the impact of the Darlan deal on this broad class of individuals. He wrote to President Roosevelt on November 16, 1942 along the following lines:

> I ought to let you know that very deep currents of feeling are stirred [here] by the arrangement with Darlan. The more I reflect upon it the more convinced I become that it can only be a temporary expedient, justifiable solely by the stress of battle. We must not overlook the serious political injury which may be done to our cause, not only in France but throughout Europe, by the feeling that we are ready to make terms with the local Quislings. . . . A permanent arrangement with Darlan or the formation of a Darlan Government in French North Africa would not be understood by the great masses of ordinary people, whose simple loyalties are our strength.[32]

He went on to add that "there is above all our own moral position. We are fighting for international decency and Darlan is the antithesis of this."

There is no question but that for all of those who saw the war as basically a conflict over values, the arrangement with Darlan was a disheartening one. It seemed to raise opportunism and cynicism to a new level, even for wartime. Here was an individual who had collaborated extensively with the Nazis, had served as premier of a government noted for its anti-Semitic legislation and crushing of political liberties, and who was now to be given supreme civil authority over all of French North Africa by the explicit *fiat* of and in cooperation with the Allied powers. It was hardly a redeeming spectacle, and its sour impact was only partially mitigated by the plea that, in order to achieve victory, a resort to unpleasant and distasteful means was almost inevitable. To what purpose all the suffering, the critics responded, if the moral purpose of the struggle was to be held hostage to the "necessities" of war?

The effects of the Darlan deal on the French resistance movement were especially disheartening. It now appeared that the Allies were prepared to treat with representatives of a regime that was seen by the resisters as complicit in the oppression of the French people. Members of the Free French forces, both within and outside France, regarded the arrangement with Darlan as a devastating (perhaps even calculated) snub, a repudiation of all their efforts and sacrifices. General De Gaulle in particular never forgave the United States for dealing with Darlan, and his resentment on this score continued even through his later period in power as president of France. The depth of antagonism that the Darlan deal, as well as other American dealings with the Vichy regime, aroused among French Republican opinion could be seen in an article appearing in the clandestine radical-socialist journal *Aurore* in June 1944, ironically entitled "The American Card":

> These Vichy gentlemen have now found the Road to Damascus. They are playing the American card. It is their supreme hope. At Vichy they go on whispering all over the place that, being afraid of the USSR, America will facilitate the creation, in the West, of an anti-Bolshevik barrier composed of France and of a Germany camouflaged to look like a democracy. . . . These gentlemen imagine, above all, that if this marvelous stunt were to come off, they would have nothing to fear from the courts-martial of a Free France, and might even take their seats in the Government![33]

As to the effect of the Darlan deal on the French people more generally, the evidence is inevitably more mixed and depends importantly on how we gauge the overall support of the French population for the Vichy regime itself. Certainly Vichy had a good many sympathizers within France, and for this group Allied support to Darlan may have given a welcome message that Vichy's commitment to "order" and "traditional values" was to be continued in North Africa (and perhaps elsewhere and in the future) even after Allied military victory. At the same time, popular support for Vichy was almost certainly declining within France by November 1942, partly because of the regime's own record but also because of ebbing German military fortunes. For the Allies to negotiate with Darlan must therefore have seemed a baffling step to many Frenchmen, and for a good number of them further evidence—if any were needed—that the Americans and British would pursue policies in their own self-interest without regard for the sentiments of those under German domination. British Foreign Secretary Anthony Eden put the case well when he observed that "our appeal to the French people, whose resistance has been steadily stiffening, is now stultified." He also addressed the wider implications of the Darlan deal:

> In Europe as a whole the "filthy race of quislings", as [Churchill] once so aptly called them, will take heart since they now have reason to think that if only they happen to be in authority when the forces of the United Nations arrive, they will be treated as being the government of the country.[34]

At the very least, the Darlan arrangement did seem to suggest that Washington and London hardly took seriously De Gaulle's Free French movement, the legitimacy of which De Gaulle had been steadily asserting in a series of overseas broadcasts to the French that seemed to be having an increasing impact. For a majority of Frenchmen, therefore, the Darlan deal undoubtedly aroused considerable confusion and doubt—qualities hardly calculated, as Eden noted, to solidify French attitudes in opposing Vichy and its German sponsors.

There were, on the other hand, two other groups whose interests can reasonably be considered to have been directly *served* by the Darlan deal. The first was the Allied troops actually involved in the TORCH operation. As we have already discussed, Darlan's order to French commanders to cease hostilities did have the effect of saving some, and perhaps a good many, lives among Allied soldiers. Assuming that one of the prime duties of leaders in wartime is to be as sparing of sacrifice among their fighting men as possible, then the deal with Darlan assumes a more positive aspect. Aside from American and British soldiers, there is also the civilian population of French North Africa to be considered. If Vichy military forces had continued to resist the Allied invasion, there is little question that civilian casualties would have escalated considerably. In order to take Casablanca, for example, the TORCH high command had planned a major assault on the city on the morning of November 11, which was to be preceded by a heavy bombing of the area, with all the attendant loss of civilian lives. Darlan's cease-fire order gave General Noguès a face-saving way of avoiding this calamity by the surrender of his forces.[35] Even earlier, it had been contemplated that a widespread bombardment of Algiers would also have to be undertaken in order to reduce the city's defenses, and Darlan's cease-fire order to French commanders in the area on November 8 undoubtedly played a role in saving its inhabitants from the casualties that would have resulted.

In considering the interests of the civilian population in North Africa, it could be argued, of course, that the continued imposition of Vichy decrees and administration that was an agreed part of the Darlan deal did violence to the rights of the citizenry, especially (for example) Jews living in the area. An equally important issue, however, is the degree to which the relatively benevolent impact of the Darlan deal on the French North African population was a *planned* or intended aspect of the arrangement. The evidence is rather murky on this score, and few references can be found in the official memoirs and other documents attesting to an overt concern with civilian casualties as a consequence of TORCH. One exception might be General Eisenhower's admission that the initial reaction of the local population to TORCH was, "Why did you bring this war to us? We were satisfied before you came to get us all killed."[36] Eisenhower was particularly concerned with the German bombing attacks on Algiers that followed the Allied landings, even though he went on to argue that the Darlan deal did help to secure Allied control of air defenses for the city, which had a significant effect in reducing civilian losses.

What net assessment of the Darlan deal is appropriate, then, in terms of the principle of universalization? One fact hanging over all our judgments is that eventually the war against the Nazis *was* won, and that this outcome was an unalloyed blessing to all the groups considered here. Thus the conclusion might be that despite all the short-term discomfiture to various parties occasioned by the Darlan deal, their *long-term* interests were eminently served by it. This assumes, of course, that the Darlan deal, on balance, produced positive (and proportionate) military results in advancing the struggle against the Germans. As we have already suggested, the record on this score may be debated, but there is no question that at least some advantages did accrue from it. From this perspective, it may be tempting to set aside the anguish that certain groups felt at the news of the Darlan deal and argue that ultimately their values were indeed served. Such a stance might receive added support from the unexpected circumstance of Darlan's death in December 1942, which should have mollified whatever rightful objections people had to Darlan's being (at least for a brief period) part of the Allied war effort.

The deeper issue here is how and to what extent the concerns of all affected parties should be taken into account by political leaders, especially in wartime. Obviously many (perhaps most) wartime decisions do violence to the legitimate needs and perspectives of various individuals and groups. Must we, or our leaders, engage in endless hand-wringing over this perennial fact? To do so may result in a virtual paralysis of decisionmaking, and, assuming the cause is a just one, a triumph of the forces of evil, or at least the demonstrably bad. At the same time, it is a standard ethical principle that even a good cause does not justify any means and that indeed the selection of bad means can dilute the very moral purpose of the struggle itself. This principle will continue to condition various attitudes toward the moral justification of the Darlan deal.

THE QUESTION OF ALTERNATIVES

In passing moral judgment on a controversial political decision, a particularly important consideration is that of the lesser of two evils. As a principle for ethical evaluation, it actually operates at two different levels. On the one hand, we want to see evidence that decisionmakers carefully weighed their alternatives with a view to picking the least bad one. This requires an awareness on their part that there *were* moral issues involved in different courses of action and that they made their final judgment only after a detailed (perhaps even agonizing) assessment of the unpalatable choices open to them. Even if they can be shown to have done so, they may of course still lay themselves open to our condemnation on the basis that they chose the patently "more evil" alternative. That they made at least a good faith effort to do relatively more good than evil, however, should soften our indictment in such a case. Statesmen become even more subject to a moral query, on the other hand, if they fail to recognize or accept that there were alternatives available to them and instead simply plunged ahead with a particular policy without giving adequate consideration to the available choices.

The principle of the lesser of two evils has a second and perhaps even more important application. Not only must decisionmakers adequately consider different policy alternatives, but they have an obligation to develop them in as full and as realistic detail as possible, and, more than this, actively to seek out and explore such alternatives. There are plenty of historical cases in which a leader, perhaps with an eye to a place in history, piously recalls that he or she was faced with unpalatable choices and was reluctantly forced to adopt a course of action that was in actuality set from the beginning. Involved here is the phenomenon of "straw men alternatives," which typically seem to come in threes. A good example is the mode of decisionmaking prominent during the Johnson administration's handling of the Vietnam War.

Memoirs of the period stress that when the president was faced with an important divide in his Vietnam policy, he was usually given three "choices":

a drastic deescalation (often referred to as "cut-and-run"), a drastic escalation (often referred to as "blow up the world"), and a middle course that involved a continuation of past policy but with a somewhat greater application of force. Not surprisingly, the last option tended to be the one chosen. This caricature of a meaningful consideration of policy alternatives was tailored by certain of Johnson's advisers to meet their president's perceived needs: he was determined to maintain his commitment to Vietnam, and at the same time wanted to feel that he was genuinely weighing all the possible choices— or at least be seen by others as doing so. In actuality, the choices presented to him, the nature of which allowed him to proceed comfortably with business as usual, hardly reflected a serious consideration of different courses of action with respect to the problem of Vietnam.[37]

The question for present purposes, then, is whether there really was a serious consideration of alternatives with respect to the Darlan deal. Assuming that American dealings with Darlan raised at the very least some troubling moral issues, did the Roosevelt administration genuinely explore different, and more morally attractive, ways of achieving an understandable and important goal: the reduction or even elimination of resistance by the French forces in North Africa to the implementation of TORCH? The answer to this question is yet another element that has to figure in any overall moral assessment we may offer of the eventual arrangement with Admiral Darlan.

The historical record in fact suggests that Darlan was more or less a last gasp alternative for the United States in dealing with the problem of potential French opposition to the Anglo-American landings in North Africa. Indeed, there was prior to November 1942 a concerted and energetic effort to identify a leading French personality who would have the authority to persuade French forces in North Africa to lay down their arms and, just as important, was relatively untainted by a deep association with Vichy, especially by a record of collaboration with the Germans. The two principal figures that became the focus of this effort were General Maxime Weygand and General Henri Giraud.

The former was a hero of the First World War who was revered in France almost as much as Marshal Pétain. He had been chief-of-staff to Marshal Foch, supreme commander of the French army, and thus was used to dealing with the intricacies of coalition politics, particularly as they involved the British and the Americans. After the war, Weygand was credited with saving Warsaw from advancing Bolshevik armies because of his professional advice to the Polish high command, and he was named chief-of-staff of the French army in 1930. Weygand was called from retirement in 1939 at age 72 in order to command French forces in the Levant, and in late

May 1940, was named supreme commander of Anglo-French forces on the western front, a desperate move taken after the battle was virtually lost due in large part to the incompetence of the previous French high command. Weygand was one of those in early June who pressured Premier Renault to seek an immediate armistice with the Germans because of the hopelessness of the French situation.

He then agreed to serve as Vichy minister of national defense, but his tenure was a very short one. Weygand was essentially apolitical and was quite uncomfortable with the intrigues that were a daily feature of life at Vichy. In order to escape this distasteful environment, he asked to be sent to command French forces in North Africa, and was subsequently named delegate general, effectively the supreme political authority in the region. At one point, Winston Churchill secretly urged him to assume De Gaulle's role as head of all French resistance forces, and in particular to lead the opposition to Vichy in North Africa. Weygand felt such an offer was an insult to his honor as a French general, and he insisted on sending a copy of Churchill's message to Pétain himself. "This confirms my distrust of Churchill's judgment," he commented. "During the battle of France, he flew over from London and told us he was waiting for a miracle to save the situation. I am a good Catholic, but in military matters I prefer not to depend upon miracles."[38]

Aside from matters of honor, Weygand evidently felt that at this point German military dominance was such that any open displays of French rebellion in North Africa would be futile. This hardly meant, however, that he was prepared to accommodate himself, as Darlan did, to Nazi demands for greater integration of French and German policy. Indeed, the enduring enmity between the two was a matter of record, and, by the fall of 1941, Berlin had grown sufficiently impatient with Weygand's stubborn insistence on protecting French interests—quite unlike the forthcoming attitude taken by Darlan—that they put pressure on Pétain to relieve him. After a veiled threat that German forces would occupy all of France unless he was dismissed, Weygand resigned under pressure on November 18.

In a memorandum he drew up at the time of his ouster, General Weygand reinforced his credentials as a French patriot, albeit one committed to caution and realism. He warned that "opening Africa to Germany means, in the last analysis, giving to Germany a unique opportunity to continue the war for ten years, and to impose her will upon France without the possibility of any reaction." He emphasized, "I moved to Africa when Britain had proved [its] ability to survive air attacks. This immensely increased the potential importance of French Africa. France possessed a trump essential in the general diplomatic situation."[39] Weygand retired to a small estate in southern France after his forced resignation, and over the following months the Roosevelt administration attempted to succeed where Churchill had failed.

Washington had always held out hopes that Weygand might be their secret weapon in driving a wedge between Vichy and the Germans, and more especially between the French possessions in North Africa and the collaborationist wing of the Pétain regime. The American ambassador to Vichy, Admiral William Leahy, was so angered by Weygand's dismissal in November 1941 that he thought it signaled the end of any prospect of working with the Vichy government at all. He urged the immediate suspension of the economic provisions of the so-called Murphy-Weygand agreement, a recommendation that was accepted by the president. This still left the possibility, however, that Weygand—particularly because of his humiliating ouster as the leading French figure in North Africa—might now be willing to enter into a formal arrangement with the Americans (if not the British).

In the event, all these hopes proved unavailing. Weygand was visited on January 20, 1942 by Douglas MacArthur II, a personal representative of the president, who offered him complete American support if he would agree to return secretly to North Africa in order to lead the opposition to the Germans and their Vichy collaborators and, not incidentally, to help deflect French resistance to an Anglo-American invasion. The response was a frosty "no," and when the American offer was repeated after the actual TORCH landings had begun, the answer remained the same. Weygand's motives in turning down the American representations evidently had to do with his straitlaced sense of what was required of him as a French officer. He had sworn fealty to Pétain as his commander in chief, and suggestions that the Vichy regime was in unholy alliance with the German enemy were dismissed as irrelevant to the demands of professional obedience and honor (which of course was an important factor in his spurning of Churchill even earlier). Such a stance might be regarded as evidence of his political naïveté, or perhaps stolid inflexibility, but it was not entirely ignoble nonetheless. In the event, such rectitude did not spare him the further displeasure of the Germans. When the Nazis occupied the remainder of France following the TORCH invasion, Weygand was promptly arrested and he spent the rest of the war years in Germany. After 1945 there was a brief attempt to try him as a member of the Vichy government, but he was quickly released, and lived on for some 20 more years in quiet retirement.[40]

The basic point behind this discussion of the trials and tribulations of General Maxime Weygand remains, in any case, that the Roosevelt administration did attempt to make an arrangement with him, not only on practical grounds (his prestige among French forces in North Africa) but also because of his relatively "clean" record. The same factors also led Washington to treat with General Henri Giraud, once it became apparent that Weygand was unprepared to cooperate in defusing French resistance to the invasion of North Africa. Giraud was a particularly attractive alternative to Weygand because he was also a well-known military leader who seemed focused entirely on prosecution of the war effort and (unlike Darlan) had few political ambitions of his own.

Giraud had a meteoric rise in the interwar period as one of the true luminaries of the French officer corps, and he was widely considered to be an inevitable choice one day to become supreme commander of the French armed forces. As a young officer in North Africa, he had developed a particularly impressive record, and he knew the Arabs and their culture better than all but a few of his military contemporaries. Part of what came to be referred to as the "Giraud legend" derived out of his reputation as a person whom no German prison camp could hold. In World War I, as a wounded captain, he had escaped from a German military hospital. Following the defeat of France in 1940, he again became a prisoner-of-war, but in the spring of 1942 he absconded from the German fortress of Königstein and eventually arrived in unoccupied France.[41] A particularly important factor in Giraud's situation was that he had never sworn allegiance to Marshal Pétain, nor had he given his word of honor not to fight the Germans again, as many other French officers (especially in North Africa) had done as a condition of their being released from prison. Under these circumstances, he seemed a promising candidate for a tacit or open alliance with the Americans in preparation for TORCH, especially since he was already involved in organizing the French resistance to the Nazis in mainland France. Moreover, certain important figures like General Charles Mast, the French military commander in Algiers, suggested (on the basis of hope rather than evidence) that the Vichy forces in North Africa would likely follow Giraud's lead.

In the fall of 1942, negotiations with Giraud developed with increasing intensity. He indicated his willingness to participate in the coming invasion of North Africa, but the terms he set for doing so were stiff ones: he demanded that the expedition consist solely of American troops, that the United States land forces somewhere in mainland France at the same time as they were coming ashore in Africa, and that he (Giraud) be given overall command of all French and American troops fighting anywhere on French soil. The impracticality of these demands were to figure prominently in the eventual deal between the Americans and Admiral Darlan. Also critical at this point was the reality that Darlan's authority over the French navy was unquestioned, and that Giraud's influence in this area was slight. Even before TORCH began, therefore, there was discussion in Washington and at Eisenhower's headquarters concerning the possibility of a joint arrangement involving both Giraud and Darlan in which the two would share the French military command in North Africa. Giraud's representatives in North Africa violently objected to this idea, and so matters remained unresolved as the day for TORCH to begin grew ever nearer.

On November 1, 1942, Giraud sent a message to Robert Murphy in Algiers to the effect that he would be unable to leave France for North Africa until November 20th at the earliest (i.e., some 12 days after the planned beginning of the invasion). Murphy then recommended to Eisenhower that the landings be postponed, but this suggestion was dismissed almost out of hand. Eventually Giraud did agree to come to Algiers a day or two before TORCH was to begin, but in an almost farcical denouement to the long string of contacts between him and the Americans, he was nowhere to be found as Allied troops began coming ashore in Morocco and Algeria. Instead he appeared at Eisenhower's headquarters at Gibraltar in order to clarify the terms of his participation in the Allied invasion. When told by Eisenhower that it would be quite impossible to give him operational command over American forces involved in TORCH, he announced his withdrawal from any participation in the affair. Giraud was eventually talked around to cooperation on the following day, but he did not arrive in Algiers until the Allied landings in North Africa had been going on for almost 36 hours. By this time Murphy, with the agreement of his superiors, had initiated alternative arrangements designed to neutralize French resistance to TORCH. As finally completed, these came to be known as the Darlan deal.[42]

Perhaps aware that he now faced the risk of being totally excluded from the march of events, Giraud, when informed of the American agreement with Darlan, agreed to join him in a dual arrangement of the sort suggested earlier by Eisenhower. Darlan's position as the principal French political authority in North Africa was confirmed, while Giraud was designated as overall military commander of the French forces in North Africa. Upon Darlan's assassination, he assumed the latter's duties as well until a so-called "shotgun wedding" was arranged between Giraud and Charles De Gaulle at the Casablanca Conference in January 1943 that provided for a sharing of authority in liberated French territory. In a relatively short period of time,

De Gaulle eased the politically inept Giraud out of any share of power, whereupon he gradually faded from the scene.

The saga of American attempts to make Giraud "their man in Algiers" was in many ways a bizarre one, characterized by cross-purposes, misunderstandings, and even outright deception. Washington, for example, never told Giraud that British troops as well as American would be participating in TORCH, lest this arouse the anti-British sentiments in Giraud that were typical of almost all French officers at the time. Nor was Giraud advised that a supplementary landing of American forces in mainland France was quite out of the question. At the same time, Giraud himself tended to display equal measures of ingenuousness and a stubborn Gallic pride that, although understandable, was quite at odds with the realities of the political–military situation at the time. His failure to appear in Algiers as promised just before the invasion represented a particularly startling example of his instinct for bad timing and the wrong move. In retrospect, the "Giraud legend" can be seen mostly as the romantic exaggeration of the talents of a brave but quite limited individual. Darlan provided a reasonably clear-headed assessment of his qualities. When informed of the American negotiations with Giraud, the French admiral shook his head and told his American counterpart, "Giraud is not your man. Politically he is a child. He is just a good divisional commander, nothing more."[43]

Even if Giraud had appeared in Algiers at the agreed moment, there remains a very real question whether his prestige and authority among the French forces in North Africa would have been sufficient to persuade them not to resist the Allied invasion. The leading French military figures in the region, after all, had sworn allegiance to Pétain and Vichy, and Giraud hardly had any cachet with either. On the other hand, there did seem to be a man who could actually perform as desired, that is, he could neutralize French resistance to TORCH—and it was Darlan with whom the Americans eventually came to deal.

But they did so only after making some reasonably energetic efforts to find an alternative. For a variety of reasons discussed above, neither a "Weygand deal" nor a "Giraud deal" ever was consummated. Still, the considerable time and effort expended on these two does suggest that there was a real concern in Washington with finding someone who could meet the practical requirements of TORCH but at the same time was relatively untarnished by past behavior and associations. Perhaps in strict moral terms Darlan can hardly be considered the lesser of two evils, but it can also be argued that right up to the morning of November 8, 1942, the United States had done its best to find a lesser evil, and had by that point effectively exhausted the possibilities of success in that endeavor.

The De Gaulle Option

Such an argument can be made, that is, if we set aside the idea that Washington *did* have another alternative to Weygand, Giraud, or, ultimately, Darlan, and that was to give its full support to General Charles De Gaulle and the Free French movement as the only legitimate voice of the French people. This would have involved a statement of support for De Gaulle *before* the TORCH operation, and a commitment to him and his supporters as the accepted French authority in North Africa.

Such a course of action had a lot of intuitive appeal, at least to many of those appalled by Washington's dealings with Darlan and other Vichy figures prior to and after November 1942. De Gaulle after all had been the first and most prominent voice calling for continued French resistance to the Nazis after the debacle of May 1940. Over a period of time he had developed an extensive organization dedicated to the fight against the Germans, and he had already managed to establish his personal authority (supplanting that of Vichy) in various areas of the French colonial empire in central Africa and the Pacific. While he did not have the military credentials of a Weygand or Giraud, he had distinguished himself in various tank battles during the German assault on France and even before the war had written several very prescient analyses of the importance of armor in modern warfare. Moreover, he was a forceful and highly intelligent individual who clearly had qualities far superior to those of, say, Henri Giraud. Above all, De Gaulle seemed to stand as a symbol of French pride and refusal to bow down to German imperialism. The British under Churchill had taken early note of this, and on June 18, 1940 recognized him as the "leader of all Free Frenchmen who would join his movement in defense of the Allied cause." A short time later De Gaulle formed a National Committee, responsible not only in the military sphere but also in civil matters having to do with transportation, finances, and information and propaganda. This too received a British imprimatur.[44] While De Gaulle did not enjoy full status as the leader of an official government-in-exile, he was clearly London's favored voice representing French resistance to the Nazis.

Many prominent people in the United States had urged the Roosevelt administration to emulate the British example and accept De Gaulle's Free French movement as the legitimate voice of the French people. The popular press was generally favorably disposed toward the Free French, as were the major veterans' organizations and such patriotic groups as the Committee to Defend America, the Fight for Freedom, and the Union for Democratic Action.[45] Why, then, did the administration not settle on De Gaulle as their French partner in organizing TORCH and in the subsequent unfolding of that campaign? Why deal with the enigmatic Weygand, the feckless Giraud, and the disreputable Darlan when De Gaulle seemed to present such an attractive—and on balance morally superior—alternative? The reasons are complex and can only be summarized here. Suffice it to say at the outset that most of those in Washington (as we have already discussed) were never as enamored of the De Gaulle mystique as were their British allies. Partly this was a matter of De Gaulle's rather imperious style. He did not easily tolerate fools, but the real problem was the way he tended to define "fools" as any who questioned his personal judgment. Churchill was able to make allowances for this arrogance because of his admiration for De Gaulle's other qualities, but the Americans were not so forgiving. President Roosevelt was particularly reluctant to deal with the French general because he regarded him for a long time as an essentially fringe figure with a talent for self-promotion but with little real impact on events. He also had doubts about De Gaulle's personal political views and seemed to feel that these were not far removed from the authoritarian ideology prevalent at Vichy itself.

It must be conceded that De Gaulle's Free French forces engaged in several operations that seemed almost calculated to exacerbate American distrust and dislike of them. One of these involved the seizure of the colony of St. Pierre and Miquelon off the coast of Newfoundland in Canada. Consisting of a group of islands with some strategic importance to Atlantic shipping, St. Pierre and Miquelon had a Vichy governor, and Washington had recently concluded an agreement with the Pétain government that recognized his authority there. De Gaulle defied this arrangement when he sent a naval force to capture the colony on Christmas Eve, 1941. American public opinion generally applauded this move as a blow to Vichy collaboration with the Germans, but President Roosevelt, and particularly his secretary of state, Cordell Hull, regarded the matter as a prime example of De Gaulle's ignoring American policy and proceeding unilaterally to serve his own interests.[46]

Even more serious, from the Roosevelt administration's perspective, was the earlier attempt by the Free French, aided by the British, to seize the important naval base at Dakar in French Senegal in September 1940. One of the principal reasons for this operation was a fear that the Germans would shortly capture the base themselves and use it as a forward staging area for their submarine campaign in the Atlantic. This was certainly Churchill's prime motivation in agreeing to the scheme. As for De Gaulle, he was keen to demonstrate that all French possessions south of the Sahara were ready to come over to his banner. A curious combination of (attempted) persuasion and force was used at Dakar. In the event, the whole exercise turned into a fiasco, and, after a few days of confused fighting, the joint Anglo-French expedition had to withdraw. The Dakar affair cemented FDR's distrust and dislike of De Gaulle, who, he thought, had used the operation mainly for his own glorification. Just as important was the evidence that details of the plan to take Dakar has leaked from the Free French organization in London. This lack of security further diminished the French leader's credentials as a possible partner in future Allied military moves.[47]

It is plain in any event that the United States never seriously considered offering De Gaulle a role in the TORCH operation. Indeed, American officials went out of their way to *conceal* their plans for invading North Africa from him and his Free French colleagues. Such a procedure could be defended on the grounds that security of information among the Free French was indeed less than might have been desired. Moreover, there was a fear that if De Gaulle were involved in TORCH, he would proceed to introduce all sorts of broader political demands and queries that would greatly complicate the operation. Above all, however, there was a perception—evidently strongly grounded—that any appeal by De Gaulle for a cessation of hostilities by French Vichy forces in North Africa would fall on mostly deaf ears. Particularly after the Dakar expedition, the hostility to his leadership among Vichy military figures in the area, especially in the French navy and air force, was pronounced, and it might even be argued that if De Gaulle had been associated with TORCH, this would have *increased* the likelihood of strong Vichy resistance to the landings.

All of this is convincing enough in its own terms, but still there remain some nagging questions about the American relationship with De Gaulle. If the United States had followed the British in giving their full support to him from the beginning, his prestige would have presumably increased, even among Vichy officials, and thus he might have had a better chance of performing usefully in the context of TORCH. Moreover, one is left with the unmistakable impression that essentially personal and idiosyncratic factors were as important in the American attitude toward De Gaulle as broader issues of strategy and politics. No doubt the French general was a difficult figure with which to deal, one who, in the classic phrase, was "a bull who always carried his own china shop with him." Nevertheless, the prime argument in favor of the Darlan deal was that it was designed to save the lives of Allied soldiers. Darlan's personal qualities were hardly more attractive than De Gaulle's, and yet in this instance Darlan's character did not seem to stand in the way of the United States doing business with him. The same standard could well have been employed in American dealings with De Gaulle.

As it happens, the American refusal to deal with De Gaulle did not last long once TORCH had achieved its initial success. At the Casablanca conference between Roosevelt and Churchill in January 1943, the two Allied leaders, as already discussed, sponsored a coming together of the forces of Giraud and De Gaulle into a common Committee of National Liberation to direct the overall resistance to the Nazis. As Roosevelt rather colorfully put it, "My job was to produce the bride in the person of General Giraud while Churchill was to bring in De Gaulle to play the role of bridegroom in a shotgun wedding."[48] It seems quite likely that Roosevelt, chastened by the public outrage over the Darlan deal and, not incidentally, freed of its obligations because of Darlan's death, now felt that recognizing De Gaulle's authority was at this point indeed the lesser of two (or several) evils. The question still remains whether an earlier move in this direction might not have paid significant dividends. Given the relative weakness of the Free French movement in North Africa prior to TORCH, the answer may well be a negative one, at least as far as the question of French resistance to the Allied landings is concerned. Yet the fact is that ultimately the United States found itself dealing with a man who was identified with collaboration with the Nazis rather than with one who was identified with resistance to the Nazis. Perhaps the reality of the situation in North Africa on the morning of November 8, 1942 dictated such an outcome, but if so it was not an easy or comfortable outcome, at least to those who saw the war as above all a struggle for certain moral principles.

THE DARLAN DEAL IN RETROSPECT

What are we left with, then, in looking back on the Darlan deal? To begin with, there is an important fact that has only been briefly alluded to but that has to weigh heavily in any final moral assessment we may offer. Admiral Jean François Darlan was assassinated in Algiers (in rather mysterious circumstances) by a young French Royalist on Christmas Eve, 1942. It is likely that our judgment on the negotiation with Darlan might be rather different if it were not for this unexpected event. Despite his supposed commitment to establishing "liberal government" in liberated French North

Africa, there is little evidence that Darlan was predisposed to any early alteration of some of the basic tenets of Vichy policy in the area, most notably in the treatment of Jews and in a generally authoritarian approach to social, political, and economic issues. His standard argument was that the immediate relaxation of earlier Vichy decrees would only provoke the Muslims of North Africa to revolt.[49]

If Darlan had lived, therefore, his approach to governing would have presented the Allies with increasingly difficult issues for resolution. Moreover, the very persona of Darlan would have continued to hang over the claims of Allied leaders to be leading an essentially moral struggle against Nazi inhumanity. Given his past record of appeasing the Germans, Darlan's continued presence on the stage would likely have been a continuing embarrassment and raised ever stronger moral queries. Even someone as focused on purely military considerations as General Mark Clark admitted to his relief at Darlan's demise: "Admiral Darlan's death was, to me, an act of Providence. . . . His removal from the scene was like the lancing of a troublesome boil. He had served his purpose, and his death solved what could have been the very difficult problem of what to do with him in the future."[50] Every human death is of course a tragedy, but it is not too much to say that at least in terms of the moral concerns of this book, nothing in Darlan's life was so becoming to him (and to others as well) as his leaving of it.

Since Darlan did depart the scene on December 24, however, it is only fair and necessary to assess the American arrangement with him within the context of the actual course of events. Considered in these terms, final judgment on the Darlan deal seems to involve a melange of negative and somewhat more positive aspects. It is unlikely that any real consensus will ever develop on the ethics of working with Darlan, but we can attempt to summarize the pros and cons of the Darlan deal and in the course of so doing arrive at some tentative conclusions. Applied ethicists, whether in international affairs or in other fields, like to speak of so-called "hard cases," that is, those situations in which the rights and wrongs are fairly evenly balanced, and well-meaning people can arrive at opposite verdicts. There is little doubt that the Darlan deal falls into the category of a "hard case."

It does not take much imagination to assemble a list of reasons why dealing with Darlan was, if not ethically reprehensible, at least highly doubtful and on balance basically wrong. There was first of all the character of the man himself and the record of his past actions. The Second World War certainly produced an impressive rogue's gallery of genuinely evil and repulsive personalities—Reinhard Heydrich deserving pride of place in this group—and it would be going too far to include Darlan among those at the top of the list. At the same time, he emerges as one of those special figures during the period who, while not totally evil in himself, *connived* in the maintenance and even spread of such evil. His fanatical hatred of the British, his own intuitive authoritarianism, and, perhaps above all, his consuming opportunism led him indeed to sup with the Devil. Particularly reprehensible was his willingness in the late spring of 1941 to coordinate Vichy military assets with those of the Germans in order to serve Nazi military interests. If Germany had eventually succeeded in winning the war, Darlan's performance would likely have been (and rightly so) the subject of even more denunciation from an oppressed humanity than it received in the actual circumstances. Even from a strictly French nationalist point of view, Darlan remains as a figure who was willing to subordinate the liberties and the independence of the French nation—values sorely fought for over previous generations—in order to curry German favor for France as a "favored" member of the New Order. From a purely pragmatic point of view, his policy in this regard suggests a man who was quite out of touch with the realities of Hitler's actual attitude toward his country. If Germany had won the war, all that Hitler had in mind for France was a succession of humiliations.

A second major mark against the Darlan deal is that the Americans did agree to the continuation of the Vichy civil and administrative structure in North Africa as the price of his cooperation. The fact is that Darlan's leverage in the early days of TORCH was hardly impressive. There was every indication that the tide of war was now beginning to swing decisively to the Allied side, and with it an undermining of the credibility of the Vichy regime itself. The Germans indeed were shortly to occupy the remainder of France that had been left to Vichy after the June 1940 armistice. Under these circumstances, it is hard to explain—or justify—why Washington should have supinely agreed to Darlan's continuing a "mini-Vichy" in North Africa. An alternative, and more morally defensible, policy would have been to convey some sort of short-term recognition to Darlan as commander-in-chief of French armed forces in the region, but at the same time insist that Vichy institutions had to be abolished forthwith, or at least substantially altered in a democratic direction. Given Darlan's prevailing opportunism, it could well have been that he would have agreed (even if reluctantly) to such an arrangement. As it was, Vichy policies, as already detailed, were to be allowed to continue for an indefinite period.

The ultimate moral indictment of the Darlan deal that can be offered, however, has to do with its reversal of the classic Clausewitzian doctrine that "war is the continuation of politics by other means." If we equate politics in some fundamental sense with the expression of *values,* and in particular the politics of World War II, then the arrangement with Darlan put things exactly backward. In order to serve essentially tactical considerations, an agreement was struck that really violated the whole political purpose of the war. It hardly seems radical to suggest that in certain instances short-term military advantages in any just war may have to be sacrificed in service to the larger point and meaning of the struggle. In this sense, the end not only does not justify any means, but actually requires that certain means be set aside.

And yet, in hard cases, there are always serious arguments that can be offered for and against, and so it is in the instance of the Darlan deal. In evaluating the conduct of the decisionmakers at the time of TORCH, it is only fair to take into account the pressures of time and circumstance. The arrangement with Darlan was struck during a period of maximum tension for the Allies: the opening hours and days of the invasion of North Africa. General Giraud had, with his typical ineptness, decided to visit Gibraltar to parlay with Eisenhower instead of coming to Algiers as he had promised, and where his presence on the morning of the invasion had been counted on. In the event, Darlan *was* in Algiers visiting his ill son. The aim of preventing any widespread resistance by French forces in North Africa to TORCH was certainly an understandable and legitimate one, and it was thus also understandable that Murphy and others should decide that, *faute de meilleur,* it was necessary to treat with Darlan.

This decision is even more defensible in terms of the relative ability of Giraud versus Darlan to command the allegiance of Vichy officers in North Africa. Certainly there had been hopes prior to TORCH that Giraud, given his past military record, would be accorded respect and obedience by these officers. A good deal of evidence had accumulated by November 8, however, that such was not likely to be the case. Thus even if Giraud had been in Algiers on the agreed date, the question remains as to how effective he would have been. Darlan, on the other hand, despite his dubious past, seemed clearly to have the loyalty of almost all the principal Vichy commanders in North Africa. Given the extreme pressures of the moment, this rather valuable bird in the hand obviously seemed more compelling than the one in the bush.

Then there is the issue of what the principal Allied figures in the Darlan deal really knew about the murky particulars of French politics. A claim of ignorance cannot be offered as a full rebuttal to a charge of immoral decisionmaking, but it can perhaps be regarded as at least a mitigating circumstance. Certainly there were some Americans—notably the ubiquitous Murphy—who had reason to know a lot not only about Darlan's background but about the other principal Vichy figures and their policies as well, but it seems safe to say that for most of the major American participants in the politics of TORCH, there was only a hazy sense of who the French players were and what they stood for. General Mark Clark, for example, openly admitted that while Murphy was unfamiliar with military matters, "I should make it clear that I was in the same position in regard to politics, particularly the complex, involved and intriguing sort of politics that the French practiced in North Africa."[51] This type of ignorance helps to explain the appointment of Marcel Peyrouton as an important official in the French administration in North Africa in early 1943. The point here is not to excuse the American government for its insensitivities to French politics. It is merely to say that an accusation of unethical conduct has its ultimate force only if it can be shown that the decisionmakers were consciously aware that they were embarked on a morally dubious course.

When all is said and done, however, the ultimate evaluation of a controversial political judgment, especially in wartime, has to be heavily influenced—once again—by the perennial principle of proportionality: was the bad done outweighed by the good? We have already offered a general assessment of the apparent consequences of the Darlan deal, but it might be well here to reemphasize that the saving of lives—even those of the enemy but especially of those fighting in a just cause—has to be regarded as a principal aspect of considerations of proportionality. Certainly the deal with Admiral Darlan did have a number of unfortunate side effects, especially in terms of the overall moral character of the Allied struggle against the Nazis, but it does seem unmistakable that many lives, both Allied and Vichy French, were spared by the arrangement. It is impossible to calculate the exact number (General Marshall, as noted, estimated it as being on the order of 10,000 on the Allied side alone), but in any case it was far from insignificant. Perhaps the ultimate issue in gauging proportionality, then, is what value we assign to the saving of lives at the expense of other considerations.

Winston Churchill put special emphasis on this factor in his analysis of the Darlan deal, and in the process perhaps applied a necessary corrective to the moral outrage of the critics. As already noted, Churchill himself had doubts about the arrangement with Darlan, and he recalled that many of his "best friends" were appalled at what they regarded as a "base and squalid deal" with one of Britain's true enemies. "Many of those with whom I was in closest mental and moral harmony were in extreme distress. 'Is this then what we are fighting for?' they asked." His own foreign secretary, Anthony Eden, was prominent among those offering such a query. At the same time, Churchill eventually came to regard such attitudes as "unreasonable and not sufficiently considerate of the severities of the struggle and the lives of the troops. As their criticisms became sharper I

grew resentful and also somewhat contemptuous of their sense of proportion."[52] There is no question but that perspectives on the Darlan deal tended
to vary considerably depending on whether the individual involved was
carrying a rifle on the road between Algiers and Tunis or attending an
intellectual salon in London or Washington.

None of what has been written here has been very complimentary about
the character and attitudes of Admiral Jean François Darlan, but there is yet
another other aspect of the Darlan deal that merits at least brief mention in
any ethical evaluation of it. Darlan may have been a genuinely unsavory
character, and especially so because of his transparent cynicism. But this
quality was matched in some considerable degree on the American side as
well. President Roosevelt's statement of November 17 was a prime example,
suggesting as it did that Darlan was simply a "temporary expedient" in
carrying out TORCH. Even those intensely hostile to Darlan might be prepared
to admit that he had considerable cause to complain that he was simply a
"lemon to be squeezed" by the Americans until he had lost his usefulness.
The South African leader Jan Smuts, one of Churchill's closest confidants,
made the not unreasonable case that "nothing could be worse than [the]
impression that we were merely using leaders to discard them as soon as they
have served our purpose."[53] To be sure, Smuts had practical concerns in
advancing such an argument, chief among them being the future willingness
of other French officials to cooperate with the Allies if they thought they
would be treated like Darlan. Still, there is an argument to be made that when
democracies deign to treat with villains, assuming they have judged this to
be necessary, they ought to show a certain becoming consistency and avoid
the impression that their cynicism, even hypocrisy, is equal to that of those
with whom they are dealing. Such values seemed to be largely absent in the
case of the American arrangement with Darlan.

Finally, a basic fact overhanging the Darlan deal is that the Allies did
succeed in clearing North Africa of Axis forces, and in this sense TORCH was
an unqualified military success. Under these circumstances, moral doubts
about a particular action inevitably become rather more muted than if the
overall goal to which that action was designed to contribute itself remains
unfulfilled. General Mark Clark, perhaps rather surprisingly, admitted to the
basic proposition. "In hindsight, the fact that we won takes away a lot of
onus, whatever one might wish to say about the ethics of doing business with
people of Darlan's stamp."[54] Certainly one of the main reasons that British
area bombing of Germany has subsequently been subject to so much moral
criticism is that it seemed to have had little effect in reducing the Nazi war
effort (German arms production, for example, increased steadily during the

main period of the bombing).[55] The results of ANTHROPOID were also distinctly problematical as far as affecting German control over Czechoslovakia was concerned. The Darlan deal, on the other hand, is historically placed within a far happier military outcome.

Still, all of these arguments do have to contend with the shadow of what happened at the Vélodrome D'Hiver on July 16, 1942. A certain Sarah Castel, then five years old, later recalled her experiences on that day: "Those cries of grief, of horror, of fear, in my spirit as a young child, the memory is of those cries, that horrible odor, the tears of children and that constant blue light day and night."[56] Sarah was luckier than the young Marie Šroubokov´a of Lidice, since she actually survived *jeudi noir* and lived to tell of it. Moreover, it would be unfair to connect Darlan as closely to the events of July 1942 as Beneš was tied to the destruction of Lidice. But the French admiral was not totally removed from it either. His general policies even before *jeudi noir* laid the groundwork for this particular atrocity. At the end of the day, the leaders of the democracies felt it necessary to deal with such a man. Their conduct may be defended on various grounds, and perhaps convincingly so, but the anguished memories of Sarah Castel, and the last words of Marie Šroubokov´a, emphasize the ethical dilemmas facing political leaders who accept to take on dirty hands in the performance of their duties. Mark Clark argued in connection with the Darlan deal that "at the time there was only one objective, winning the war; we had little time to think of ethics." It might well be asked, however, what is the purpose of just wars if not to sustain a vision of ethics, and in particular the value and dignity of a single human being?

Conclusion

In introducing this book, we made the point that our primary goal here was not to level easy condemnations at the actions of statesmen, but rather to make a reasonable effort at understanding the complexities and dilemmas that confronted them in carrying out their duties. Such an effort is particularly important when it is a question of the statesmen having dirty hands, whether it involves the destruction of a small Czech village or a deal with a dubious representative of a discredited regime. In a somewhat paradoxical sense, the real purpose of this essay has been to rescue the study of ethics and political conduct, especially in wartime, from the simplicities and clichés that are often attendant on it.

It might be well here to reconsider one of the central issues that continues to bear on discussions of the role of morality in foreign policy decisionmaking. For some, the concept of "political morality" is essentially an oxymoron, and time spent on examining it an exercise in futility. They associate themselves with the old principle from Thucydides's Melian dialogues that the strong will do what they will and the weak what they must.[1] From this perspective, it is idle to speak of restraints on the actions of powerful individuals, except insofar as there may be an entirely prudential reason for not adopting brutal measures to their fullest. Part of the basis for such a bleak vision has to do with a general pessimism about the nature of the human condition itself. The Hobbesian assertion that relations between individuals and between nations are in effect a war of all against all provides the (often unstated) intellectual underpinning for such an attitude. What may be called the pure fatalist approach to political morality also derives, however, out of a prevailing cynicism about the political process itself. The assumption is that politicians are basically creatures entirely driven by self-interest, perennially ready to abandon principle or the real needs of their constituencies should their personal ambition so dictate.

A curious manifestation of the above attitudes may be found in the continuing controversy over the legitimacy of the Nuremberg trials that followed World War II. It is hardly surprising that there were and are even today certain voices out of Germany that regard the trials as being simply an example of "victors' justice," a reflection of the vengefulness of the triumphant side in a great war, based not on any real legal precedent but merely on a desire to humiliate the losers. What is more striking is how so many *outside* Germany continue to suggest that the whole Nuremberg proceeding was indeed a doubtful enterprise. Thus one of the best-known analyses of the trials by an American author refers to "mistakes piled on follies" and states categorically that the actions of the prosecutors at Nuremberg were "replete with blindness, miscalculation and a suicidal passion for complexity. . . . the whole notion of Allied action to bring justice to a war-torn world ran headlong against the main thrust of the war itself."[2] Some have gone so far as to argue that if Germany had won the war, it would have been able to—and have the right to—place certain Allied figures on trial, for example, those who were involved in the bombing of Dresden and other German cities.[3] This seems to be an exceptionally bizarre interpretation of what was, after all, an attempt to deal with a quite unprecedented assault on basic human values in the twentieth century and to hold to account those who were most closely connected with this effort. It might also be observed that the Nuremberg defendants were given extensive legal protections, and that as a consequence three of them were actually acquitted of the charges levied against them.

Quite in contrast to the pure fatalist approach to political ethics is the position adopted by what may be called the pure moralists. The latter share a curious premise with the former in that they tend to view most (or all) politicians simply as scoundrels attendant only to their own self-interests. The difference between the two schools of thought is that the fatalists accept the politicians' immorality with a shrug as only a reflection of the conditions of social life itself, whereas the moralists wax indignant over the fact that politicians *could* do good but for their own reasons do not. Clearly there is a fundamental contradiction in these respective theories: the former holds that ethically attractive political action is basically a chimera, whereas the latter suggests that the world is indeed open to moral improvement if only the relevant will existed.

It need hardly be emphasized that, given their basic orientations, the pure moralists tend to be an angry and often embittered lot. The achievement of good is on the horizon, but the obstinacy and selfishness of political leaders continues to confound the potential for progress. A good example of the moralists' approach to political action may be found in a recent book dealing with the tragedy in Bosnia. Certainly the suffering of the Bosnian people has constituted a grave humanitarian challenge to the world community, and there are legitimate questions that can be raised about the relative ineffectiveness, or perhaps even lack of will, of that community in dealing with the challenge. Yet any reasonable analysis of the situation in Bosnia would suggest that there are a host of complications and ambiguities that make a morally appropriate (and productive) approach to that issue hardly a simple matter for consideration. In the book referred to, however, we are treated to the following sweeping summation:

> The story of Bosnian defeat is the story of Western European and North American disgrace. What has taken place in Bosnia has revealed the bankruptcy of every European security institution, from the North Atlantic Treaty Organization to the Conference on Security and Cooperation in Europe, exposed the fact that nowhere in these great structures was there either intellectual preparedness or moral fortitude for dealing with the crises of the post-cold war world.[4]

It will come as no surprise that from my own perspective neither the approach of the "pure fatalists" nor that of the "pure moralists" seems very satisfactory in arriving at a fair judgment on the problem of the dirty hands of political leaders. The former is especially troubling because of its almost casual dismissiveness of the notion that there is actually any issue to discuss; the latter is off-putting because it implies that the problem of moral choice in politics is in fact relatively easy to resolve. Even so, there are a few concluding issues that need addressing in weighing the problem of dirty hands and political decisionmaking.

It is important to recognize that the choices made by the Czech government-in-exile and by American officials in our two case studies were arrived at in atmospheres of great stress and tension. Eduard Beneš was rightly appalled by the increasing success of Reinhard Heydrich in crushing resistance to Nazi rule in Czechoslovakia, and under the circumstances it can hardly be wondered at that he cast around for some step that might have the effect of mitigating German oppression of his fellow Czechs. Equally, the Allied invasion of North Africa was regarded by American planners as a scheme replete with difficulty and even the possibility of failure because of the various unknown factors that bore on it. This was, after all, to be the first major encounter of American forces with the formidable German enemy, and under these circumstances as well, it is not surprising that any step that might contribute to the success of TORCH would be eagerly grasped.

Given the pressure bearing on the decisionmakers in both instances, it is tempting to give them a generous benefit of the doubt and stay whatever moral quibbles we might have about their conduct. There is obviously some merit in such an approach, and indeed—as we have already said—this essay has made a particular effort to understand the circumstances in which the political leaders under examination had to operate. At the same time, the notion that if a decision is made under great stress, our ethical evaluation of it has to be especially forgiving can be carried too far. The fact is that all the really "hard cases" in applied ethics in international affairs will inherently *involve* situations of great complexity and tension. If these circumstances are absent, then we do not normally have a hard case, and it is these cases that are the real testing ground of the appropriate interaction between ethical principle and political conduct. The plea of the decisionmaker for understanding simply because he or she faced an exceptionally difficult problem thus can stand as only a partial defense for morally dubious actions.

In considering the execution of ANTHROPOID and the development of the Darlan deal, there is a further important point to be made. None of the individuals involved in these cases (on the Allied side) can be considered "bad men" in any commonly accepted definition of the term. This apparently jejune observation has a special application when it is a matter of analyzing the dirty hands of decisionmakers. As discussed in an earlier part of this essay, if a leader is a reprehensible person as an individual, the problem of dirty hands becomes much less compelling. These repugnant personal characteristics may simply find their way into a set of repugnant public policies, the latter being a reflection of the former. What we had here, however, was a collection of individuals who presented some generally attractive qualities of character: a commitment to the defeat of the Nazis, a steadfastness in attempting to overcome all obstacles, and a belief that they were serving the basic needs of an oppressed humanity. They may not have been saints, but they were very far from being villains either.

The real query that can perhaps be leveled at them is not whether they were bad men, but whether they ignored what Thomas McCollogh's calls "moral imagination," that is, an ability to consider their actions in terms of their total effect.[5] Especially important to an appropriate moral imagination is an empathy for the just rights of others, and the likely impact of decisions taken on those rights. Thus Eduard Beneš certainly saw the assassination reasonably convincing argument that can be made for its being an ethically defensible action. Not everyone would agree, but the evident contribution that the arrangement with Darlan made to the success of TORCH does seem to overshadow what the theory of proportionality would consider the evil side effects of the Allies dealing with so disreputable a figure. Particularly important to such a judgment is that the Darlan deal, unlike ANTHROPOID, undoubtedly had the effect of saving lives rather than leading to an unnecessary sacrifice of them.

Whatever final view one may take of either of these cases, in considering them we are led to perhaps the most profound of all the questions raised in the course of this essay, which has to do with the possibility of ethical conduct even during (or especially during) times of great crisis. As noted earlier, it is easy enough to adopt the high moral ground during periods of tranquillity when taking a moral stance involves relatively little prospect of dire consequences. Far more difficult and challenging are those situations in which to do right potentially has the gravest of consequences. Consider, for example, the conduct of one Stella Goldschlag compared with that of one Oskar Schindler.

Because of the film by Steven Spielberg, many will be familiar with the story of how Schindler, at great personal risk, managed to save over a thousand Polish Jews from the extermination camps.[7] Given the numbing figures of those consumed by the Holocaust, this might seem like a modest achievement, but in fact it stands out as one gleam of light in an otherwise dark landscape. What is critical about the Schindler saga is that by most conventional standards he was hardly a model of personal virtue: a womanizer, a drinker, an expert player on the black market, and for a long time a callous user of Polish slave labor in his Krakow factory. Through some mysterious metamorphosis, however, he eventually did embrace one virtue of the most fundamental kind, that is, compassion in the face of human suffering. His decision to do so represents almost an ideal example of the capacity of a single person, even in the most drastic of circumstances, to follow what one writer has called the "pathway of individual conscience."[8]

The story of Stella Goldschlag is rather different. Born into a prominent family and possessing a multitude of talents, as well as great personal beauty, she was almost a legendary figure in the eyes of her envious classmates in the Jewish high school in Berlin that she attended before the outbreak of the war in 1939. Once the war began, however, a transformation took place with Stella Goldschlag that was in its own way as dramatic as what occurred with Oskar Schindler—but in the opposite direction. After her arrest by the Gestapo, she agreed to become a *greifer,* or chaser, one of the handful of of Reinhard Heydrich as an important statement of continuing Cze⟨ resistance to Nazi domination of his homeland. The American officia⟨ who supported the Darlan deal clearly dwelled on the practical contribu⟨ tions of this arrangement to the success of TORCH. In each instance⟨ however, the ancillary effects of their actions seem to have been largely⟨ ignored, whether it was the likely scope of Nazi reprisals against the Czech⟨ people or the dismay that so many opponents of Hitler would feel at the⟨ spectacle of the Allies doing business with a man who had effectively⟨ consorted with Hitler prior to November 1942.

This failure on the part of the relevant individuals to exercise the⟨ needed moral imagination may be counted as a general—and disturbing—⟨ phenomenon of our times. What is involved is an increasing *abstraction*⟨ in the making of important political decisions. The large numbers of people⟨ to be affected by those decisions recede ever more over the horizon, and⟨ actions are taken on the basis of a cold calculation of strategy with the⟨ human element being largely absent. C. S. Lewis vividly described this⟨ phenomenon some years ago.

> The greatest evil is not done now in those sordid "dens of crime" that
> Dickens loved to paint. It is not even done in concentration and labor
> camps. In those we see its final result. But it is conceived and ordered
> (moved, seconded, carried and minuted) in clean, carpeted, warmed and
> well-lighted offices, by quiet men with white collars and cut fingernails
> and smooth-shaven cheeks who do not need to raise their voice.[6]

Lewis was writing with particular regard to Nazi atrocities in Europe, and there is no suggestion that our two case studies bear any resemblance to those outrages. Nevertheless, it is unmistakable that in both instances decisions were taken in "clean, carpeted, warmed and well-lighted offices" that were to have consequences not exactly ignored but given rather subsidiary status nonetheless on the part of those involved.

This is not to say that ANTHROPOID and the Darlan deal should be considered in exactly the same light. Indeed the ethical verdict that we have rendered here with respect to these two cases has obviously been rather different. Beneš's decision to order the assassination of Reinhard Heydrich resulted in so much suffering for the Czech people—notably the destruction of Lidice—and had so little practical utility for the war effort that it is not hard to conclude that his dirty hands in this instance were quite beyond justification. As to the Darlan deal, however, a moral conclusion inevitably seems more complex, and on balance there is a

Jews at the time in Berlin who connived in the Holocaust by seeking out their religious compatriots in hiding and handing them over to the police. In return for her cooperation, Stella was spared being sent East to the extermination camps. The estimate is that Stella Goldschlag eventually was responsible for the arrest and deportation of over a thousand Jews in Berlin. She managed to survive the war, and after serving a period of imprisonment, lives a quiet and lonely existence even today in a small town in Bavaria.[9]

Now it is true that neither Oskar Schindler nor Stella Goldschlag were powerful political figures—the subjects of this essay—but their contrasting behavior nevertheless stands as an object lesson in the alternative paths that can be taken by those who are presented with ethical dilemmas in a time of great tension. The whole point of the discussion here has been to suggest that at even at the level of great political responsibility, there is always an opportunity for melding conscience with power, and that such a coming together is not only attainable but, even more, a responsibility. Some may shrink from the challenge because of their despair (or cynicism) about doing perfect good in an imperfect world. Yet it has rightly been said that the most morally objectionable individuals are those who do nothing because they feel they cannot do enough.

There has been grim material enough in this book, but in closing perhaps it is possible to finish on a somewhat more positive note. Politicians may legitimately be accused of occasional indifference about their dirty hands, and even of attempting to explain away their sins as being in service to a "higher cause." For a good many, however, the nagging pull of conscience does seem to exist alongside their pursuit of self-interest. Perhaps the voice of morality speaks in muted tones when compared with their other concerns, but it can hardly be said to be totally absent. It will be recalled that President Truman, in his public utterances, appeared to be immune to the moral queries raised about the dropping of the atomic bomb on Hiroshima and Nagasaki. At the same time, we also suggested that in his private ruminations, he may have been more affected by these queries than might be supposed. One other piece of evidence indicates that this may have been so. After the attack on Nagasaki, Truman evidently directed that no more atomic bombs be dropped on Japan. Henry Wallace, his secretary of commerce, wrote in his diary that the president "had given orders to stop the atomic bombing. He said the thought of wiping out another 100,000 people was too horrible. He didn't like the idea of killing 'all those kids.'"[10]

That Japan surrendered almost immediately after the bombing of Nagasaki—and that there may not actually have been any more atomic bombs immediately available for use—may render somewhat irrelevant Truman's pangs of conscience. Yet it is the fact that he felt them at all that remains as a central point here. The Talmud teaches that "he who saves a single life saves the world entire." Such a standard may rightly be applied to the actions of all the world's leaders: even though they may regularly be guilty of wicked acts, even one step taken by them for its own sake to alleviate human suffering should be the occasion for at least modest applause from an otherwise questioning humanity.

Notes

Preface

1. Merle Miller, *Plain Speaking* (New York: Berkley Publishing Corporation, 1973).
2. Ibid., 245.
3. Cited in Michael Walzer, *Just and Unjust Wars* (New York: Basic Books, 1977), 290.
4. Jean-Paul Sartre, *Dirty Hands,* in No Exit and Three Other Plays, trans. Lionel Abel (New York: Vintage, 1960), 224.
5. G. M. Trevelyan, *Garibaldi and the Making of Modern Italy* (London: Longmans, Green, 1948), 23.
6. Peter Singer, *Practical Ethics* (Cambridge: Cambridge University Press, 1979), 2.
7. Cited in Alberto R. Coll, "Normative Prudence as a Tradition of Statecraft," *Ethics and International Affairs* 5 (1991), 45.
8. Arnold Wolfers, "Statesmanship and Moral Choice," in *Discord and Collaboration* (Baltimore: The Johns Hopkins University Press, 1965), 51.
9. Miller, *Plain Speaking,* 248.

Chapter 1

1. Sissela Bok, *A Strategy for Peace* (New York: Pantheon Books, 1989), 118-25.
2. An attempt to sort out the actual moral issues raised by the Vietnam War may be found in my *Ideals and Reality* (Washington, DC: University Press of America, 1978).
3. Dean Acheson, "Ethics in International Relations Today: Our Standard of Conduct," *Vital Speeches of the Day* 31 (Pelham, NY: City News Publishing Company, 1965), 228.
4. Robert W. McElroy, *Morality and American Foreign Policy.* (Princeton: Princeton University Press, 1992), 8-13.
5. These "primordial demands," moreover, are innately selfish and even brutal when compared to the sort of aspirations considered admirable in individual life. Reinhold Niebuhr's *Moral Man and Immoral Society* (New York: Charles Scribner, 1932) still

constitutes one of the classic treatments of the notion that "collectives" cannot be held to the same moral standards as individuals.

6. E. M. Forster, *Two Cheers for Democracy* (New York: Harcourt Brace, 1951).

7. Niccolo Machiavelli, *The Prince and the Discourses,* Chapter 5 (New York: The Modern Library, 1940), 56.

8. Max Weber, "Politics as a Vocation," in *Max Weber,* trans. and ed. by H. H. Gerth and C. Wright Mills (New York: Oxford University Press, 1946), 125-6.

9. Immanuel Kant, "Eternal Peace," in *The Philosophy of Kant,* ed. Carl J. Friedrich (New York: Random House, 1949), 469.

10. Cited in Donald G. Jones, "Introduction," in Donald G. Jones, ed., *Private and Public Ethics* (New York: The Edwin Mellen Press, 1978), x.

11. Elie Abel, *The Missile Crisis* (Philadelphia: J.B. Lippincott Company, 1966), 64. In a subsequent comment on the air strike issue, Kennedy said that intelligence sources had estimated that 25,000 Cubans would be killed in a major attack on the missile silos and air bases. But, Kennedy said, the president had rejected the idea of a "Pearl Harbor in reverse" because of his "belief in what is right and what is wrong."

12. *Thirteen Days* (New York: W. W. Norton, 1971). Theodore Sorensen states that Robert Kennedy had planned to issue a revised version of Thirteen Days in which the basic ethical questions presented by the Cuban Missile Crisis would be examined. He was to be the victim of an assassination before he could do so.

13. Hans Morgenthau, *Politics Among Nations,* 2nd ed. (New York: Alfred A. Knopf, 1956), 200.

14. Jimmy Carter, *Why Not the Best?* (Nashville, TN: Broadman Press, 1975). Emphasis added.

15. On this point, see Henry Feingold, *The Politics of Rescue: The Roosevelt Administration and the Holocaust 1938-1945* (New Brunswick, NJ: Rutgers University Press, 1970).

16. Cited in Michael Walzer, *Just and Unjust Wars* (New York: Basic Books, 1977), 240.

17. Arnold Wolfers, *Discord and Collaboration* (Baltimore: The Johns Hopkins University Press, 1962), 60.

18. J. David Singer, "The Level-of-Analysis Problem in International Relations," *World Politics* (October 1961).

19. This discussion owes a great deal to Dennis Thompson's *Political Ethics and Public Office* (Cambridge, MA: Harvard University Press, 1987), especially Chapter 2 on "The Moral Responsibility of Many Hands," 40-65.

20. Weber, "Politics as a Vocation," 95.

21. Thomas Hobbes, *Leviathan,* ed. Michael Oakeshott (New York: Macmillan, 1962), 192-3.

22. On Rostow's role in Vietnam policymaking, see David Halberstam, *The Best and the Brightest* (New York: Random House, 1969), particularly 635-39.
23. I try to summarize the basic moral arguments with respect to area bombing in my *Ethics and Airpower in World War II* (New York: St. Martin's Press, 1993).
24. Ibid., 331-6.
25. Freeman Dyson, *Weapons and Hope* (New York: Harper and Row, 1984), viii.
26. Ibid., 120.
27. Dennis Thompson carefully considers the problem of "democratic dirty hands" in his *Political Ethics and Public Office*, 11-39.
28. The best single treatment of this affair is William Shawcross, *Sideshow* (New York: Simon and Schuster, 1979).
29. Dennis Thompson, *Political Ethics and Public Office*, 44-7.

Chapter 2

1. J. E. Hare and Carey B. Joynt, *Ethics and International Affairs* (New York: St. Martin's Press, 1982), 4-5.
2. Cited in Alberto R. Coll, "Normative Prudence as a Tradition of Statecraft," *Ethics and International Affairs* 5 (1991), 41.
3. Paul Edwards, editor-in-chief, *The Encyclopedia of Philosophy*, vol. 2 (New York: The Macmillan Company and The Free Press, 1967), 343; see also, Dagobert D. Runes, ed., *Dictionary of Philosophy* (Totowa, NJ: Littlefield, Adams and Co., 1975), 76, 150.
4. Peter Singer, *Practical Ethics* (Cambridge: Cambridge University Press, 1979), 3 Singer argues as well that deontology can lead to two different assessments of an individual's values: the person who behaves according to a value system of which we disapprove, and one who seems to have no value system at all We may give a begrudging approval to the former (as suggesting at least some type of moral consciousness) while dismissing the latter as essentially morally anarchic.
5. Hans Morgenthau, *Politics Among Nations*, 4th ed. (New York: Alfred A. Knopf, 1967), 235-41.
6. Michael Walzer, *Just and Unjust Wars* (New York: Basic Books, 1977) 29, 136.
7. Rushworth Kidder, "The Three Great Domains of Human Action," *Christian Science Monitor* (January 29, 1990), 13 For Lord Moulton's original essay, see "Law and Manners," *Atlantic Monthly* (July 1924), 1-5.
8. Robert W. McElroy, *Morality and American Foreign Policy* (Princeton: Princeton University Press, 1992), 54.
9. Mark Moore, "Realms of Obligation and Virtue," in *Public Duties: The Moral Obligations of Government Officials*, eds. Joel Fleishman et al. (Cambridge, MA: Harvard University Press, 1981), 10.

10. Singer, *Practical Ethics,* 3.

11. Garrett Hardin is one of the best-known critics of the presumed morality of massive food aid programs For a representative sample of his arguments in this regard, see *Promethean Ethics* (Seattle: University of Washington Press, 1980) and *Living Within Limits* (New York: Oxford University Press, 1993).

12. J. Fred Buzhardt, legal counsel to President Nixon, addressed this principle in his own fashion when he asked rhetorically (presumably with reference to Nixon himself) whether the average citizen would "rather have a competent scoundrel or an honest boob in the office [of the presidency]?" Donald Jones, "Introduction," in *Private and Public Ethics,* ed., Donald Jones (New York: The Edwin Mellen Press, 1978), xi.

13. Coll, "Normative Prudence as a Tradition of Statecraft," 33-50.

14. The above points are adapted in part from Robert Jackson, "The Situational Ethics of Statecraft." Paper prepared for the Ethics and Statecraft Conference (Vancouver, Canada: October 1993).

15. Quoted in L. I. Bredvold and R. G. Ross, eds., *The Philosophy of Edmund Burke* (Ann Arbor: University of Michigan Press, 1967), 38.

16. For an interesting discussion of this principle, see G. Elfstrom and N. Fotion, *Military Ethics* (London: Routledge and Kegan Paul, 1986).

17. Singer, *Practical Ethics,* 11.

18. For a thorough discussion of cosmopolitanism, see Charles Beitz, *Political Theory and International Relations* (Princeton: Princeton University Press, 1979), 148 et seq.

19. Immanuel Kant, "Religion within the Limits of Reason Alone," in *The Philosophy of Kant,* Carl J. Friedrich, ed. (New York: Random House, 1949), 406

20. Aristotle, *Nicomachean Ethics,* Martin Ostwald, trans. (Indianapolis: Bobbs-Merrill, 1962), VI, 1143a, 17-33.

21. Thomas McCollogh, *The Moral Imagination and Public Life* (Chatham, NJ: Chatham House Publishers, 1991), 16-17.

22. Thomas Nagel, "Ruthlessness in Public Life," in *Public and Private Morality,* Stuart Hampshire, ed. (Cambridge: Cambridge University Press, 1978), 75.

23. Immanuel Kant, "Eternal Peace," in *The Philosophy of Kant,* 459.

24. Garrett, *Ethics and Airpower in World War II,* 30-34.

25. Again, I am indebted to Dennis Thompson for several of the basic ideas in this particular discussion See his *Political Ethics and Public Office* (Cambridge, MA: Harvard University Press, 1987), 49-65.

26. John Rawls, *A Theory of Justice* (Cambridge, MA: Harvard University Press, 1971), 379.

27. Max Hastings, *Bomber Command* (New York: Simon and Schuster, 1987), 124.

28. Hare and Joynt, *Ethics and International Affairs,* 70.

29. Michael Walzer, "Political Action: The Problem of Dirty Hands," *Philosophy and Public Affairs* 2 (Winter 1973), 174-80.

30. A very interesting review of these and other cases may be found in Istvan Deak's "Misjudgment at Nuremberg," *New York Review of Books* (October 7, 1993), 46-52.

31. John Robert Greene, *The Limits of Power* (Bloomington: Indiana University Press, 1992), 222-30.

32. Garrett, *Ethics and Airpower in World War II*, 34-37 Vera Brittain, a well-known British writer of the period, strongly opposed Winston Churchill's condoning and even sponsorship of area bombing, and suggested that he may have been directly "punished" as a result by the British people. Commenting on his defeat in the British general election of July 1945, she offered the following: "It [the election] gave the British people the first opportunity to voice their mute revolt against the evils committed in their name. Most of them had regarded these evils as 'necessary', but that did not mean that they approved or wanted any longer to be led by the men responsible for political vengeance." Vera Brittain, *Testament of Experience* (London: Victor Gollancz, 1957), Perhaps Brittain's analysis of the reasons for Churchill's defeat was off the mark (domestic social and economic policy was probably an even more important factor), but her analysis still raises some interesting questions about the British people's attitude toward Churchill's own dirty hands.

33. Despite his stern public image, MacNamara admitted, "I have always been a very emotional person, ever since I can remember having emotions." Deborah Shapley, *Promise and Power: The Life and Times of Robert McNamara* (Boston: Little, Brown and Company, 1993), 586.

34. Robert McNamara, *In Retrospect: The Tragedy and Lessons of Vietnam* (New York: Times Books, 1995).

35. Robert Massie, *Dreadnought* (New York: Random House, 1991).

36. The Vance resignation is discussed in Thompson, *Political Ethics and Public Office* 18-19. For Vance's own thoughts on the matter, see his *Hard Choices* (New York: Simon and Schuster, 1983).

37. For a review of the relevant facts here, see Edward Weisband and Thomas Franck *Resignation in Protest* (New York: Grossman Publishers, 1976).

38. Ball's memoirs of this period provide some interesting insight into his attitude toward the President and his own role as "house dissenter." George Ball, *The Past | Another Pattern* (New York: W. W. Norton, 1982).

39. I have drawn on Mike Nicoson's unpublished study of the State Department "revolt" over American policy toward Bosnia for some of the facts enumerated here. See Eric Schmitt, "US Aide Who Quit Calls Yugoslav Policy Ineffective," *New York Times* (August 27, 1992), A10.

40. For details of the von Weisacker case, see Sanford Levinson, "Responsibility for Crimes of War," *Philosophy and Public Affairs* 2 (1973).

41.	Sissela Bok, *Secrets* (New York: Vintage Books, 1989), 173.

42.	John Stuart Mill, "Considerations on Representative Government," in *On Liberty and Considerations on Representative Government,* ed. R. B. McCallum (Oxford: Clarendon Press, 1946), 34.

43.	Bok, *Secrets,* 199.

44.	Gilbert Murray, *Tradition and Progress* (Boston: Houghton Mifflin, 1922), 199.

45.	Thomas Nagel, "Ruthlessness in Public Life," in *Public and Private Morality,* Stuart Hampshire, ed., (Cambridge: Cambridge University Press, 1978), 90.

46.	The above arguments are adapted from Walzer, "Political Action: The Problem of Dirty Hands," 169-74.

47.	S. I. Benn, "Wickedness," in *Ethics and Personality,* ed. John Deigh (Chicago: University of Chicago Press, 1992), 197.

48.	Ibid., 199.

49.	The details of this episode are taken from Lou Cannon's *President Reagan: The Role of a Lifetime* (New York: Simon and Schuster, 1991), 400-1.

50.	McElroy, *Morality and American Foreign Policy,* 40-1.

51.	Robert Jervis, *The Logic of Images in International Relations* (Princeton: Princeton University Press, 1970), 71.

52.	Bok, *Secrets,* 193.

Chapter 3

1.	Ivan Cigánek, *Lidice* (Prague: Orbis Press Agency, 1982), 9-10.

2.	J. F. N. Bradley, *Lidice: Sacrificial Village* (New York: Ballantine Books, 1972), 87-90.

3.	Ibid., 94-100, 111-15.

4.	Alan Burgess, *Seven Men At Daybreak* (New York: E. P. Dutton and Company, 1960), 187.

5.	Herman Rauschning, *The Revolution of Nihilism* (New York: Alliance Books Corporation, 1939).

6.	J. F. N. Bradley, *Czechoslovakia* (Edinburgh: University of Edinburgh Press, 1971), 156-59.

7.	Vojtech Mastny, *The Czechs Under Nazi Rule* (New York: Columbia University Press, 1971), 101.

8.	Ibid., 66.

.	Callum MacDonald, *The Killing of SS Obergruppenführer Reinhard Heydrich* (New York: The Free Press, 1989), 62-3.

	Ihor Gawdiak, ed., *Czechoslovakia: A Country Study* (Washington, DC: Department of the Army, 1989), 49

11.	Bradley, *Lidice: Sacrificial Village,* 33.

12. Ibid., 42

13. Gunther Deschner, Heydrich: *The Pursuit of Total Power* (London, 1981), 192.

14. Lucy S. Dawidowicz, *The War Against the Jews 1933-1945* (New York: Holt, Rinehart and Winston, 1975), 78.

15. J. B. Huták, *With Blood and Iron* (London: Robert Hale Limited, 1957), 45.

16. He had impregnated the young woman but had refused to marry her, arguing that he could not do so because anyone who gave herself to a man before marriage was unfit to become a German naval officer's bride. G. S. Graber, *History of the SS* (New York: David McKay Company, 1978), 69-71.

17. Vojtech Mastny, *The Czechs Under Nazi Rule*, 185.

18. Burgess, *Seven Men At Daybreak*, 70.

19. Deschner, *Heydrich*, 227.

20. Graber, *History of the SS*, 142.

21. Deschner, *Heydrich*, 197.

22. Miroslav Ivanov, *Target: Heydrich*, trans. Patrick O'Brien (New York: Macmillan Publishing Company, 1973), 39. Emphasis in original. Heydrich's position was, not surprisingly, a close reflection of that of Hitler's himself. The Führer stated at one point that "by firmly leading the Protectorate, it ought to be possible to push the Czech language in about twenty years back to the importance of a dialect."

23. MacDonald, *The Killing of SS Obergruppenführer Reinhard Heydrich*, 112-14.

24. Ibid., 48.

25. Eduard Beneš, *Memoirs of Dr. Eduard Beneš*, trans. Godfrey Lias (London: George Allen and Unwin, 1954), 64.

26. Bradley, *Czechoslovakia*, 162-63.

27. František Moravec, *Master of Spies* (London: The Bodley Head, 1975), 164.

28. Edward Táborský, "Politics in Exile," in *A History of the Czechoslovak Republic*, eds. Radomir Luza and Victor S. Mamatey (Princeton: Princeton University Press, 1973), 324.

29. Beneš, *Memoirs*, 197.

30. Ibid., 209.

31. Compton MacKenzie, *Dr. Beneš* (London: George Harrap and Company, 1946), 329.

32. Moravec, *Master of Spies*, 198.

33. If the Czechs had resisted the Germans militarily in the fall of 1938, there is considerable evidence that the outcome would not have been the rout that Beneš evidently contemplated. General Erich von Manstein, one of the top German military commanders, stated flatly at the Nuremberg trials that "there is no doubt whatsoever that had Czechoslovakia defended herself, we would have been held up by her fortifications, for we did not have the means to break through." He and others on the German General Staff also assumed that Britain, France, and perhaps even Ru' would have then become involved in the fighting, and that Germany wou'

suffered a catastrophic defeat as a result. William L. Shirer, *The Rise and Fall of the Third Reich* (New York: Simon and Schuster, 1960), 423-24.

34. Bradley, *Czechoslovakia*, 163-4.

35. Bradley, *Lidice: Sacrificial Village*, 20-21.

36. Deschner, *Heydrich*, 212-13.

37. Ibid., 210.

38. The SOE seems to have had its own reasons for supporting ANTHROPOID, since the success of the operation would validate its own role in the war effort and allay the skepticism that so many in the British government felt at the time about its activities.

39. Jan Wiener, *The Assassination of Heydrich* (New York: Grossman Publishers, 1969), 97-8.

40. A considerably less-known atrocity shortly followed that at Lidice. On June 24, 1942, the SS surrounded the village of Ležáky in eastern Bohemia and shot all of its 24 adult inhabitants (both men and women in this case). Eleven children from the town suffered the same fate as those from Lidice. One difference between Ležáky and Lidice was that there was far more tangible evidence that the citizens of Ležáky had in fact given real assistance to the assassins of Heydrich. Mastny, *The Czechs Under Nazi Rule*, 220.

Chapter 4

1.   Compton MacKenzie, *Dr. Beneš* (London: George Harrap and Company, 1946), 273.

2.   Ibid., 255.

3.   Bruce Lockhart, *Comes the Reckoning* (London: Putnam, 1947), 64.

4.   František Moravec, *Master of Spies* (London: The Bodley Head, 1975), 166.

5.   Recalling the time he spent in the United States, for example, Beneš made much of the fact that "[I] visited and lectured at all the important universities. A number of universities offered me honorary degrees, a number of others tried to tempt me to leave Chicago University [sic]." Eduard Beneš, *Memoirs of Dr. Eduard Beneš*, trans. Godfrey Lias (London: George Allen and Unwin, 1954), 62, 74-75.

6.   MacKenzie, *Dr. Beneš,* 15.

7.   Piotr Wandycz, "The Foreign Policy of Eduard Beneš," in *A History of the Czechoslovak Republic,* eds. Radomir Luza and Victor Mamatey (Princeton: Princeton University Press, 1973), 219.

8.   Edward Táborský, "Politics in Exile, 1939-1945," in *A History of the Czechoslovak Republic,* eds. Luza and Mamatey, 322.

9.   Vojtech Mastny, *The Czechs Under Nazi Rule* (New York: Columbia University Press, 1971), 141.

10. MacKenzie, *Dr. Beneš,* 268.

11. Beneš, *Memoirs,* 59. Emphasis in original.

12. Ibid., 278.
13. Moravec, *Master of Spies,* 223.
14. Mastny, *The Czechs Under Nazi Rule,* 208.
15. Ibid., 209.
16. Callum MacDonald, *The Killing of SS Obergruppenführer Reinhard Heydrich* (New York: The Free Press, 1989), 119.
17. Mastny, *The Czechs Under Nazi Rule,* 214.
18. Ibid., 212.
19. Gotthold Rhode, "The Protectorate of Bohemia and Moravia," in *A History of the Czechoslovak Republic,* eds. Luza and Mamatey, 298.
20. Beneš, *Memoirs,* 285.
21. MacDonald, *The Killing of SS Obergruppenführer Reinhard Heydrich,* 204.
22. Mastny, *The Czechs Under Nazi Rule,* 201.
23. Rhode, "The Protectorate of Bohemia and Moravia," in *A History of the Czechoslovak Republic,* eds. Luza and Mamatey, 315-16.
24. In arriving at this accounting, it is only right to recognize that about three-fourths of Czech Jewry did not survive, which equated to some 70,000 deaths.
25. Mastny, *The Czechs Under Nazi Rule,* 217.
26. Gunther Deschner, *Heydrich* (London: Orbis Publishing, 1981), 246.
27. Beneš, *Memoirs,* 158.
28. Ibid., 215.
29. Moravec, *Master of Spies,* 167.
30. MacKenzie, *Dr. Beneš,* 237.
31. Moravec, *Master of Spies,* 216.
32. Miroslav Ivanov, *Target: Heydrich,* trans. Patrick O'Brien (New York: Macmillan Publishing Company, 1974), 80-1.
33. Alan Burgess, *Seven Men At Daybreak* (New York: E. P. Dutton and Company, 1960),187-8.
34. Ivanov, *Target: Heydrich,* 204.
35. Karel Čurda, one of the parachutists sent from London and the man who eventually betrayed Gabčík and Kubiš as well as others in the resistance, later said himself that he had gone to the Gestapo because he "could not watch the murdering of innocent people." The Nazis released his mother and sister from custody in the aftermath of his turning against his comrades. One should not exaggerate Čurda's tender sentiments, however: he received a reward of five million Czech crowns from the German authorities, later changed his name and adopted German citizenship, and married the sister of an SS official. He spent the remaining war years touring the Protectorate as a Gestapo spy, posing as a parachutist and fingering other members of the resistance. Čurda was hanged after the war for his actions. Jan Wiener, *The Assassination of Heydrich* (New York: Grossman Publishers, 1969), 154.

36. Ivanov, *Target: Heydrich*, 109. Emphasis added.

37. Ibid., 142.

38. Mastny, *The Czechs Under Nazi Rule*, 209.

39. Ivanov, *Target: Heydrich*,145.

40. Wiener, *The Assassination of Heydrich*, 160.

41. Ibid., 161.

42. Ibid., 143.

43. Deschner, *Heydrich*, 262.

44. Charles Wighton, *Heydrich—Hitler's Most Evil Henchman* (London: Macmillan, 1962), 270.

45. Stanislav F. Berton, "Das Attentat auf Reinhard Heydrich von 27 Mai 1942," 33 *Vierteljahreshefte für Zeitgeschichte* (1985), 673-706, as quoted in MacDonald, *The Killing of SS Obergruppenführer Reinhard Heydrich*, 207.

46. Deschner, *Heydrich*, 252.

47. MacDonald, *The Killing of SS Obergruppenführer Reinhard Heydrich*, 207.

48. Moravec, *Master of Spies*, 223.

49. Ivanov, *Target: Heydrich*, 208.

50. Moravec, *Master of Spies*, 211.

51. MacDonald, *The Killing of SS Obergruppenführer Reinhard Heydrich*, 205.

52. Moravec, *Master of Spies*, 234, 238.

53. J. F. N. Bradley, *Lidice: Sacrificial Village* (New York: Ballantine Books, 1972), 165.

54. Ivanov, *Target: Heydrich*, 283.

55. Moravec, *Master of Spies*, 223.

56. MacDonald, *The Killing of SS Obergruppenführer Reinhard Heydrich*, 202. Beneš's foreign minister, Jan Masaryk, echoed this line of argument as well. "I was in the US at the time of Lidice and making no progress in our propaganda, having exhausted all the possibilities of the situation. Then came Lidice, and I had a new lease of life. Czechoslovakia was put on the map again and we had an easy time." Ibid., 200.

57. Moravec, *Master of Spies*, 223.

58. Ibid., 223-4.

59. Josef Korbel, *Twentieth-Century Czechoslovakia* (New York: Columbia University Press, 1977), 112-19.

60. Táborský, "Politics in Exile, 1939-1945," 337.

61. Beneš, *Memoirs*, 221. Emphasis in original.

62. MacDonald, *The Killing of SS Obergruppenführer Reinhard Heydrich*, 202.

63. Susan Zuccotti, *The Holocaust, the French and the Jews* (New York: Basic Books, 1993).

64. Burgess, *Seven Men At Daybreak*, 182.

65. Mastny, *The Czechs Under Nazi Rule*, 198.

66. Ibid., 161, 197.
67. Deschner, *Heydrich,* 225.
68. Ivan Cigánek, *Lidice* (Prague: Orbis Press Agency, 1972), 32.

Chapter 5

1. For the details of the round-up of Jews on July 16, I have relied on Susan Zuccotti's brilliant study of wartime French complicity in the Holocaust. See *The Holocaust, the French and the Jews* (New York: Basic Books, 1993), 103-17. All of the subsequent quotations and information, unless otherwise indicated, are taken from her work.

2. Claude Lévy and Paul Tillard, *Betrayal at the Vel d'Hiv,* trans. Inéa Bushnaq (New York: Hill and Wang, 1969), 27.

3. Serge Klarsfeld, *Memorial to the Jews Deported from France* (New York: Beate Klarsfeld Foundation, 1983), 60.

4. Ibid., 166-9.

5. Zuccotti, *The Holocaust, the French and the Jews,* 115.

6. Winston S. Churchill, *Their Finest Hour* (Boston: Houghton Mifflin Company, 1949), 42.

7. Maurice Larkin, *France Since the Popular Front* (Oxford: Clarendon Press, 1988), 80-1.

8. Cited in Alexander Werth, *France* (New York: Henry Holt and Company, 1956), 16.

9. The recognition of this fact led to a sort of historical amnesia settling over France following the end of the war, in which the efforts of the *maquis* were now elevated to the status of a myth whereby virtually all Frenchmen had (supposedly) participated in their activities. The reality that relatively few had done so was exposed—to considerable controversy—by films such as *The Sorrow and the Pity,* directed by Claude Chabroul, and by "revisionist" writings such as Peter Novick's study *The Resistance Versus Vichy* (New York: Columbia University Press, 1968).

10. Lucy Dawidowicz, *The War Against the Jews, 1939-1945* (New York: Holt, Rinehart and Winston, 1975), 361.

11. Larkin, *France Since the Popular Front,* 98-101.

12. Ibid., 102.

13. Robert Paxton, *Vichy France* (New York: Alfred A. Knopf, 1972), 298. In February 1944, Darnand became Vichy Minister of the Interior. He was executed after the war for his collaboration with the Nazis.

14. Cordell Hull, *Memoirs of Cordell Hull,* Vol. 1 (New York: The Macmillan Company, 1948), 805.

15. William Leahy, *I Was There* (New York: Whittlesey House, 1950), 8.

16. Hull, *Memoirs of Cordell Hull,* Vol. 1, 804.

17.   Robert Murphy, *Diplomat Among Warriors* (Garden City, NY: Doubleday and Company, 1964), 48, 65.

18.   William Langer, *Our Vichy Gamble* (New York: Alfred A. Knopf, 1947), 212.

19.   The Neutrality Act (or Acts) prohibited the shipment of munitions to any wartime belligerent, banned American loans to such countries, and stated that any trade between the United States and them could only be on a "cash and carry" basis, that is., American goods would have to be paid for in cash and transported on the ships of the country purchasing them. The legislation was designed in response to the supposed lessons of American "entrapment" in hostilities in World War I. As of late June 1940, of course, Vichy was technically no longer a "belligerent" in the war.

20.   *The New Republic* (November 16, 1942); *Washington Post* (November 12, 1942).

21.   Langer, *Our Vichy Gamble,* 217.

22.   Murphy, *Diplomat Among Warriors,* 56.

23.   Ibid., 86.

24.   Langer, *Our Vichy Gamble,* vii.

25.   Peter Calvocoressi and Guy Wint, *Total War* (Hammondsworth, Middlesex, England: Viking Penguin, 1972), 366.

26.   Louis Snyder, *The War* (New York: Dell Publishing Company, 1960), 354-60.

27.   Murphy, *Diplomat Among Warriors,* 101.

28.   David S. Bell, Douglas Johnson and Peter Morris, eds., *Biographical Dictionary of French Political Leaders Since 1870* (New York: Simon and Schuster, 1990), 103-4.

29.   Alec De Montmorency, *The Enigma of Admiral Darlan* (New York: E. P. Dutton, 1943).

30.   Churchill was to recall that his decision to authorize an attack on the French fleet was among the "most hateful" he had to make during the entire war. For a thorough discussion of his attitude toward the matter, see Churchill, *Their Finest Hour,* 231-41.

31.   Calvocoressi and Wint, *Total War,* 307.

32.   Werth, *France,* 88.

33.   Langer, *Our Vichy Gamble,* 70.

34.   Susan Zuccotti, *The Holocaust, the French and the Jews,* 67.

35.   United States, Department of State, *Foreign Relations of the United States 1941,* Vol. 2 (Washington, DC: GPO, 1967),189.

36.   Mark Clark, *Calculated Risk* (New York: Harper and Brothers, 1950), 106. Clark also suggests that if his French counterparts had not agreed to what he wanted, he would have proceeded to arrest them all and lock them up aboard one of the ships in Algiers harbor.

37.   Arthur Layton Funk, *The Politics of TORCH* (Lawrence, KS: The University Press of Kansas, 1974), 43.

38.   Murphy, *Diplomat Among Warriors,* 114.

39. Arthur Layton Funk, *Charles de Gaulle: The Crucial Years, 1943-1944* (Norman, OK: University of Oklahoma Press, 1959), 42.

40. Robert Dallek, *Franklin D. Roosevelt and American Foreign Policy, 1932-1945* (New York: Oxford University Press, 1979), 364.

41. Warren Kimball, ed., *Churchill and Roosevelt: The Complete Correspondence*, Vol. 2 (Princeton: Princeton University Press, 1984), 7.

42. Dallek, *Franklin D. Roosevelt and American Foreign Policy, 1932-1945*, 364.

43. Murphy, *Diplomat Among Warriors*, 158.

44. Robert Sherwood, *Roosevelt and Hopkins* (New York: Harper and Brothers, 1950), 675.

45. As it happened, Peyrouton became governor general of Algeria some four weeks *after* Darlan was no longer on the scene. The French admiral was the victim of an assassin's bullet on Christmas Eve, 1942. Peyrouton managed to hang on until the following June, when De Gaulle's increasing ascendancy in French North Africa made it impossible for him to remain. He was later subjected to a war crimes trial by French courts after the war, but the charges were eventually dismissed. The issues presented by the Darlan and Peyrouton cases are to be sure rather different. The arguments for dealing with the former essentially derived out of considerations of military expediency. The appointment of the latter seemed to reflect a certain kind of moral inertia.

46. Clark, *Calculated Risk*, 125, 132.

47. Winston S. Churchill, *The Hinge of Fate* (Boston: Houghton Mifflin Company, 1950), 635.

Chapter 6

1. Mark W. Clark, *Calculated Risk* (New York: Harper and Brothers, 1950), 106, 132.

2. Robert Murphy, *Diplomat Among Warriors* (Garden City, NY: Doubleday and Company, 1964),140-3.

3. Ibid., 32-35.

4. Cited in Robert Sherwood, *Roosevelt and Hopkins* (New York: Harper and Brothers, 1950), 678.

5. Dwight D. Eisenhower, *Crusade in Europe* (Garden City, NY: Doubleday and Company, 1948), 106-7.

6. Ibid., 129-30.

7. Harold Macmillan, *The Blast of War* (New York: Harper and Row, 1967), 174.

8. Eisenhower, *Crusade in Europe,* 128.

9. Ibid., 131.

10. Ed Cray, *General of the Army* (New York: W. W. Norton, 1990), 351.

11. Larry Bland, ed., *The Papers of George Catlett Marshall,* Vol. 3 (Baltimore: The Johns Hopkins University Press, 1991), 445.

12. Cray, *General of the Army,* 351.

13. Forrest C. Pogue, *George C. Marshall: Ordeal and Hope* (New York: Viking, 1966), 422.

14. Bland, ed., *The Papers of George Catlett Marshall,* Vol. 3, 446.

15. Cordell Hull, *The Memoirs of Cordell Hull,* Vol. 2 (New York: The Macmillan Company, 1948), 1133.

16. Ibid., 1194.

17. Ibid., 1199, 1201.

18. Robert Dallek, *Franklin D. Roosevelt and American Foreign Policy, 1932-1945* (New York: Oxford University Press, 1979), 363.

19. Sherwood, *Roosevelt and Hopkins,* 654.

20. Samuel Rosenman, *Working with Roosevelt* (New York: Harper and Brothers, 1952), 364.

21. Dallek, *Franklin D. Roosevelt and American Foreign Policy, 1932-1945,* 365.

22. William Langer, *Our Vichy Gamble* (New York: Alfred A. Knopf, 1947), 371.

23. Ibid., 373.

24. William Leahy, *I Was There* (New York: Whittlesey House,1950), 132.

25. United States, Department of State, *The Conferences at Washington, 1941-1942 and Casablanca, 1943* (Washington, DC: GPO, 1968), 608.

26. Ibid. Such attitudes could be found in many places, including within Eisenhower's own staff. When a local American official questioned the morality of the Darlan deal, given Vichy's record of anti-Semitism, one of Eisenhower's aides responded as follows: "Art, old fellow, if you have nothing better to do in Africa than to worry about those Jews and Communists who helped us, why don't you go home?" David Schoenbrun, *Soldiers of the Night* (New York: E. P. Dutton, 1980), 231.

27. Langer, *Our Vichy Gamble,* 371.

28. Clark, *Calculated Risk,* 125-26.

29. Cray, *General of the Army,* 350.

30. To be fair, the early planning for TORCH had anticipated that Allied forces would land in Tunisia itself as well as in Algeria and Morocco. When this idea was eventually dropped, it put Estéva in an almost impossible position, given the substantial German presence in that area already.

31. Eisenhower, *Crusade in Europe,* 105.

32. Warren Kimball, ed., *Churchill and Roosevelt: The Complete Correspondence,* Vol. 2 (Princeton: Princeton University Press, 1984), 7.

33. Alexander Werth, *France* (New York: Henry Holt and Company, 1956), 91.

34. Anthony Eden, *The Reckoning* (Boston: Houghton Mifflin, 1965), 409-410.

35. Arthur Funk, *The Politics of TORCH* (Lawrence, KS: The University Press of Kansas, 1974), 242.

36. Eisenhower, *Crusade in Europe,* 112.

37. One of the most perceptive analyses of the procedure described here is James C. Thompson, "How Could Vietnam Happen: An Autopsy," in *At Issue,* ed. Steven Spiegel (New York: St. Martin's Press, 1973), 268-78. Thompson was a participant himself in many of the most important meetings having to do with Vietnam.

38. Murphy, *Diplomat Among Warriors,* 77.

39. Ibid., 93-4.

40. David S. Bell, Douglas Johnson, and Peter Morris, eds., *Biographical Dictionary of French Political Leaders Since 1870* (New York: Simon and.Schuster, 1990), 437.

41. Ibid., 178-80.

42. Langer, *Our Vichy Gamble,* 334-40.

43. Murphy, *Diplomat Among Warriors,* 131.

44. Raoul Aglion, *Roosevelt and De Gaulle* (New York: The Free Press, 1988), 52.

45. Langer, *Our Vichy Gamble,* 173.

46. Peter Calvocoressi and Guy Wint, *Total War* (Harmondsworth, Middlesex, England: Viking Penguin, 1972), 315-17.

47. Murphy, *Diplomat Among Warriors,* 75-6.

48. Louis Snyder, *The War* (New York: Dell Publishing, 1960), 365.

49. Cray, *General of the Army,* 351.

50. Clark, *Calculated Risk,* 130. Even before Darlan's assassination, Clark had suggested to the French admiral that he might want to make an early departure from North Africa. On December 23, he had held out the prospect that Darlan might be able to accompany his son to Georgia. Clark said he made the offer "with the ulterior hope of getting a reaction from Darlan on his removal from the North African political scene."

51. Ibid., 107.

52. Winston S. Churchill, *Hinge of Fate* (Boston: Houghton Mifflin Company, 1950), 632, 637.

53. Ibid., 635. Churchill himself in his memoirs offers a surprisingly generous summary verdict on Darlan, considering his earlier detestation of the man: "It is not for those who benefited enormously from his accession to our side to revile his memory."

54. Clark, *Calculated Risk,* 125.

55. Stephen A. Garrett, *Ethics and Airpower in World War II* (New York: St. Martin's Press, 1993), 162, 166-7.

56. Susan Zuccotti, *The Holocaust, the French and the Jews* (New York: Basic Books, 1993), 111.

Conclusion

1. As Thucydides put it somewhat more formally, "They that have odds of power exact as much as they can, and the weak yield to such conditions as they can get." Cited in Michael Walzer, *Just and Unjust Wars* (New York: Basic Books, 1977), 5.

2. Bradley F. Smith, *Reaching Judgment at Nuremberg* (New York: Basic Books, 1977), 301.

3. For a sense of how controversial the Nuremberg trials continue to be in some quarters, see the letters to the editor in the *New York Review of Books* that followed Istvan Deak's largely favorable review of Telford Taylor's recent book on the trials, *The Anatomy of the Nuremberg Trials* (New York: Alfred A. Knopf, 1992). Taylor himself was, of course, one of the main American figures at Nuremberg, and he continues to insist that the proceedings there were right and necessary. For Deak's review, see "Misjudgment at Nuremberg," *New York Review of Books* (October 7, 1993).

4. David Rieff, *Slaughterhouse: Bosnia and the Failure of the West* (New York: Simon and Schuster, 1994).

5. Thomas McCollogh, *The Moral Imagination and Public Life* (Chatham, NJ: Chatham House Publishers, 1991).

6. C. S. Lewis, *The Case for Christianity* (New York: The Macmillan Company, 1945).

7. Steven Spielberg's achievement in directing *Schindler's List* is obviously one to be admired, but the full context and meaning of the Schindler case can only be gleaned from a reading of Thomas Keneally's book of the same title (New York: Simon and Schuster, 1982), upon which the film was based.

8. Robert W. McElroy, *Morality and American Foreign Policy* (Princeton: Princeton University Press, 1992).

9. For the extraordinary story of Stella Goldschlag, see Peter Wyden's *Stella* (New York: Simon and Schuster, 1992). Wyden was a schoolmate of Stella's in the prewar Berlin days.

10. Cited in Richard Rhodes, *The Making of the Atomic Bomb* (New York: Simon and Schuster, 1986), 743.

Bibliography

Abel, Elie. *The Missile Crisis*. Philadelphia: J. B. Lippincott Company, 1966.

Acheson, Dean. "Ethics in International Relations Today: Our Standard of Conduct," *Vital Speeches of the Day* 31 (Pelham, NY: City News Publishing Company, 1965).

Aglion, Raoul. *Roosevelt and De Gaulle*. New York: The Free Press, 1988.

Ahrenfeldt, Robert H. *Psychiatry in the British Army*. New York: Columbia University Press, 1958.

Aristotle. *Nicomachean Ethics*. Trans. Martin Ostwald. Indianapolis: Bobbs-Merrill, 1962.

Aron, Robert. *The Vichy Regime*. New York: The Macmillan Company, 1958.

Ball, George. *The Past Has Another Pattern*. New York: W. W. Norton, 1982.

Beitz, Charles. *Political Theory and International Relations*. Princeton: Princeton University Press, 1979.

Bell, David S., Johnson, Douglas, and Morris, Peter, eds. *Biographical Dictionary of French Political Leaders Since 1870*. New York: Simon and Schuster, 1990.

Beneš, Eduard. *Memoirs of Dr. Eduard Beneš*. Godfrey Lias, trans. London: George Allen and Unwin, 1954.

Bernstein, Barton. "Why We Didn't Use Poison Gas in World War II," *American Heritage* 46 (August-September, 1985).

Blackett, P. M. S. *Political and Military Consequences of Atomic Energy*. London: Turnstile Press, 1948.

Bland, Larry, ed. *The Papers of George Catlett Marshall*. Vol. 3. Baltimore: The Johns Hopkins University Press, 1991.

Bok, Sissela. *A Strategy for Peace*. New York: Pantheon Books, 1989.

————. *Secrets*. New York: Vintage Books, 1989.

Boyle, Joseph, Finnis, John and Grisez, Germain, eds. *Nuclear Deterrence, Morality and Realism*. Oxford: Clarendon Press, 1987.

Bradley, J. F. N. *Czechoslovakia*. Edinburgh: University of Edinburgh Press, 1971.

————. *Lidice: Sacrificial Village*. New York: Ballantine Books, 1972.

Bredvold, L. I., and R. G. Ross, eds. *The Philosophy of Edmund Burke*. Ann Arbor: University of Michigan Press, 1967.

Brittain, Vera. *Testament of Experience*. London: Victor Gollancz, 1957.

Burgess, Alan. *Seven Men At Daybreak*. New York: E. P. Dutton and Company, 1960.

Calder, Angus. *The People's War*. New York: Pantheon Books, 1969.

Calvocoressi, Peter and Wint, Guy. *Total War*. Harmondsworth, Middlesex, England: Viking Penguin, 1972.

Cannon, Lou. *President Reagan: The Role of a Lifetime*. New York: Simon and Schuster, 1991.

Carter, Jimmy. *Why Not the Best?* Nashville, TN: Broadman Press, 1975.

Casey, Lord Richard. *Personal Experience 1939-1945*. London: Constable, 1962.

Churchill, Winston S. *The Grand Alliance*. Boston: Houghton Mifflin Company, 1951.

————. *Closing the Ring*. Boston: Houghton Mifflin Company, 1951.

————. *The Hinge of Fate*. Boston: Houghton Mifflin Company, 1950.

————. *Their Finest Hour*. Boston: Houghton Mifflin Company, 1949.

Ciganek, Ivan. *Lidice*. Prague: Orbis Press Agency, 1972.

Clark, Mark W. *Calculated Risk*. New York: Harper and Brothers, 1950.

Coll, Alberto R. "Normative Prudence as a Tradition of Statecraft," *Ethics and International Affairs* 5 (1991).

Collier, Basil. *The Second World War: A Military History*. New York: William Morrow and Company, 1967.

Colville, John. *The Fringes of Power*. New York: W. W. Norton and Company, 1985.

Cowan, Howard. "Allies Decide on New Policy of Terror Raids," *St. Louis Post Dispatch* (February 18, 1945).

Cray, Ed. *General of the Army*. New York: W. W. Norton, 1990.

Dallek, Robert. *Franklin D. Roosevelt and American Foreign Policy, 1932-1945*. New York: Oxford University Press, 1979.

Davidowicz, Lucy. *The War Against the Jews*. New York: Holt, Rinehart and Winston, 1975.

Deak, Istvan. "Misjudgment at Nuremberg," *New York Review of Books* (October 7, 1993).

Deigh, John ed. *Ethics and Personality*. Chicago: University of Chicago Press, 1992.

Deschner, Gunther. *Heydrich: The Pursuit of Total Power*. London: Orbis Publishing, 1981.

Dyer, Gwynne. *War*. Homewood, IL: Dorsey Press, 1985.

Dyson, Freeman. *Weapons and Hope*. New York: Harper and Row, 1984.

Eden, Anthony. *The Reckoning*. Boston: Houghton Mifflin, 1965.

Edwards, Paul, editor-in-chief. *The Encyclopedia of Philosophy*. Vol. 2. New York: The Macmillan Company and The Free Press, 1967.

Eisenhower, Dwight D. *Crusade in Europe*. Garden City, NY: Doubleday and Company, 1948.

Elfstrom, G. and N. Fotion. *Military Ethics*. London: Routledge and Kegan Paul, 1986.

Farmer, Paul. *Vichy: Political Dilemma*. New York: Columbia University Press, 1955.

Feingold, Henry. *The Politics of Rescue: The Roosevelt Administration and the Holocaust 1938-1945*. New Brunswick, NJ: Rutgers University Press, 1970.

Fleishman, Joel et al. *Public Duties: The Moral Obligations of Government Officials*. Cambridge: Harvard University Press, 1981.

Forster, E. M.. *Two Cheers for Democracy*. New York: Harcourt Brace, 1951.

France During the German Occupation, 1940-1944. Trans. Philip W. Whitcomb, vol. 2. Stanford: Stanford University Press, 1957.

Frankland, Noble and Webster, Charles. *The Strategic Air Offensive Against Germany 1939-1945.* London: Her Majesty's Stationary Office, 1961.

Friedrich, Carl J. ed. *The Philosophy of Kant.* New York: Random House, 1949.

Funk, Arthur Layton. *Charles De Gaulle: The Crucial Years, 1943-1944.* (Norman, OK: University of Oklahoma Press, 1959).

————. *The Politics of TORCH.* Lawrence, KS: The University Press of Kansas, 1974.

Garrett, Stephen A. *Ethics and Airpower in World War II.* New York: St. Martin's Press, 1993.

————. *Ideals and Reality.* Washington, DC: University Press of America, 1978.

Gawdiak, Ihor. *Czechoslovakia: A Country Study.* Washington, DC: Department of the Army, 1989.

Gilbert, Martin. *The Second World War.* New York: Henry Holt and Company, 1989.

Graber, G.S. *History of the SS.* New York: David McKay Company, 1978.

Greene, John Robert. *The Limits of Power.* Bloomington, IN: Indiana University Press, 1992.

Halberstam, David. *The Best and the Brightest.* New York: Random House, 1969.

Hampshire, Stuart, ed. *Public and Private Morality.* Cambridge: Cambridge University Press, 1978.

————. *Morality and Conflict.* Oxford: Basil Blackwell,1983.

Handel, Michael, ed.. *Leaders and Intelligence.* London: Frank Cass, 1989.

Hardin, Garrett. *Living Within Limits.* New York: Oxford University Press, 1993.

————. *Promethean Ethics.* Seattle, WA: University of Washington Press, 1980.

Hare , J. E. and Carey B. Joynt. *Ethics and International Affairs.* New York: St. Martin's Press, 1982.

Hastings, Max. *Bomber Command.* New York: Simon and Schuster, 1987.

Hobbes, Thomas. *Leviathan.* Ed. Michael Oakeshott. New York: Macmillan, 1962.

Hull, Cordell. *The Memoirs of Cordell Hull.* 2 vols. New York: The Macmillan Company, 1948.

Huták, J. B. *With Blood and Iron.* London: Robert Hale Limited, 1957.

Ivanov, Miroslav. *Target: Heydrich.* Trans. Patrick O'Brien. New York: Macmillan Publishing Company, 1974.

Jackson, Robert. "The Situational Ethics of Statecraft." Paper prepared for the Ethics and Statecraft Conference. Carnegie Institute of Ethics and International Affairs. (Vancouver, Canada: October 1993).

Jervis, Robert. *The Logic of Images in International Relations.* Princeton: Princeton University Press, 1970.

Jones, H. A. *The War in the Air.* London: Oxford University Press, 1937.

Jones, R. V. *Most Secret War.* London: Hamish Hamilton, 1978.

Jones, Donald G., ed. *Private and Public Ethics.* New York: The Edwin Mellen Press, 1978.

Keneally, Thomas. *Schindler's List.* New York: Simon and Schuster, 1982.

Kennedy, Robert. *Thirteen Days* (New York: W. W. Norton, 1971).

Kidder, Rushworth. "The Three Great Domains of Human Action." *Christian Science Monitor* (January 29, 1990).

Kimball, Warren, ed. *Churchill and Roosevelt: The Complete Correspondence.* 3 vols. Princeton: Princeton University Press, 1984.

Klarsfeld, Serge. *Memorial to the Jews Deported from France.* New York: Beate Klarsfeld Foundation, 1983.

Korbel, Josef. *Twentieth-Century Czechoslovakia.* New York: Columbia University Press, 1977.

Langer, William. *Our Vichy Gamble.* New York: Alfred A. Knopf, 1947.

Larkin, Maurice. *France Since the Popular Front.* Oxford: Clarendon Press, 1988.

Leahy, William. *I Was There.* New York: Whittlesey House,1950.

Levinson, Sanford. "Responsibility for Crimes of War," *Philosophy and Public Affairs* 2 (1973).

Lévy, Claude and Tillard, Paul. *Betrayal at the Vel d'Hiv.* Trans. Inéa Bushnaq. New York: Hill and Wang, 1969.

Lewin, Ronald ed. *Churchill as Warlord.* New York: Stein and Day, 1973.

Lewis, C. S. *The Case for Christianity.* New York: The Macmillan Company, 1945.

Liddell Hart, Basil. *History of the Second World War.* New York: G. P. Putnam's Sons, 1970.

Lockhart, Bruce. *Comes the Reckoning.* London: Putnam, 1947.

Luza, Radomir and Victor S. Mamatey, eds. *A History of the Czechoslovak Republic.* Princeton: Princeton University Press, 1973.

MacDonald, Callum. *The Killing of SS Obergruppenführer Reinhard Heydrich.* New York: The Free Press, 1989.

Machiavelli, Niccolo. *The Prince and the Discourses.* New York: The Modern Library, 1940.

MacKenzie, Compton. *Dr. Beneš.* London: George Harrap and Company, 1946.

Macmillan, Harold. *The Blast of War.* New York: Harper and Row, 1967.

Massie, Robert. *Dreadnought.* New York: Random House, 1991.

Mastny, Vojtech. *The Czechs Under Nazi Rule.* New York: Columbia University Press, 1971.

McCollogh, Thomas. *The Moral Imagination and Public Life.* Chatham, NJ: Chatham House Publishers, 1991.

McElroy, Robert. W. *Morality and American Foreign Policy.* Princeton: Princeton University Press, 1992.

McNamara, Robert. *In Retrospect: The Tragedy and Lessons of Vietnam.* New York: Times Books, 1995.

Messenger, Charles. *'Bomber' Harris.* New York: St. Martin's Press, 1984.

Bibliography   191

Mill, John Stuart. "Considerations on Representative Government," in *On Liberty and Considerations on Representative Government,* ed. R. B. McCallum. Oxford: Clarendon Press, 1946.

Miller, Merle. *Plain Speaking.* New York: Berkley Publishing Corporation, 1973.

Montmorency, Alec De. *The Enigma of Admiral Darlan.* New York: E. P. Dutton, 1943.

Moravec, František Moravec. *Master of Spies.* London: The Bodley Head, 1975.

Morgenthau, Hans. *Politics Among Nations.* 2nd ed. New York: Alfred A. Knopf, 1956.

———. *Politics Among Nations.* 4th ed. New York: Alfred A. Knopf, 1967.

Murphy, Robert. *Diplomat Among Warriors.* Garden City, NY: Doubleday and Company, 1964.

Murray, Gilbert. *Tradition and Progress.* Boston: Houghton Mifflin Company, 1922.

Nicolson, Sir Harold. *The War Years 1939-1945.* New York: Atheneum, 1967.

Niebuhr, Reinhold. *Moral Man and Immoral Society.* New York: Charles Scribners, 1932.

Novick, Peter. *The Resistance Versus Vichy.* New York: Columbia University Press, 1968.

Paxton, Robert. *Vichy France.* New York: Alfred A. Knopf, 1972.

Pogue, Forrest C. *George C. Marshall: Ordeal and Hope.* New York: Viking, 1966.

Rauschning, Herman. *The Revolution of Nihilism.* New York: Alliance Books Corporation, 1939.

Rawls, John. *A Theory of Justice.* Cambridge, MA: Harvard University Press, 1971.

Rhodes, Richard. *The Making of the Atomic Bomb.* New York: Simon and Schuster, 1986.

Rieff, David. *Slaughterhouse: Bosnia and the Failure of the West.* New York: Simon and Schuster, 1994.

Rosenman, Samuel. *Working with Roosevelt.* New York: Harper and Brothers, 1952.

Rostow, W. W. *Pre-Invasion Bombing Strategy.* Austin: University of Texas Press, 1981.

Runes, Dagobert D., editor. *Dictionary of Philosophy.* Totowa, NJ: Littlefield, Adams and Company, 1975.

Sartre, Jean-Paul. *No Exit and Three Other Plays.* Trans. Lionel Abel. New York: Vintage, 1960.

Saward, Dudley. *Bomber Harris.* Garden City, NY: Doubleday, 1985.

Schoenbrun, David. *Soldiers of the Night.* New York: E. P. Dutton, 1980.

Shapley, Deborah. *Promise and Power: The Life and Times of Robert McNamara.* Boston: Little, Brown and Company, 1993.

Shawcross, William. *Sideshow.* New York: Simon and Schuster, 1979.

Sherwood, Robert. *Roosevelt and Hopkins.* New York: Harper and Brothers, 1950.

Shirer, William L. *The Rise and Fall of the Third Reich* (New York: Simon and Schuster, 1960).

Singer, J. David. "The Level-of-Analysis Problem in International Relations." *World Politics* (October, 1961).

Singer, Peter. *Practical Ethics.* Cambridge: Cambridge University Press, 1979.

Smith, Bradley. *Reaching Judgment at Nuremberg.* New York: Basic Books, 1977.

Snyder, Louis. *The War.* New York: Dell Publishing, 1960.

Táborský, Edward. *President Eduard Beneš Between East and West 1938-1948*. Stanford: Stanford University Press, 1981.

Taylor, Telford. *The Anatomy of the Nuremberg Trials*. New York: Alfred A. Knopf, 1992.

"The Hague Rules of 1923," *American Journal of International Law* 17 (October 1923).

Thompson, Dennis. *Political Ethics and Public Office*. Cambridge, MA: Harvard University Press, 1987.

Thompson, James C. "How Could Vietnam Happen: An Autopsy," in *At Issue*, ed. Steven Spiegel. New York: St. Martin's Press, 1973.

Tompkins, Peter. *The Murder of Admiral Darlan*. New York: Simon and Schuster, 1965.

Trevelyan, G. M. *Garibaldi and the Making of Modern Italy*. London: Longmans, Green, 1948.

Unites States, Department of State, *Foreign Relations of the United States 1941*, vol. 2. Washington, DC: GPO, 1967.

———. *The Conferences at Washinton, 1941-1942 and Casablanca, 1943*. Washington, DC: GPO, 1968.

Vance, Cyrus. *Hard Choices*. New York: Simon and Schuster, 1983.

Walzer, Michael. *Just and Unjust Wars*. New York: Basic Books, 1977.

———. "Political Action: The Problem of Dirty Hands," *Philosophy and Public Affairs* 2 (Winter, 1973).

Weber, Max. "Politics as a Vocation," in *Max Weber*. Trans. and Eds. H. H. Gerth and C. Wright Mills. New York: Oxford University Press, 1946.

Weisband, Edward and Thomas Franck. *Resignation in Protest*. New York: Grossman Publishers, 1976.

Werth, Alexander. *France*. New York: Henry Holt and Company, 1956.

Wiener, Jan. *The Assassination of Heydrich*. New York: Grossman Publishers, 1969.

Wighton, Charles. *Heydrich—Hitler's Most Evil Henchman*. London: Macmillan, 1962.

Wolfers, Arnold. *Discord and Collaboration*. Baltimore: The Johns Hopkins University Press, 1965.

Wyden, Peter. *Stella*. New York: Simon and Schuster, 1992.

Zuccotti, Susan. *The Holocaust, the French, and the Jews*. New York: Basic Books, 1993.

Index

Acheson, Dean, 4
Acton, Lord, 5
Allied bombing of Germany in World War II,
  moral criticism of, 37
  and search for scapegoats after the war,
    40-41
ANTHROPOID (operation to assassinate
  Reinhard Heydrich), ix, 63-5
  actual success of in killing Heydrich, 65
  and disillusionment of agents assigned
    to carry it out, 85-6
  and need to secure support for Czech
    cause from the Allies, 74-5, 78,
    95-6
  assessment of broader results of, 72-80
  better alternatives to, 79-80
  British support for, 64
  effect of in causing collapse of Czech
    resistance movement, 77-8
  effect of on the Czech people, 83-90
  influenced by considerations of Czech
    relations with Stalin, 73-4, 78-9
  intuitive values of Eduard Beneš and,
    71-2
  principle of universalization and, 83-90
  pure desire for revenge as possible fac-
    tor in planning of, 73-4
  use of principle of proportionality in
    judging, 93-7
applied ethics
  and the importance of case studies in
    examining, xi
  and the significance of "hard cases",
    157
  definition of, ix
  see also ethics and statesmanship
Aquinas, Saint Thomas, 22-3
Aristotle, 31

Bach-Zelewski, Erich von dem, 79
Ball, George, dissent of against Vietnam War,
  43
Bank, Lord Moulton of, 25
Bartoš, Josef, 87
Beneš, Eduard, 61, 77, 84
  and early British doubts about, 62

and knowledge of conditions in the
  Czech homeland, 81
argued that death of Heydrich secured
  Allied support for Czech cause,
  95
attitude of concerning minorities problem in Czechslovakia, 69
denial after the war of responsibility
  for ANTHROPOID, 90
early political experience of, 61
general character of, 67-9
intuitive values of, 71-2
obsession with Munich agreement of,
  62-3
personal political stake in development
  of ANTHROPOID, 70-71
  see also Czech government-in-exile
Benn, S. I., 46-7
Bethman Hollweg, Theobold von, 11
Böhme, Horst, 53, 55
Boisson, General Pierre, 139
Bok, Sissela, 3, 45, 48-9
Bonaparte, Napoleon, 25
Bosnia
  denunciation of Western inaction to-
    ward as immoral, 165
  protest by State Department officials
    against American policy on, 43
Bradley, John, 94
Brittain, Vera, 175
Burke, Edmund, x, 29
Butcher, Commander Harry, 131

Carter, President Jimmy, 9-10
Casablanca Conference (1943), 156
Castel, Sarah, 162
Cavour, Count Camillo di, ix
Central Intelligence Agency, 37-8
Chamberlain, Joseph, 42
Churchill, Prime Minister Winston, 95, 107
  attempt by to get General Weygand to
    commit to Allied cause, 148
  criticizes formation of Vichy govern-
    ment, 115
  eventual impatience of with criticism
    of Darlan deal, 160-1